Ward Coldridge, Cyril Vyvyan Hawksford

The Law of Gambling

Civil and Criminal - With Forms

Ward Coldridge, Cyril Vyvyan Hawksford

The Law of Gambling
Civil and Criminal - With Forms

ISBN/EAN: 9783337232733

Printed in Europe, USA, Canada, Australia, Japan

Cover: Foto ©Suzi / pixelio.de

More available books at **www.hansebooks.com**

THE

LAW OF GAMBLING

CIVIL AND CRIMINAL.

𝔚𝔦𝔱𝔥 𝔉𝔬𝔯𝔪𝔰.

BY

WARD COLDRIDGE, M.A.,

OF LINCOLN'S INN AND THE WESTERN CIRCUIT,

AND

CYRIL V. HAWKSFORD, B.A.,

OF THE MIDDLE TEMPLE,

BARRISTERS-AT-LAW.

LONDON:

REEVES AND TURNER,

100, CHANCERY LANE, AND CAREY STREET,

𝔏𝔞𝔴 𝔅𝔬𝔬𝔨𝔰𝔢𝔩𝔩𝔢𝔯𝔰 𝔞𝔫𝔡 𝔓𝔲𝔟𝔩𝔦𝔰𝔥𝔢𝔯𝔰.

———

1895.

LONDON :
PRINTED BY C. F. ROWORTH, GREAT NEW STREET, FETTER LANE, E.C.

PREFACE.

GAMBLING is not a term of precise and defined meaning, but it sufficiently indicates the subject-matter with which this book deals (namely), speculating, wagering, and gaming. This book is divided into two parts, civil and criminal. The civil portion commences with a detailed discussion of wagering contracts as such; the attitude of the common law towards wagers, games, and gaming is then shown. From that point the civil portion traces the development of illegal transactions and obligations connected therewith, and subsequently the Act 8 & 9 Vict. c. 109, introduces the void transactions and the obligations arising therefrom. The effect of the Gaming Amendment Act, 1892, is stated, and the authorities are collated. The law relating to gaming securities is traced and illustrated by reference to all classes of securities. Speculation on the Stock Exchange forms the subject-matter of a separate chapter. The criminal portion commences with a succinct account of criminal procedure, and it is hoped that that chapter will form a useful introduction to the subsequent matters. The Betting House Act and its difficulties, together with the present authorities thereon, have been examined in Chapter XIII., and on the questions of the legality of betting on race-courses, the probable influence of the decision in the Albert Club Case (*Downes* v. *Johnson*) is, with submission, indicated.

The book has been written primarily for the use of members of the legal profession; at the same time it is hoped that it may be of service to others interested in the subject. The Authors, in endeavouring to state the present law, have been compelled to trace its development and exhibit the different phases through which it has passed.

W. C.
C. V. H.

New Square, Lincoln's Inn.
November, 1895.

CONTENTS.

Part I.—CIVIL.

CHAPTER I.

CHAPTER II.

CHAPTER III.

CHAPTER IV.

CHAPTER V.

CHAPTER VI.

CHAPTER VII.

CHAPTER VIII.

CHAPTER IX.

CHAPTER X.

CONTENTS. vii

Part II.—CRIMINAL.

CHAPTER XI.

CONTENTS. vii

Part II.—CRIMINAL.

APPENDIX.

TABLE OF CASES.

b 2

The Law of Gambling.

Part I.—CIVIL.

CHAPTER I.

WAGERING CONTRACTS.

THERE are two essential characteristics of a wagering contract: first, an unascertained event; secondly, the parties to the contract must stand respectively either to gain or lose, according as the uncertainty shall be determined in the one way or in the other. ^{Characteristics of wagering contracts.}

The consideration for the contract consists in the mutual promises to pay made by the parties one to the other, according to the event of the uncertainty. Such mutual promises would be lacking in the following instance :—A. promises B. that if B. makes one hundred runs in a certain cricket match, he (A.) will give him a present. Either B. will make one hundred runs or he will fail to do so; if he succeeds he becomes entitled to the present, but if he fails he has not promised to make a payment to A. Such a contract does not involve in each event a necessary winner and a loser; if B. fails, he suffers merely the negation of a gain, and A. wins nothing. ^{The consideration.}

The event involved must be uncertain, although it may at the time of contracting be either past or future. ^{The uncertain event.}

G.   B

If it is past in time, then, in so far as it has happened, it is certain, and beyond the control of the parties; but if the result has not been ascertained by the parties, then, *quoad* them, it is uncertain, and as between them can be properly made the subject of a wager (*a*). With regard to future events, their uncertainty is a matter of degree, for whilst, on the one hand, the event is absolutely certain to no one, yet, on the other hand, it may be more or less controllable. An engineer can control the event of whether an engine he is constructing shall be of more or less than two hundred horse-power. A builder has more or less control over the date of the completion of a house which he is building. Such instances are different from those of races, where one competitor can have no honest control over another. When the uncertain event is clearly under the control of one of the parties, it is highly improbable that any contract by those parties in relation to such an event will be a wagering one.

Carlill v. *The Carbolic Smoke Ball Company.*
The essentials of a wagering contract were considered in the recent case of *Carlill* v. *The Carbolic Smoke Ball Company* (*b*). The defendants, who were the proprietors and vendors of a medical preparation called the "Carbolic Smoke Ball," inserted in the newspapers the following advertisement :—"£100 reward will be paid by the Carbolic Smoke Ball Company to any person who contracts the increasing epidemic influenza colds, . . . after having used the ball three times daily for two weeks, according to the printed directions supplied with

(*a*) *Pugh* v. *Jenkins*, 1 Q. B. 631; 1 G. & D. 40; 5 Jur. 1082.
(*b*) *Carlill* v. *The Carbolic Smoke Ball Company*, (1892) 2 Q. B. 484; 61 L. J. Q. B. 696; 56 J. P. 665; affirmed, (1893) 1 Q. B. 256; 62 L. J. Q. B. 257; 4 R. 176; 67 L. T. 837; 41 W. R. 210; 57 J. P. 325.

each ball. . . . During the last epidemic of influenza many thousand carbolic smoke balls were sold as preventatives against this disease, and in no ascertained case was the disease contracted by those using the carbolic smoke ball. . . ." The plaintiff, having read the advertisement, bought, on the faith of it, one of the defendants' carbolic smoke balls, and used it as directed, and, whilst so doing, was attacked by influenza. She thereupon sued to recover the 100*l*. The defendants, amongst other pleas, pleaded that the contract was a wagering one. Hawkins, J., said :—" It is not easy to define with precision what amounts to a wagering contract, nor the narrow line which separates a wagering from an ordinary contract ; but, according to my view, a wagering contract is one by which two persons, professing to hold opposite views touching the issue of a *future* (c) uncertain event, mutually agree that, dependent upon the determination of that event, one shall win from the other, and that other shall pay or hand over to him, a sum of money or other stake, neither of the contracting parties having any other interest in that contract than the sum or stake he will so win or lose, there being no other real consideration for the making of such contract by either of the parties. It is essential to a wagering contract that each party may under it either win or lose, whether he will win or lose being dependent on the issue of the event, and therefore remaining uncertain until that issue is known. If either of the parties may lose but cannot win, it is not a wagering contract." One of the essential elements of a wagering contract was, therefore, in this case absent. The defendants promised to pay the 100*l.* in the event

(c) But see p. 2.

B 2

of the plaintiff contracting the influenza. But if the plaintiff did not contract the disease, the defendants gained nothing, for there was no promise on the plaintiff's part to pay or do anything if the ball had the desired effect. In this judgment it is noticed that in some instances the question of the intention of the parties is at issue, and for a wagering contract both parties must intend to make the gain or loss involved in the second essential characteristic. This element of intention is denoted by the term mutuality, and will be discussed in connection with difference transactions, where it is of much importance.

Non-wagering contracts: i. Warranties and liquidated damages.

Many contracts involving elements of uncertainty are found, when tested by the essential characteristics of a wager, not to be wagering contracts. As ancillary to a contract for sale and purchase, the vendor warrants the article to the purchaser, and agrees with him to pay liquidated damages for a breach of the warranty. An engineer agrees with a mine owner to make an engine for a certain price, with not less than a certain pumping power. If the engine, when made and delivered, shall be of less power, then the engineer agrees to pay the mine owner a fixed sum (——l.) by way of liquidated damages. Here the unascertained event is the power of the engine, and on that event will depend whether or not the engineer will be obliged to pay the mine owner the ——l. The unascertained event is controllable by the engineer, and the transaction involves neither a winner nor a loser. In any event, the mine owner obtains an engine, and pays the agreed price; if the engine is of less power than stipulated for, he is compensated by the liquidated damages; but presumably the engineer has spent less money in making the inefficient engine than he would have done in making an efficient one, and cannot therefore be said to lose by being compelled to make the payment of the ——*l.* Of a similar character are contracts of guarantee. A. en- Contracts of guarantee. gages B. to render personal services of a fiduciary character : C. guarantees A. against loss from the dishonesty of B.; B. may, in the event, prove dishonest, and whether he will or will not is, at the time of making the contract, uncertain. But though C. may lose money by having to make a payment to A. on account of that dishonesty, yet, if B. had continued honest, A. would not have had to pay anything to C.; therefore C. may lose, but he cannot win under his contract with B., and the contract is, of course, no wager. C. may be induced to incur the risk of that contract, because he is morally certain that the risk is, in fact, nothing. On the other hand, if C. and B. are strangers, and C. only enters into the contract of guarantee with A. because B. undertakes to make certain annual payments to C., then certainly C. stands either to win or to lose according to the event; but B. stands to lose his annual payments, but he does not stand to win anything from C. In no event will C. pay anything to B.; his payment to A. will be under his separate contract of guarantee with A., and will not be made as the agent of B. and on behalf of B. The case approximates to, but does not amount to a wager between B. and C.

Again, in contracts for sale and purchase the price ii. Sales conditional as to price. may be made conditional on a future event. For example: A mine owner has a mine of great value, provided that not less than 200 gallons of water per minute are pumped out of it, but worthless if the water is removed at the rate of 190 gallons per minute only; he therefore agrees with an engineer to purchase an engine which, when made, shall be powerful enough to pump and raise 200 gallons of water per minute, and it is made a condition of the contract that if the engine reaches the required standard that the price shall be 1,000*l.*, but if it falls short of the requirements of the mine owner that the price shall be only 5*l.* (*d*). The event whether or not the engine reaches the standard is under the control of the engineer, and the aim of the contract is to minimize the uncertainty. In the one event, the mine owner obtains what he wants, and pays the 1,000*l.*, which presumably is a reasonable price. In the other event, he obtains that which will not make the mine valuable, and pays the 5*l.* as the price. His gain (if any) would depend on a possible re-sale. The engineer's loss (if any) is a result of his own default. Such a transaction would not be a wagering contract.

iii. Speculative sales.

The fact that a contract of sale and purchase is of a highly speculative character, involving elements of future uncertainty, does not make the contract a wagering one. Lord Tenterden, it is true, at a time of grave commercial depression, held, in *Lorimer* v. *Smith* (*e*), that a man could not validly bargain to deliver corn not then in his possession, and rely on making a future purchase in time to fulfil his undertaking; and four years later, in 1826, in the case of *Bryan* v. *Lewis* (*f*), the learned judge laid down the principle, "If a man sells goods to be delivered on a future day, and neither has the goods at the time, nor has entered into any prior contract to buy them, nor has any reasonable expectation of receiving them by consignment, but means to go into the market and to buy the goods

(*d*) *Brogden* v. *Marriott*, 3 Bing. N. C. 88; 2 Scott, 712; 2 Hodges, 136.

(*e*) *Lorimer* v. *Smith*, 1 B. & C. 1; 2 D. & R. 23.

(*f*) *Bryan* v. *Lewis*, Ry. & M. 386.

which he has contracted to deliver, he cannot maintain an action upon such a contract. Such a contract amounts on the part of the vendor to a wager on the price of the commodity, and is attended with the most mischievous consequences."

But in the case of *Hibblewhite* v. *M'Morine* (g) this principle was pleaded by way of defence to a declaration on a contract of sale for future delivery of certain shares. The Court (Parke, B., Alderson, B., Maule, B.) were unanimously of opinion that the principle was justifiable neither in law nor on the grounds of commercial expediency. Parke, B., said :—" Such a contract does not amount to a wager, inasmuch as both the contracting parties are not cognizant of the fact that the goods are not in the vendor's possession "; thereby recognizing that a wager must be a wager on the part of both parties to the contract, or it will not be a wager. In the case of *Martin* v. *Gibbon* (h), where the validity of the sale of prospective dividends was decided on, Bramwell, B., said :—" Of course, a man may sell a prospective dividend, and so fix his uncertainty, and I do not think such transaction is within the Wager Act." And Blackburn, J., said :—" On the other point, that a contract to sell a dividend not declared was a wagering contract, I would say that a contract to pay for all the oil in a whaling ship, although you cannot tell how many whales the ship will bring back, is not wagering." Again, no wager is involved in a contract to sell next year's crop of the apple trees growing in a specified orchard (i). An effective instance of speculative transactions, the enter-

(g) *Hibblewhite* v. *M'Morine*, 5 M. & W. 462 ; 3 Jur. 509.
(h) *Martin* v. *Gibbon*, 33 L. T. N. S. 561 ; 24 W. R. 87.
(i) See *post*, p. 11.

ing into which would commonly be described as
"gambling on the Stock Exchange," is afforded by
the case of *Forget* v. *Ostigny* (*k*), which, on appeal from
a judgment of the Supreme Court of Canada, came
before the Privy Council. The appellant, Mr. Forget,
was a stockbroker at Montreal. During the years
1882, 1883, and 1884, the respondent instructed him
to carry out certain transactions in stocks and shares,
and accordingly the appellant effected certain purchases
and sales in Montreal. After giving credit to the respondent for profit on one transaction, and including
interest and commission in respect of them all, there
was, on June 3rd, 1890, a considerable sum due and
payable to the appellant by the respondent upon the
balance of the account. The respondent had pleaded
that the transactions were not serious ones, but were
fictitious, and in the nature of gambling transactions
upon the rise and fall of stocks; that they were made
upon margin, and without any intention of the real
purchase of the stocks; and that they were therefore
illegal, and could not form the basis of an action.
Herschell, L. C., in delivering the judgment, stated
that it might well be that the appellant was aware that
in directing a purchase to be made the respondent—a
clerk with small means—did not intend to keep the
shares purchased, but to sell them when, as he antici-
pated, they should have risen in value; that his object
was not investment, but speculation. To enter into
such contracts was sometimes spoken of as "gambling
on the Stock Exchange," but it certainly did not follow
that the transactions involved any gaming contract.
A contract could not properly be so described, because

(*k*) *Forget* v. *Ostigny*, (1895) Ap. Cas. 318; 72 L. T. 399; 43
W. R. 509.

it was entered into in furtherance of a speculation. To buy a commodity in the expectation that it will rise in value, and with the intention of realizing a profit by its re-sale, is a legitimate commercial transaction, and one of every-day occurrence. The legal aspect of the case was the same whatever be the nature of the commodity—whether it be a cargo of wheat, or the shares of a joint stock company. Such purchases and sales did not become "gaming contracts" because the person purchasing was not possessed of the money required to pay for his purchases, but obtained the requisite funds in a large measure by means of advances on the security of the stocks or goods he purchased.

Having thus indicated the essentials of a wagering contract, and having in the foregoing instances, by reference to transactions involving future uncertainty, and perhaps highly speculative characteristics, exhibited the absence of those essentials, it now remains to consider instances of wagering contracts. Such instances may conveniently be grouped in connection with three subject matters: first, sports and games; secondly, stocks and shares; thirdly, insurance.

It is hardly necessary to exemplify wagering contracts in connection with horse races and such like sports, and in the course of the book numerous examples will occur. A simple instance would be :—A. backs Tortoise with B. for 100*l.* to win the Derby. B. lays 10 to 1 against him, that is 1,000 to 100. How the event will turn out is uncertain until the race is over. Until then A. may win 1,000*l.* or he may lose 100*l.*; B. may win 100*l.* or he may lose 1,000*l.*: but each must be a winner or a loser on the event. Under the wager neither has any interest except in the money he may win or lose

I. Wagers in sports, &c.

by it (*l*) ; but it would be none the less a wager if B. were the owner of the horse, and by laying against his horse were merely hedging as against his expenses or other wagers. Again, several persons may arrange a horse race on the terms that 50*l.* shall be contributed towards the stakes to be raced for by each person entering a competing horse. Each subscriber under such a contract stands either to lose the portion of the stakes subscribed by him or to win the contributions thereto of the others, according to the happening of the uncertain event (*m*). It is the same where A. and B. agree to walk a match for 200*l.* a-side, and deposit the money with a stakeholder (*n*) ; though, of course, the actual deposit is not essential to the wager. Where, however, the contribution to the stake is made by some person other than a competitor, and such contributor makes a gift, the result to him is the same however the event may happen—in either or any event he is the poorer in so far as he has made the gift; such contribution, then, is clearly distinguishable from the payments of the competitors (*o*).

II. Wagers connected with stocks and shares.

Wagering contracts on the future rise or fall in price of stocks and shares are rarely in such simple form as follows:—A. backs the shares of a certain company

(*l*) *Carlill* v. *The Carbolic Smoke Ball Co.*, (1892) 2 Q. B. 484; 61 L. J. Q. B. 696; 56 J. P. 665; affirmed, (1893) 1 Q. B. 256; 62 L. J. Q. B. 257; 4 R. 176; 67 L. T. 837; 41 W. R. 210; 57 J. P. 325.

(*m*) *Bentinck* v. *Connop*, D. & M. 538; 8 Jur. 336; 5 Q. B. 693; 13 L. J. Q. B. 125; *Varney* v. *Hickman*, 5 D. & L. 364; 17 L. J. C. P. 102; 5 C. B. 271; *Martin* v. *Hewson*, 10 Exch. 737; 24 L. J. Ex. 174; 1 Jur. N. S. 214.

(*n*) *Diggle* v. *Higgs*, 2 Ex. Div. 422; 46 L. J. Ex. 721; 37 L. T. 27; 25 W. R. 777, C. A., reversing, 25 W. R. 607.

(*o*) *Applegarth* v. *Colley*, 12 L. J. Ex. 34; 10 M. & W. 723; 7 Jur. 18.

with B. for 100*l.* that the shares will rise in market
price 10*s.* per share within a fortnight, and B. lays the
odds of 10 to 1 that such a rise will not occur within
the time. More commonly the transaction would be
that A., being of the opinion that certain shares will
rise in price, and B. being of the contrary opinion, A.
promises B. that if the shares (say 1,000) shall have
fallen in price at the end of the fortnight, A. will pay
to B. the amount of the fall; but if the contrary shall
happen, then B. promises that he will pay to A. the
amount of the rise (*p*). Such a contract is a simple
wagering contract both in form and substance. Without
changing the substance of the transaction its form might
be varied as follows:—A. agrees to purchase from B.
the 1,000 shares at the then current price on condition-
that B. shall at the end of a fortnight repurchase from
A. the said shares at the then current price. No real
transfer of the property in the shares is contemplated
by either A. or B.; the contracts for sale and purchase
are purely fictitious (*q*). Such a transaction is known
under the name of a time bargain or difference transaction, and is in its nature a purely wagering contract.
Of the two designations the term "difference transaction" is preferable to that of a "time bargain." For
a speculative sale, such as the next year's crop of the
apple trees growing in a specified orchard, is a time
bargain, as was pointed out by Bramwell, L.J., in
Thacker v. *Hardy* (*r*), but does not, as heretofore seen,

(*p*) See the plea in *Knight* v. *Cambers*, 15 C. B. 562; 3 C. L.
R. 565; 24 L. J. C. P. 121; 1 Jur. N. S. 525.

(*q*) See the plea in *Knight* v. *Fitch*, 3 C. L. R. 567; 24 L. J.
C. P. 122; 1 Jur. N. S. 526; 15 C. B. 566.

(*r*) *Thacker* v. *Hardy*, 4 Q. B. D. 685; 48 L. J. Q. B. 289;
39 L. T. 595; 27 W. R. 158. See Benjamin on Sales, 4th ed.,
p. 526.

amount to a wagering contract. Substituting for the term "time bargain," the term "difference transaction," the same is described by Lindley, J., in the case of *Thacker* v. *Hardy*, as follows :—"But what are called difference transactions are, in fact, the result of two distinct and perfectly legal bargains, namely, first, a bargain to buy and sell ; and, secondly, a subsequent bargain that the first shall not be carried out ; and it is only when the first bargain is entered into upon the understanding that it is not to be carried out, that a difference bargain, in the sense of an unenforceable bargain, is entered into ;" which is to the same effect as the statement by Bramwell, L.J., in the Court of Appeal in the same case: "But if the term *difference transaction* is understood to mean an agreement to pay the difference between the price at the time when the bargain is made and the price at the subsequent time, that agreement is perhaps in the nature of a wager." The only obligation that could arise under a " difference transaction," if the same were enforceable, would be a payment of money from one of the parties to the other. It has been in connection with difference transactions that mutuality has been said to be of the essence of a wagering contract. Suppose that A. has certain shares for sale, and that B. desiring to speculate in those shares, buys them from A. simply with a view to realize a profit. B. may subsequently re-sell those shares, at a profit or loss, either to A. or to some third person. In the case of a re-sale to a third person no question, it is clear, can arise as to a wagering transaction ; and even though the re-sale be to A., yet the fact that B. always intended to deal with these shares in a speculative manner, will not, in the absence of a similar intention on the part of A. (whose original intention in substance and

Difference transaction.

Mutuality.

in fact was to part with his property once and for all, and whose repurchase of the same was an entirely independent action), render the combination of the two contracts impeachable as a difference or wagering contract.

Difference transactions have been before the courts on many occasions, and questions of fact of much nicety arise in connection therewith. In the case of *Grizewood* v. *Blane* (s), Jervis, L. C. J., left the questions of fact to the jury, by directing them to find "what was the plaintiff's intention and what was the defendant's intention at the time of making the contracts, and whether either party really meant to purchase or sell the shares there in question;" telling them that if neither party intended to sell or purchase, the contract was, in his opinion, a gambling transaction. On a motion for a new trial, this direction was upheld. The evidence disclosed the fact that the plaintiff was a stock and share jobber in London; that the defendant, through his broker, contracted to sell and to repurchase the shares mentioned in the declaration; and that there had been former dealings between the parties of the same character, in which there had been no passing of shares, but merely settlements of differences. It was objected, on the part of the defendant, that the contract was a wagering one. The jury, on the facts, found for the defendant. If, however, they had not taken into account the custom which had existed between the parties for a long series of years, and had not gone behind the form of the transaction, viz., a sale for future delivery, followed subsequently by an alleged separate contract for repurchase, their conclusion must have been to the contrary. But in all these cases the

Question for the jury.

(s) *Grizewood* v. *Blane*, 11 C. B. 526; 12 L. J. C. P. 46.

jury must determine the substance of the transaction, and the direction of Jervis, L. C. J., correctly directs their attention to essential questions.

In every case where there is an allegation that the transactions were merely difference transactions, the documentary evidence may, of course, be highly important ; but it is not conclusive, for the documents may be a mere blind. Lord Shand, in his judgment in the case of *Shaw* v. *The Caledonian Railway Company* (t), said :—" That if it appears clearly that the contracts and dealings between the parties were for differences only, and were not intended in any sense to be real transactions, then they must be regarded as gambling transactions, and the Court will not give effect to them. And I may say further, that if it appears that any writings which passed between the parties in the form of sale notes or otherwise were a mere form, intended by both parties to give a colour to the transactions, and to have no legal effect of any kind, then I do not think that writings in such circumstances would take the case out of the rule I have mentioned. Transactions carried through by writings of that kind would be colourable merely, the transactions in themselves being truly for differences, and for nothing else (u). But, on the other hand, I think it appears from the authorities, and on sound principle, that if contracts for the sale of stock, or shares, or goods, as the case may be, are entered into so as to create mutual obligations upon the parties on the one hand to give, and on the other to take, delivery of shares, or stock, or of goods, as the case may be : if

Shaw v. *The Caledonian Railway Company.*

Written documents may be fictitious.

The contract of sale and purchase may be specifically enforceable.

(t) *Shaw* v. *The Caledonian Railway Company*, 17 C. S. C. 466 (4th Series).

(u) *Strachan* v. *Universal Stock Exchange*, 43 W. R. 611; (1895) 2 Q. B. 329.

the obligation is such as can be enforced if either of the parties think fit to do so, then I think we get out of the region of arrangements for mere differences of the nature of betting or gambling. If either one or both parties may, as and when he thinks fit, demand or give delivery of stock, and ask payment of the price under the contract—if that be so as to one of the parties—then I think the transaction has the mark or stamp of a real transaction, and is inconsistent with the notion of a transaction for mere differences. I have said that the writings may not be conclusive upon the matter. For example, if both parties on oath were to admit, and it appeared quite clear upon the evidence, that the writings were a mere blind, and that both parties understood their contract, and were prepared to act upon their contract as one for payment of differences only, then I should be disposed to hold that that was a gambling transaction. But unless the case could be brought up to that, and if it did appear that the contracts·did create obligations which could be enforced, then I think the case would no longer be in the region of a contract for the payment of mere differences, but would be out of the rule as to gambling contracts."

Mr. Rayner, who had entered into the transactions with the pursuer, stated that it never was intended and was no part of his bargain with Shaw that stock should be delivered, and that he had no contract save for the payment of differences. He stated that he looked upon the series of transactions in which he engaged from the autumn of 1886 down to the end of June, 1887, as gambling transactions. On the other side two witnesses were called, who described the particulars of the transactions and the general course of the dealings. In the pursuer's office there was a telegraphic instrument, which

The evidence describing the cover system as worked in a bucket-shop.

ran off a tape which supplied information as to the value
of stocks. With regard to the stocks named, it disclosed
two prices, viz., those at which the dealer on the Stock
Exchange was willing to buy or to sell, the lower being
that at which he was willing to buy, the higher at which
to sell. Shaw, although not a member of the Stock
Exchange, was, like the dealers on the Stock Exchange,
ready to buy at the lower, and to sell at the higher
price appearing on the tape. Mr. Rayner coming in,
judged whether he would purchase or sell certain stocks,
and he bought or sold accordingly. These were, so far
as mere externals were concerned, just ordinary purchases and sales for investment. They were generally
purchases, but sometimes sales, and it appeared that,
unless the stock was carried over to another settling day
to be continued, there was either a re-sale or a re-purchase
of stock, which enabled Mr. Rayner to avoid making
delivery of the stock on the one hand, or taking it on
the other, and he merely met the result by paying or
receiving the differences. Mr. Rayner deposited cover,
the purpose of which was, on the one hand, to put Mr.
Shaw, in dealing with Mr. Rayner, in such a position
that if the stock which had been sold by Rayner rose
in price he was in a position to avoid losing through
Mr. Rayner's inability to fulfil his contract, because he
was entitled, and, indeed, bound under the contract,
immediately to provide stock to meet Mr. Rayner's
obligation. But while the cover operated in the way of
preventing a loss, either by the dealer in the shares, or,
beyond a certain limit, by Mr. Rayner, who had bought
them, on the other hand, if Mr. Rayner's transactions
were turning out favourably, then undoubtedly he was
entitled to hold by his sale or purchase, whichever it
might happen to be. The contracts in every case were

written. There was a slip authorizing the transaction to be entered into, and signed by Mr. Rayner ; and there was, secondly, a bought or sold note, as the case might be, which was issued by the pursuer and received by Mr. Rayner, recording the transaction.

Lord Shand was of opinion that the transactions severally did create obligations. He pointed to two passages in the evidence : " Every transaction between Rayner and the pursuer was accompanied by a contract note, which bound pursuer either to sell or to buy a certain stock, as the case might be ; " and again, " If the stock goes against Rayner, to the extent of the cover specified in the slips, pursuer is authorized by Rayner to make an opposite transaction, so as to allow that transaction to close as far as Rayner is concerned. That does not at all affect the original transaction, namely, that pursuer is obliged to deliver the stock if called upon. So long as a man keeps his stock covered he can always have delivery of it, and he can at any time increase his cover so long as the stock has not been actually closed, and when he takes it up he is given credit for his cover. In a case where Rayner had sold and pursuer bought, if Rayner had come upon the settling day with the stock in his hand, pursuer would have accepted it." Lord Shand concluded therefrom that the transactions did create real obligations to give and to take delivery respectively.

A very similar case to the last mentioned one is also a Scotch case, *Lowenfeld* (*Liquidator of the Universal Stock Exchange Company, Limited*) v. *Howat* (*v*). The Lord President, in the course of his judgment, said : " It is unnecessary to say that the fact that the trans-

(v) *Lowenfeld* (*Liquidator of the Universal Stock Exchange Company, Limited*) v. *Howat*, 17 C. S. C. 128 (4th Series).

actions are evidenced by writing would not at all preclude the possibility of establishing that the writings
are merely simulate, and represent another and totally
different transaction from that which was really entered
into. Our law knows cases of that kind, where writings
are used merely as a cloak, and for collateral purposes,
and where the substance of the transaction is entirely
contrary to what is set out in the writings. But where
writings evidencing a contract are to be so dealt with,
and to be shown not to set forth the truth of the transaction, but to be merely a device, it is necessary that
some very definite and plain evidence should be brought
for that purpose." The bought and sold notes were
similar to those in the last case. Included in the printed
terms of business was the following :—" Every purchase
or sale of stock or shares contracted by the company is
a *baná fide* transaction for delivery, the company always
being prepared to deliver or take up, on the settling day
specified in the contract, any and every stock or share
which it may have bought or sold. Clients may, if it
suits their convenience, repurchase or re-sell to the company, or any other stock dealers, any stocks or shares
which they may have previously bought or sold. The
company shall, however, have no power to compel them
to do so, the company's intention on entering into any
and every transaction being to deliver or take up the
stocks bought or sold by them." The defenders' evidence that there had been an original agreement that
the dealings were to be for differences only did not
suffice, in the presence of the contrary testimony, to
upset the documents (*x*).

(*x*) See also *Universal Stock Exchange (Limited)* v. *Stevens*, 40
W. R. 494 ; 66 L. T. 612 ; *Shaw* v. *Balley*, 24th Jan., Times
Newspaper, 1893.

In the case of *In re Chapple, Ex parte Cochrane and Sons* (*y*), on appeal from the Barnstaple County Court, Vaughan Williams and Wright, JJ., admitted that if one party had a right to call for delivery, the contract would be within the principle which Lord Shand enunciated, and the contract would not be a wagering one. But the Court held in that case that the contract was a composite one, and that its terms were to be gathered, not only from the bought and sold notes, but also from the circular issued by Messrs. Cochrane and Sons. Having regard to the whole of the contract, it was decided that neither party had the right to demand delivery, and that the contract was a mere wagering one.

The same allegation has been raised where the transactions have been conducted on the Stock Exchange. But there the rules of the Stock Exchange, as will ·be seen subsequently in Chapter X., are strongly against the contention that a transaction conducted on the Exchange is a fictitious and not a real sale or purchase. It may be noticed that in *Grizewood* v. *Blane* (*z*) the jury did find, as a fact, that the transactions were mere difference transactions. A new trial, however, may be obtained on the ground that the verdict of the jury was unsatisfactory. In the case of *Cooper* v. *Neil* (*a*), the jury had found that certain contracts entered into by a broker on behalf of the defendant with a jobber were wagering contracts; thereupon the Court of Appeal directed a new trial.

Transactions on the Stock Exchange.

New trial.

(*y*) *In re Chapple, Ex parte Cochrane and Sons*, 9th and 10th Aug. 1895. Leave to appeal was given.

(*z*) *Grizewood* v. *Blane*, 11 C. B. 526; 12 L. J. C. P. 46.

(*a*) *Cooper* v. *Neil*, W. N. (1878) 128.

Reggio v. Stevens & Co.

In the case of *Reggio* v. *Stevens & Co.* (b), the defendants, the outside brokers, had set up the plea of wagering contracts. The jury found for the plaintiff. The defendants sought to set aside the verdict. The Court applied the crucial test : Was there any evidence on which the jury might have found, as a fact, that either party had intended that the shares should be taken up? The plaintiff stated that he had had no intention to take up the stock, and the defendants were positive to the same effect. The Court does not appear to have considered the question whether the plaintiff and the defendants, or either of them, had a right to call for delivery; whether they intended to exercise that right or not being a second question. Evidence that the parties did not intend to exercise the right would tend to establish the conclusion that such right was merely formal, and had not an existence in substance and in fact.

Substance not form in all cases.

Brogden v. Marriott.

It is not only with regard to alleged difference transactions that it has been held that the substance of the transaction must prevail over the form. In *Brogden* v. *Marriott* (c), the form of the transaction was an out and out sale of a horse, but the substance was held to be a wager on a trotting match against time. In this case the defendant agreed to sell his horse Partington to the plaintiff for the sum of 200*l.*, provided that he trotted eighteen miles within one hour; but if the horse failed, then he was thereby sold to plaintiff for the sum of one shilling. The plaintiff obtained a verdict; but the judgment was subsequently arrested. Tindal, C. J., said it would depend on the event of a trotting match

(b) *Reggio* v. *Stevens & Co.*, 4 T. L. R. 326.
(c) *Brogden* v. *Marriott*, 3 Bing. N. C. 88; 2 Scott, 712; 2 Hodges, 136.

against time whether the plaintiff should gain a horse for one shilling, which, according to his own agreement, was worth 200*l.* if he performed the task, and, on the other hand, the defendant's property was staked on the bargain. Park and Vaughan, JJ., concurred, and Gaselee, J., said it was a question for the jury. Here there is an uncertain event, and of a nature uncontrollable by the parties : in the one event, *i. e.*, of the horse failing, the plaintiff stood to win the difference between the fair value of the horse and one shilling, and the defendant stood to lose that amount ; but the difficulty in the case, it is submitted, arises from the fact that it is not stated that 200*l.* was beyond the value of a horse of such trotting power, so that it is not clear that in the other event, *i. e.*, of the horse succeeding, the plaintiff would have lost or the defendant won. This case is in clear contrast to *Crofton* v. *Colgan* (*d*), where the plaintiff sold to the defendant a racing mare for a fixed sum, and also half of whatever she should win within a fixed time. The converse proposition that though the transaction was in form a wager, yet in substance it was a sale, was raised in the case of *Rourke* v. *Short* (*e*). In that case the plaintiff and the defendant held contrary opinions as to the price per cwt. at which the plaintiff had on a previous occasion sold rags to the defendant. The plaintiff asserted that the price had been 5*s.* 9*d.* per 112 lbs., and the defendant asserted that the price had been 6*s.* They agreed that if the plaintiff's assertion should prove correct, then the defendant should pay to the plaintiff the price of one gallon of best brandy, and should also receive from the plaintiff

(*d*) *Crofton* v. *Colgan*, 10 Ir. R. C. L. 133.
(*e*) *Rourke* v. *Short*, 5 E. & B. 904; 25 L. J. Q. B. 196; 2 Jur. N. S. 352.

similar rags at the price of 6s. for every 112 lbs., such
price being more than the real value; and that, on
the contrary, if the defendant's assertion should prove
correct, then the plaintiff should pay to the defendant
the price of one gallon of the best brandy, and should
also sell and deliver to the defendant the goods at
the price of 3s. per 112 lbs., being less than the real
value of the rags. Campbell, C. J., said that on the
terms employed, and not employed merely colourably,
the previous price was the point on which the wager
was to turn, and the stake was the difference in price
now to be paid. Coleridge, J., held that it was merely
a stipulation for the sale and purchase of goods at a
price to be regulated by ascertaining a past event or a
wager on that event. Hence the motion for a new
trial, on the ground that the jury, who had found that
the transaction was a wagering one, had been mis-
directed, was dismissed.

**III. Insur-
ance wagers.** Insurance at one period was made the instrument of
wagering and gambling to an appalling extent. Other
men's lives and property were insured by strangers
to enormous amounts, and insurance, thus abused,
was in danger of becoming, and in fact did develop
into, a public evil. But the history of that phase and
the law of insurance to-day are outside the scope of
this book. At the same time, however, it is pertinent
to illustrate the subject of wagering contracts and their
essentials by reference to the topic.

**Marine and
fire insurances
contracts of
indemnity.** Marine and fire insurances are contracts of indemnity.
The owner of the ship or of the property is liable to
loss by the perils of the sea or by fire, as the case may
be. He indemnifies himself against the happening of
that future uncertain event by insurance, and of such
contract of indemnity the main principle of law is that

thereunder he can only be compensated to the extent of his actual loss. It will therefore be seen that the assured does not gain in the same sense as that in which the winner of a wagering contract does. If there be no interest in respect of which an actual loss could be sustained, then a contract to pay a sum certain of money on the happening of the uncertain event in consideration of the payment of premiums is a simple wager; for the parties thereto stand respectively either to win or to lose according to the happening or non-happening of the event. The law first took cognizance of such wagering contracts after the Revolution; and they were subsequently prohibited by the statute 19 Geo. II. c. 37. An instance of such a wagering policy is found in the case of *Kent* v. *Bird* (*f*), where the contract between the plaintiff and defendant was that the plaintiff gave so much to the defendant in consideration that the ship should save her passage to China; and if not, then upon her returning to England the plaintiff was to receive a much larger sum from the defendant. Lord Mansfield said :—" If the first of these events happened, the defendant won: but he could not lose unless both happened. Is not this gaming? Is not this wagering? If there is no interest, it is gaming and wagering." In the case of *Lowry* v. *Bourdieu* (*g*), the plaintiff had advanced 26,000*l.*, on the security of a common bond, to the captain of a ship. Whilst the ship was on its voyage the plaintiff obtained a policy of insurance underwritten by the defendant. The amount insured for was 26,000*l.* Under the policy it was provided that in case of loss no other proof of interest was to be

(*f*) *Kent* v. *Bird*, Cowper, 583.
(*g*) *Lowry* v. *Bourdieu*, 2 Doug. 468.

required than the exhibition of the bond, warranted free from average, and without benefit of salvage to the insurer. Lord Mansfield said :—" There are two sorts of policies of insurance : mercantile and gaming. The first sort are contracts of indemnity and indemnity only. The second sort may be the same in form, but in them there is no contract of indemnity, because there is no interest on which a loss can accrue. They are mere games of hazard, like the casts of a dice. In the present case the nature of the insurance is known to both parties. The plaintiff says : ' I mean to game, but I give my reasons for it : Captain L. owes me a sum of money, and I want to be secure in case he should not be in a position to pay me.' It was a hedge. But he had no interest, for if the ship had been lost, and the insurer had paid, still the plaintiff would have been entitled to recover the amount of the bond from L. This, then, is a gaming policy."

Life assurance wagers. Life assurance differs from marine and fire insurance in so far as it is not essentially a contract of indemnity. The decision of Lord Ellenborough, holding that life assurance, like every other insurance valid in law, was essentially a contract of indemnity (h), was unanimously overruled in the case of *Dalby* v. *The India and London Life Assurance Company* (i), where Parke, B., said :— " The contract commonly called life assurance is, when properly considered, a mere contract to pay a certain sum of money on the death of a person in consideration of the due payment of a certain annuity for his life, the amount of the annuity being calculated in the first instance according to the probable duration of the life,

(h) *Godsall* v. *Boldero*, 9 East, 72.
(i) *Dalby* v. *The India and London Life Assurance Company*, 15 C. B. 365 ; 3 C. L. R. 361 ; 24 L. J. C. P. 2 ; 18 Jur. 1024.

and when once fixed it is constant and invariable."
The following succinct definition was given by Jessel,
M. R., in *Fryer* v. *Morland* (*j*):—"It is a purchase of
a reversionary sum in consideration of a present payment of money, or, as is generally the case, on the
payment of an annuity during the life of the person
insuring." These two definitions suggest that life
assurance is of the nature of a speculative sale; the
annual payments (an uncertain number) correspond
to the uncertain crop of apples, and the sum to be
paid by the insurer to the price of the crop. But the
analogy would be closer if the insurer paid at once
the agreed price in consideration of the subsequent
payment by the assured during his life of an agreed
annuity. As a matter of fact, the policy of life assurance does not fix an uncertainty as is done in the instance of a speculative sale such as is mentioned by
Blackburn, J., in *Martin* v. *Gibbon* (*k*); the ultimate
payment of the reversionary sum is conditional on the
annual payments by the insured. When a person
insures his own life, in substance he and the insurer
enter into a series of wagering contracts. In each year
the insured lays his annual payment against the amount
assured, minus the premium of the year, that he will
die within the year, and the insurer backs that he will
not so die by the amount assured, minus the premium
of the year, to the annual premium. Sometimes the
uncertain event is not the date of a man's death, but
the contingency of one man surviving another, *c. g.*,
of A. surviving B. If in such an instance A. dies before
B., the insurer will gain the premiums, plus the accre-

(*j*) *Fryer* v. *Morland*, 3 Ch. Div. 675; 45 L. J. Ch. 817;
35 L. T. 458; 25 W. R. 21.
(*k*) *Martin* v. *Gibbon*, 33 L. T. N. S. 561; 24 W. R. 87.

tions of interest, and the insured will lose the same ; or if, on the other hand, A. survive B., then, if at the time of final settlement the said premiums with their interest amount to less than the sum assured, the insurer will lose the difference, and the insured will win the same; whilst, if at final settlement the annual premiums and the interest exceed the amount assured, the insurer will win, and the insured lose. Life assurance, then, is a wagering contract (*l*), or, more accurately, a series of wagering contracts. Since the Gambling Act (14 Geo. III. c. 48), every insurance on lives or other events, unsupported by an interest, is by way of gaming and wagering, and as such is null and void. Where there is an interest, the contract is valid within the meaning of the Act, even though it be, as shown above, a wagering contract inherently. The third section of the Act limits the amount recoverable to the value of the interest of the insured in such life or lives or other event or events. A man, however, may insure his own life for any sum, and the same will be recoverable, because he thereby protects his estate from the loss of his future gains or savings uncertain in amount which might result from his death.

Conclusion. The reader will appreciate the dictum of Mr. Justice Hawkins, that it is not easy to define, with precision, what amounts to a wagering contract, nor the narrow line which separates a wagering from an ordinary contract. The two essentials are the uncertain event, and the certainty for each party of loss or gain, which chance of gain or loss must be respectively contemplated and aimed at by each party to the contract. If, in substance, such elements are present, then, in fact, the contract is a wagering one.

(*l*) See Bunyon on Life Assurance.

CHAPTER II.

AT common law, a wagering agreement was an enforceable contract. The existence of this general rule is emphasized by the exceptions which were made thereto on the grounds of public policy, and by the various statutes which were passed for the purpose of limiting the legality of wagers. The question which came before the Courts for decision in early cases was as to the proper frame and form of an action for the enforcement of a wager, as is exemplified in the following cases:—One Bovey agreed with one Castleman that if the Duke of Savoy made an incursion into the Dauphine within such a time, then Bovey should give Castleman 100*l.*; but if the duke did not, then Castleman was to pay Bovey 100*l.*; in the result Bovey became entitled to the 100*l.* Bovey thereupon sued Castleman, but since he framed his action as follows, *i.e.*, that in consideration that the plaintiff had won 100*l.* of the defendant on a wager, the defendant had promised to pay the 100*l.*, it was held that the action would not lie. A wager would not support an *indebitatus assumpsit*; the only assumpsit that would lie was a special one based upon the mutual promises to pay, so that Bovey might have claimed the 100*l.* from Castleman, pursuant to the latter's promise, in consideration of Bovey's promise to Castleman (*a*).

Wagers valid at common law.

Form of action.

Special assumpsit.

(*a*) *Bovey* v. *Castleman*, 1 Ld. Raymond, 69. See also *Andrews* v. *Hearne*, 1 Lev. 33 ; *Walker* v. *Walker*, 5 Mod. 13.

The action when thus framed clearly shows the consideration moving from the one party to the other.

At a later date, when the Courts were sifting out wagering contracts which were not legal from those that were, many instances occur in which wagering contracts were successfully sued on. In the leading case of *Da Costa* v. *Jones* (b), Lord Mansfield laid down the principle, "Indifferent wagers upon indifferent matters without interest to either of the parties are certainly allowed by the law of this country." A year previously, in the case of *Jones* v. *Randall* (c), where the wager was for 50l. that a decree of the Court of Chancery would be reversed on appeal to the House of Lords, the defendant admitted that the contract was against no positive law, and that no authority could be cited to show that it was illegal. The plaintiff in the last case was interested in the result of the appeal, and the wager being without fraud, upon equal terms, and on a very nice question of law, the plaintiff was held entitled to recover the money he had won. As an instance of a wager in which neither party had an interest, that in the case of *Good* v. *Elliott* (d) may be cited, and it will also serve to illustrate the frivolous nature of the cases brought before the Courts: the defendant wagered the plaintiff the sum of 5l. that Susan Tye had, before the time of the conversation, bought a certain waggon. The action was maintained. In the case of *Hussey* v. *Crickitt* (e), the plaintiff sued the defendant on a wager of a rump and a dozen (that is, a good dinner and plenty of wine for all present), that

(b) *Da Costa* v. *Jones*, 2 Cowp. 729.
(c) *Jones* v. *Randall*, 1 Cowp. 37; Lofft, 383, 428.
(d) *Good* v. *Elliott*, 3 T. R. 693.
(e) *Hussey* v. *Crickitt*, 3 Camp. 168.

the defendant was older than the plaintiff. The defendant was found to be six years older; but although he
had notice of the settlement of the dispute and of the
dinner he did not come; thereupon the plaintiff paid for
the dinner, and sued the defendant for 18*l.* so expended.
The plaintiff showed that the wager was not void for
uncertainty, and supported its morality by a passage
from the Digest (*f*). Thereupon he succeeded. In the
case of *The Earl of March* v. *Pigot* (*g*), a curious point
arose. Two gentlemen at Newmarket agreed to run
their fathers each against the other; one retired, and
the plaintiff took up the wager, which then stood that
the defendant should pay the plaintiff 500 guineas if
the defendant's father died before Sir William Codrington, but if the defendant's father survived Sir
William Codrington, then plaintiff was to pay the defendant 1,600 guineas. As a fact, though unknown to
the parties, the defendant's father was at the time of
the wager actually dead. The plaintiff recovered the
amount of the wager—500 guineas.

The judges from time to time complained strongly *Complaints of the judges.*
of the extent to which wagers were brought before the
courts, as Lord Mansfield did in the case of *Da Costa*
v. *Jones* (*h*). Again, in *Hussey* v. *Crickitt* (*i*), he said,
"While we were occupied with these idle disputes parties
having large debts due to them and questions of great
magnitude to try were grievously delayed," and Cham-
bers, J., in the same case, suggests that it would have
been better if courts of justice had refused altogether

(*f*) Quod in convivio viscendi causa ponitur, in eam rem
familiæ ludere permittitur : Dig. lib. xi. t. v.
(*g*) *March (Earl of)* v. *Pigot*, 5 Burr. 2802.
(*h*) *Da Costa* v. *Jones*, 2 Cowp. 729.
(*i*) *Hussey* v. *Crickitt*, 3 Camp. 168.

to entertain actions upon bets. In *Evans* v. *Jones* (k), it was submitted in argument that there was a class of wagers which a judge might refuse to try on the ground of their being unlawful and improper, and distinguishable from the class, hereafter to be mentioned, of wagers illegal because contrary to public policy. The submission was based on *Thornton* v. *Thackray* (l). But the contention was disapproved of, and it was stated that the judge was bound to try them at some time, though he might postpone them until cases of more importance had been tried.

Exception to general validity at common law.

The general validity under the common law of wagering contracts was limited by a concurrent exception of wide and somewhat indeterminate extent. The basis of that exception is exemplified in Lord Mansfield's judgment in the above cited case of *Da Costa* v. *Jones* (m). The wager was on the sex of Mons. Le Chevallier D'Eon, whereunder the plaintiff was to pay twenty-five guineas down to the defendant, and the defendant was to pay the plaintiff 300*l*., if at any time D'Eon should prove to be a female. Lord Mansfield having stated the general rule, continued: "There must be a variety of instances where the voluntary act of two indifferent parties by laying a wager *shall not be permitted to form a ground of action in a court of justice*. Suppose a wager between two people that one of them or that a third person shall do a criminal act. To go from stronger cases to those that are less strong, 'I lay you a wager you do not beat such a person, you lay that you will.' Such a wager would be *void*, because it is an incitement to a breach of the peace. Suppose the

Tending to a breach of the peace.

(k) *Evans* v. *Jones*, 5 M. & W. 77; 2 H. & H. 67; 3 Jur. 318.
(l) *Thornton* v. *Thackray*, 2 Y. & J. 156.
(m) *Da Costa* v. *Jones*, 2 Cowp. 729.

subject-matter were a violation of chastity or an im- Immorality.
moral action, 'I lay I seduce such a woman.' Would
a court of justice entertain an action upon such a
wager? Most clearly not, because it is an incitement
to immorality. Suppose a wager upon a subject *contra
bonos mores*, as in the case of Sir Charles Sedley:
would a court try a wager that incites to such in-
decency? It may be said *there are no adjudged cases;
but you offend, you misbehave by laying such a wager.*
To come nearer the point, suppose a wager that affects Interests of
the interest or the feelings of a third person, which is third persons.
one of the grounds upon which a motion for a new
trial in this case has been argued. For instance, that
such a woman has committed adultery; would a court
of justice try the adultery in an action upon such a
wager? Or a wager that an unmarried woman has
had a bastard, would you try that? Would it be en-
dured? Most unquestionably it would not, because it
is not only an injury to a third person, but it *disturbs
the peace of society*, and in either of these two last cases,
the party to be affected by it would have a right to say,
How dare you bring my name in question? If a husband complains of adultery he shall be allowed to try it,
because he is a party injured. So if it be necessary to
justice to try whether such an one is a bastard, it shall
be tried. But third persons, merely for the purpose of
laying a wager, shall not then wantonly expose others
to ridicule and libel them under the form of an action."
The wager for the last-mentioned reason was, therefore,
held to be *illegal*, and the action was accordingly dismissed. A wager which is injurious to a third person
will not be enforced, even though the third person
courts the inquiry. In *Ditchburn* v. *Goldsmith* (*n*), the

(*n*) *Ditchburn* v. *Goldsmith*, 4 Camp. 152.

Court held that no action could be maintained upon
the wager whether or not an unmarried woman has
had a child, even though the woman desires inquiry, and
asserts that she is a witch, and that the conception was
immaculate.

The contract in *Eltham* v. *Kingsman* (*o*) affords another
instance of an illegal wager, because it tended to subject
a third person to inconvenience. The plaintiff and
defendant wagered their respective watches that a certain Colonel Longford would go in the plaintiff's *Fly
by Night*, and no other, that evening to the assembly
rooms. The importunities of the proprietors of the
vehicles would be inconvenient to the third party.

Illegal on
grounds of
public policy.
Public policy was frequently a ground for holding
wagers to be illegal. An examination of such cases
exemplifies that as a basis for the decisions public policy
was elastic and uncertain. It was held in *Hartley* v.
Rice (*p*), that a wager of fifty guineas that the plaintiff
would not marry within six years was void, for although
the restraint was partial, yet the immediate tendency of
such a contract, as far as it went, was to discourage
marriage, and no circumstances appeared to show that
in the particular instance the restraint was prudent and
proper. A bet of 5*l*. whether the Canterbury collection
on the hop duties for 1786 would be greater than in
the preceding year was held illegal, on the ground, as
stated by one of the learned judges, that Parliament is
the proper place in which these questions are to be
discussed, and that the same would be improper subject-
matter for discussion elsewhere (*q*). A wager was held
to be void whereunder A. was to pay B. 100 guineas if

(*o*) *Eltham* v. *Kingsman*, 1 B. & Ald. 683.
(*p*) *Hartley* v. *Rice*, 10 East, 22.
(*q*) *Atherfold* v. *Beard*, 2 T. R. 610.

Napoleon Bonaparte died on or before the 31st May, 1802, and if he did not, then B. was to pay A. one guinea for every day he lived. B. paid the money for some considerable time, but at the date of the action brought by A. was in arrear 2,296*l*. Lord Ellenborough, C. J., based his decision on the ground that the tendency of such a wager was towards public mischief and inconvenience (*r*). Again, a wager on the result of a criminal trial was held illegal as tending to interfere with the course of justice (*s*). This last case is distinguishable from *Jones* v. *Randall*, where it was pointed out that the bet was not with anyone who could in any way influence the decision of the House of Lords: *secus*, if a bet were made with an influential member of the Archbishop's Court that "I do not get that bishopric that is now vacant," such a bet would be corrupt. Again, a wager which might tend to impair the fair exercise of the privileges of an elector, and be made an instrument of corruption, was illegal (*t*). In another case, the Court declined to solve a legal conundrum as to whether a person could be lawfully held to bail on a "special original" for a debt under 40*l*., on the ground that the Court was not bound to answer whatever impertinent questions persons might think proper to ask them in the form of a wager (*u*). Yet Lord Holt, on another occasion, with the assistance of the groom porter, decided whether a person playing at backgammon, who had stirred one of his men without

(*r*) *Gilbert* v. *Sykes*, 16 East, 150; cf. *Andrews* v. *Hearne*, 1 Lev. 33, where in a similar wager the objection was not taken.

(*s*) *Evans* v. *Jones*, 5 M. & W. 77; 2 H. & H. 67; 3 Jur. 318.

(*t*) *Allen* v. *Hearn*, 1 T. R. 56.

(*u*) *Henkin* v. *Guerss*, 12 East, 247.

G.   D

moving it from the point, was bound to play it (*x*). The Court held a wager by an attorney's clerk that he would not pass his examination to be unenforceable, on the ground that he could determine the event in his own favour (*y*); but it may be suggested that it was void on the ground of public policy, as tending to hinder the promotion of legal knowledge.

Wagers for excessive amounts. Amongst the cases decided according to the common law, there does not appear to be any in which wagers were held to be contrary to public policy merely because the amounts involved were excessive. There is an authority of Lord Chief Justice Hale's time in which an action on a wager on a foot-race for an excessive amount was not dismissed as unenforceable, but protection was given to the defendant by allowing liberty from time to time to imparl. The defendant was protected because those great wagers proceeded from avarice, and were founded in corruption (*z*).

Games. At common law the playing at any game was lawful and permissible. In the case of *Bell* v. *The Bishop of Norwich* (*a*), the defendant had refused a clerk because he was a haunter of taverns and unlawful games, but a plea stating this ground of refusal was held bad, "because the faults alleged were not evill in their own nature" (*b*). In the case of *Monopolies* (*c*), where the case in Dyer is cited, it is stated—" And the playing at

---

(*x*) *Pope* v. *St. Leger*, 1 Salk. 344. Cf. *Brown* v. *Leeson*, 2 H. Bl. 43.

(*y*) *Fisher* v. *Waltham*, 4 Q. B. 889; D. & M. 142; 12 L. J. Q. B. 330; 7 Jur. 625.

(*z*) Reg. Lib. 1687, A., fol. 219, a case between Sir Charles Bishop and Sir John Staples.

(*a*) *Bell* v. *Bishop of Norwich*, Dyer, Mich. Term, 8 & 9 Eliz., fol. 254 b.

(*b*) Goldsb. p. 35; Mich. Term XXIX. Anno Eliz., case 10.

(*c*) *Monopolies*, 11 Co. Rep. 87 b.

dice and cards is not prohibited by the common law
(unless a man is deceived by false dice and cards, for
then he who is deceived shall have an action on his case
for the deceit) (d), and therefore playing at cards, dice,
&c., is not *malum in se.*"

As any game was permissible at common law, it
would follow that money won at play could be recovered
by action. Thus, in *Sherborn* v. *Colebach* (e), it was
allowed that on a properly constituted action the sum
of 20l. lost by the defendant to the plaintiff at a certain play called hazard, could be recovered. As in the
case of actions on wagers, so in actions for money won
at games, the action had to be framed as a special
assumpsit, and not as an *indebitatus assumpsit* (f) ; as
Holt, C. J. said, in the case of *Smith* v. *Aiery* (g), " No
way in the world to recover money won at play but by
special assumpsit."

The validity of games played for excessive stakes, and Gaming for
the enforcement of obligations arising thereunder, is a excessive
question of some difficulty. There does not appear to
be any old authority to show that the mere excess of
the stakes would make the play illegal : though doubtless the Court would view the matter with abhorrence.
The case of *Bishop* v. *Staples* (h), exemplifies the attitude of the Court towards an excessive wager. In
Eggleton v. *Lewin* (i), it was stated by the judges that

(d) The case of *Holyday* v. *Oxenbridge*, Cr. Chas. 234, cited in
the marginal note (f), is an authority to show that a private
person may arrest a common cheating gambler ("*molliter manus
imposuit*").
(e) *Sherborn* v. *Colebach*, 2 Vent. 175.
(f) *Anonymous*, Salk. 100 ; *Whitgrave* v. *Chancey*, Lut. 100.
(g) *Smith* v. *Aiery*, 6 Mod. 128.
(h) *Bishop* v. *Staples*, Reg. Lib. 1687, A., fol. 219.
(i) *Eggleton* v. *Lewin*, 3 Lev. 118.

they would be cautious of giving encouragement to actions for money won at play " more than needs must." In an instance where an excessive amount had been won fairly at play, it may be surmised that the Court would have given discouragement by granting the defendant liberty from time to time to imparl. But the Court of equity declared that if such discouragement was given at common law, it ought much more to be done in a Court of equity. The question was raised in the case of *Firebrass* v. *Brett* (k). The defendant and Sir William Russell dined with the plaintiff. After dinner the defendant fell into play at hazard with the plaintiff, and won of him about 900*l.*; the plaintiff being somewhat drunk, fetched a further sum of 1,500*l.*, and the defendant won that also. As the defendant was leaving, the plaintiff and his servants seized the 1,500*l.*, but the defendant carried away the 900*l.* The defendant commenced an action at law for trespass against the plaintiff: the plaintiff caused the defendant to be tried on an information for cheating with loaded dice, but on that charge the defendant was acquitted. The plaintiff by his bill asked to be relieved in respect of the 1,500*l.*, and likewise against the action for trespass. On a motion, the Chancellor granted an interim injunction until the trial of the action (l). At the trial the Chancellor stated that he thought it a very exorbitant sum to be lost at play at one sitting between persons of their rank, and that he would discourage as much as in him lay such excessive gaming, and he cited with approval the case of *Staples* v. *Bishop* (m).

(k) *Firebrass* v. *Brett*, 2 Vern. 70.
(l) *Firebrass* v. *Brett*, 1 Vern. 489.
(m) *Staples* v. *Bishop*, Reg. Lib. 1687 A., fol. 219.

This strong expression of opinion led the defendant to accept a compromise, and an order was taken by consent, whereunder the parties respectively retained the 1,500*l.* and the 900*l.* If a game played for an exces- sive stake had been illegal at law or at equity, one would have expected a statement to that effect. In the case of *Woodroffe* v. *Farnham* (*n*), the plaintiff and defen- dant, apprentices within the City of London, played whist, with the result that, at two sittings, the defendant won of the plaintiff about 100*l.* For securing 50*l.*, part of this sum, the plaintiff gave the defendant a bond, against which the plaintiff in his suit sought to be relieved. The Court granted the relief, and affirmed that gaming in all instances ought to be discouraged, and especially amongst apprentices, as it put the master in danger to have his cash wasted, and his shop and house robbed to supply the extravagance of an appren- tice who frequents gaming.

In Bacon's Abridgment, sub-tit. Gaming, the common law is purported to be declared as follows:—" By the common law the playing at cards, dice, &c., when practised innocently and as a recreation, and the better to fit a person for business, is not unlawful, nor punish- able as any offence whatsoever;" but later it is stated " that, from the destructive consequences of excessive gaming, both courts of law and equity have shown abhorrence to it." The accuracy of the first excerpt has recently been questioned by Hawkins, J., in the case of *Jenks* v. *Turpin* (*o*), but the second excerpt is

Bacon's
Abridg.
Gaming.

Jenks v.
Turpin.

(*n*) *Woodroffe* v. *Farnham*, 2 Vern. 290. It appears that the apprentices for playing whist would have been subject to a penalty of 40*s.*, under sect. 16 of 33 Hen. VIII. c. 9; hence the illegality of the bond in the above case.

(*o*) *Jenks* v. *Turpin*, 13 Q. B. D. 505; 53 L. J. M. C. 161; 50 L. T. 808; 49 J. P. 20; 15 Cox, C. C. 486.

supported by the authorities hereinbefore cited. It would appear that the second statement is somewhat destructive of the limitation contained in the first; for, if it be suggested that a lawful game became, when no longer played "innocently as a recreation, the better to fit a person for business," at once unlawful by the common law, one would not expect devices of imparlance, or in a court of equity suggestions that gaming ought to be discouraged. Hawkins, J., states that he does not find the qualification, *when practised innocently and as a recreation, the better to fit a person for business*, recognized in any reported case or in any of the other old text books (*p*).

R. v. Rogier.   In *R.* v. *Rogier* (*q*) there is a dictum of Abbott, C. J., that the playing for large and excessive sums of money would of itself make any game unlawful; but that principle is not supported by any authority, and was enunciated at a time when statutes were in force under which games for excessive stakes were illegal. Smith, J., in the before-mentioned case of *Jenks* v. *Turpin*, approves of the dictum in question, and thinks it still good law, and therefore common sense, even though the statutes against excessive gaming have been repealed. It is, however, submitted that the balance of the authorities is against its validity otherwise than as explained by Hawkins, J. Beyond question, the playing of a game for an excessive stake would be most material evidence to prove the keeping a common gaming house.

Gaming.   Gaming does not consist merely in the playing of a game; it consists essentially in playing a game for money or some other valuable thing. To play dominoes

---

(*p*) *Jenks* v. *Turpin*, 13 Q. B. D. at p. 516.

(*q*) *R.* v. *Rogier*, 1 B. & C. at p. 275; 2 D. & R. 431.

is not to game, but to play it for money is gaming (*r*). Anyone who, in the course of gaming, was guilty of cheating, as, for instance, by playing with false cards, dice, &c., could be indicted for it at common law, and fined and imprisoned according to the circumstances of the case (*s*). At common law an indictable nuisance was constituted by keeping a common gaming house, Common gaming that is to say, a house where a large number of persons houses. are invited habitually to congregate for the purpose of gaming. In Hawkins' Pleas of the Crown, book 1, c. 75, s. 6, it is said :—"There is no doubt but that common bawdy houses are indictable as common nuisances : also it hath been said, that all common stages for rope dancers, and also all common gaming houses, are nuisances in the eye of the law, not only because they are great temptations to idleness, but also because they are apt to draw together great numbers of disorderly persons, which cannot but be very inconvenient to the neighbourhood ; " and in section 7, " a common play house may be a nuisance if it draws together such numbers of coaches or people as prove generally inconvenient to the places adjacent ; " but the learned author then distinguishes " nuisances so occasioned and such nuisances as bawdy houses and common gaming houses," stating that " play houses are not nuisances in their own nature, but may only become such by accident, whereas the others cannot but be nuisances."

Blackstone, in his Commentaries, Book iv., p. 171, in a section on the offence of gaming, advances considerations which, though not therein restricted to gaming houses, give reasons why common gaming houses are

(*r*) *R*. v. *Ashton*, 1 E. & B. 286; 22 L. J. M. C. 1; 17 Jur. 501.
(*s*) 2 Roll. Abridg. 78 ; *Holyday* v. *Oxenbridge*, Cr. Chas. 234.

public nuisances: "Next to that of luxury, naturally follows the offence of gaming, which is generally introduced to supply or retrieve the expenses occasioned by the former; it being a kind of tacit confession that the company engaged therein do in general exceed the bounds of their respective fortunes, and therefore they cast lots to determine upon whom the ruin shall at present fall, that the rest may be saved a little longer. But, taken in any light, it is an offence of the most alarming nature, tending by necessary consequence to promote public idleness, theft, and debauchery among those of the lower class; and among persons of a superior rank it hath been frequently attended with the sudden ruin and desolation of ancient and opulent families, an abandoned prostitution of every principle of honour and virtue, and too often hath ended in self murder. . . . It is the gaming in high life that demands the attention of the magistrate; a passion to which every valuable consideration is made a sacrifice " (t). Again, in Russell on Crimes, vol. i. p. 428, the principle on which a common gaming house is a public nuisance is stated as follows :—" They are detrimental to the public, as they promote cheating and other corrupt practices, and incite to idleness and avaricious ways of gaining property great numbers whose time might otherwise be employed for the good of the community." In *R.* v. *Rogier* (u), the general principle is enunciated that "any practice which has a tendency to injure public morals is a common law offence." It has been held that it is not necessary that the neigh-

(t) Blackstone cites Tacitus, De Mor. Germ. c. 24, and suggests that the tendency to gaming is inherited from those ancestors.

(u) See *ante*, p. 38.

bourhood should be inconvenienced by the drawing together of disorderly persons; without that public annoyance, a house may be still a common gaming house (x) and a public nuisance (y).

The freedom allowed by the common law with regard to wagers, games, and gaming was gradually restricted by a series of statutory enactments, which will form the subject-matter of the next two chapters.

(x) R. v. Rice, L. R. 1 C. C. R. 21; 35 L. J. M. C. 93; 12 Jur.. N. S. 126; 13 L. T. 382; 14 W. R. 56; 10 Cox, C. C. 155; and Hawkins, J., in Jenks v. Turpin, 13 Q. B. D. 505.

(y) Instances of indictments for public nuisances will be found in the following cases :—rope dancing booth at Charing Cross : 1 Mod. 76; 2 Keb. 846; a cock pit: 3 Keb. 464; a play house : 5 Mod. 142; 1 Vent. 169.

CHAPTER III.

GAMES INVOLVING SKILL AND CHANCE.

STATUTORY ENACTMENTS.

Section A.—*The Statute of Hen. VIII.*

Section B.—*Excessive and Deceitful Gaming.*

Section C.—*Horse Racing.*

Section D.—*Cockfighting and other Sports cruel to Animals.*

Section A.—*The Statute of Hen. VIII.*

1541   THE first steps taken by the legislature against gaming were avowedly for the purpose of preventing the subjects from wasting their time over useless games, and, as a consequence, having their attention drawn away from archery. Several statutes having this object in view had been passed previously to 1541, but in that year the 33 Hen. VIII. c. 9, came into force, and repealed all previous enactments, and laid down the law for the future.

33 Hen. VIII. c. 9. Object of.   This Act, which is intituled "An Act for the Maintenance of Artyllarie and debaringe unlawful Games," complained that, owing to the unlawful games and plays which were in vogue all over the kingdom, archery and good shooting were being

grievously injured, and that an Act, which had been passed in a previous year of the same reign (a), was defrauded by subtle, inventative, and crafty persons, who had discovered many and sundry "new and crafty games and plays, such as logitinge in the field, stydethrife, otherwise called shovegrote," and that houses and alleys were kept for their maintenance, with the result that archery was sore decayed, and was likely to become more so still; that the boywers and fletchers had left the kingdom and taught their trade to foreigners, to the great detriment of England; and that the bow-makers had, from want of work, resorted to London, thereby leaving many places in the country unfurnished with anyone to teach their craft. The Act then states that the good archers with which the kingdom had always been provided had acted not only as a defence against foreign enemies, but also had made many places obedient, and that as people were too poor to buy long bows on account of indulging in tennis play, bowles, coysh, and other unlawful games, poverty, murders, and robberies had resulted.

The statute, by section 11, enacts that for the future no one of whatever quality or condition shall by himself, factor, deputy, servant, or other person, for his or their gain, lucre, or living, keep, have, hold, occupy, exercise, or maintain any common house, alley, or place of bowling, coyting, cloysh, cayles, half bowl, tennis, dicing table or carding, or any game prohibited by any previous statute, or any unlawful new game then invented or thereafter to be invented. A penalty was inflicted both on the person keeping such house or alley and on the players. Provisions are then made as to the

Sect. 11. Keeping a place for purposes specified forbidden.

Unlawful new games.

(a) 3 Hen. VIII., made perpetual by 6 Hen. VIII.

granting of licences, and power of search is given to the officers of the shires, cities, and boroughs to enter suspected houses, and, in the event of their finding gaming being carried on, to arrest and imprison both the keepers of the houses and the people found playing.

Restrictions on certain classes of people. The statute then prohibits certain classes of people absolutely from playing at "tables, tennis, dice, cards, bowls, clash-coyting, logatinge, or any other unlawful games," except at Christmas time, and then only in their masters' houses or presence. Bowls are not to be played by anyone in any open place except a private garden or an orchard, and a penalty is imposed on anyone committing any such offence.

1729. Executive powers of last statute extended. In 1729 the 2 Geo. II. c. 28, was passed, which, after reciting that under the previous statute of Hen. VIII. the justices of the peace had not power to take sufficient security from people found playing at games contrary to the provisions of that Act, confers upon them more extended powers.

Résumé of statute. It thus appears that there is nothing in this statute of Hen. VIII. to make any game absolutely unlawful. The statute does no more than to make it unlawful, first, for any person to keep for gain any house for playing at the specified games or new games *ejusdem generis;* and, secondly, for persons to haunt or use such a house. And persons of humble rank were prohibited from playing such games out of Christmas or save with a licence, &c. The games are called unlawful, but the illegality is only conditional (*b*).

(*b*) *Jenks* v. *Turpin*, 13 Q. B. D. 505; 53 L. J. M. C. 161; 50 L. T. 808; 49 J. P. 20; 15 Cox, C. C. 486.

Section B.—*Fraudulent and Excessive Gaming.*

In 1664, an Act intituled "An Act against deceitful, disorderly, and excessive gaming" (16 Car. II. c. 7) was passed. The title suggests the evils to which it was directed, and its policy was to protect the losers against the winners. The preamble recites that, "whereas all lawful games and exercises should not be otherwise used than as innocent and moderate recreations, and not as constant trades or callings to gain a living or make unlawful advantage thereby; and whereas, by the immoderate use of them, many mischiefs and inconveniences do arise, and are daily found to the maintaining and encouraging of sundry idle, loose, and disorderly persons in their dishonest, lewd, and dissolute course of life, and to the circumventing, deceiving, cousining, and debauching of many of the younger sort, both of the nobility, gentry, and others, to the loss of their precious time and the utter ruin of their estates and fortunes, and withdrawing them from noble and laudable exercise and employment." In the first section the common law, under which it was an indictable offence to cheat at gaming, was supplemented, and penalties inflicted. In substance the section is as follows :—If any person shall "by any fraud, shift, cousenage, circumvention, deceit, or unlawful device or ill practice whatsoever, in playing at or with cards, dice, tables, tennis, bowls, skittles, shovel board, or in any cock fightings, horse races, dog matches, foot races, or other pastimes, game, or games whatsoever, or in or by bearing a share or part in the stakes, wagers, or adventures, or in or by betting

[margin notes:] 1664. 16 Car. II. c. 7.

Preamble. Aim of statute.

Sect. 1. Dishonest gaming, &c.

on the sides or hands of such as do or shall play, act, ride, or run as aforesaid," win, obtain, or acquire any money or other valuable thing, he shall for such offence forfeit treble the sum or value of the money or other thing so won, obtained, or acquired. Such forfeit was to be applied as therein mentioned, and if the loser did not within six months from the date of the offence sue for the penalty, then provisions were made for strangers so to sue.

Sect. 3. Honest, but excessive gaming, &c. The third section was directed at excessive and immoderate and not at dishonest gaming, and the mode of restriction adopted was to limit play otherwise than with or for ready money. The section was as follows: —" If any person shall play at any of the said games or any other pastime, game, or games whatsoever (other than with or for ready money), or shall bet on the sides or hands of such as do or shall play thereat, and shall lose any sum or sums of money, or other thing or things so played for, exceeding the sum of 100*l.* at any one time or meeting upon ticket or credit or otherwise, and shall not pay down the same at the time when he or they shall lose the same, the party or parties who loseth or shall lose the said moneys or other thing or things so played or to be played for above the said sum of 100*l.*, shall not in that case be bound or compelled or com-

Where limit exceeded the contract and securities, both void. pellable to pay or make good the same ; *but the contract and contracts for the same and for every part thereof, and all and singular judgments, statutes, recognizances, mortgages, conveyances, assurances, bonds, bills, specialties, promises, covenants, agreements, and other acts, deeds, and securities whatsoever, which shall be obtained, made, given, acknowledged, or entered into for security or satisfaction of or for the same or any part thereof, shall be utterly void* *and of no effect;* and that the person or persons so winning the said moneys or other things shall forfeit and lose treble the value of all such sum or sums of money which he shall so win, gain, obtain, or acquire above the said sum of 100*l.*" The remainder of the section dealt with the application and recovery of the penalties.

In 1710 a further statute was passed, having the same policy in view, but much more drastic in its measures. 9 Ann. c. 14, was entitled, "An Act for the better preventing excessive and deceitful gaming," and after reciting that the laws in force were insufficient to prevent the mischiefs which happen by gaming, it went on to enact, "that all notes, bills, bonds, judgments, mortgages, or other securities or conveyances whatsoever given, granted, drawn, or entered into or executed by any person or persons whatsoever, where the whole or part of the consideration of such conveyances or securities shall be for any money or other valuable thing whatsoever *won by gaming or playing at cards, dice-tables, tennis, bowles, or other game or games whatsoever, or by betting on the sides or hands of such as do game at any of the games aforesaid, or for the reimbursing or repaying any money knowingly lent or advanced for such gaming or betting as aforesaid, or lent or advanced at the time and place of such play* to any person or persons so gaming or betting as aforesaid, or that shall during such play so play or bet, *shall be utterly void, frustrate, and of none effect to all intents and purposes whatsoever.*" The statute then particularizes, and enacts, though the provisions have since been entirely repealed (*c*), that " where such mortgages, securities, or other convey-

1710.

9 Ann. c. 14. Extending the policy of the statute of Charles II.

Avoidance of securities.

(c) 5 & 6 Will. IV. c. 41.

ances shall be of lands, tenements, or hereditaments, or shall be such as encumber or affect the same, such mortgages, securities, or other conveyances shall endure and be to and for the sole use and benefit of, and shall devolve on such person or persons as should or might have or be entitled to such lands, tenements, or hereditaments in case the said grantees or grantors thereof, or other person or persons so encumbering the same, had been naturally dead, and as if such mortgages, securities, or other conveyances had been made to such person or persons so to be entitled after the decease of the person or persons so encumbering the same, and that all grants or conveyances to be made for the preventing of such lands, tenements, or hereditaments from coming to or devolving upon such person or persons hereby intended to enjoy the same as aforesaid shall be deemed fraudulent and void, and of none effect to all intents and purposes whatsoever." Having thus dealt with securities, the statute next lowers the limit of the amount of money that might be lawfully won

Excessive play.

or lost: "Any person or persons whatsoever who shall at any one time or sitting by playing at cards, dice-tables, or other game or games whatsoever, or by betting on the sides or hands of such as do play at any of the games aforesaid, lose to any one or more person or persons so playing or betting in the whole

Limit lowered.

the sum or value of 10*l.*, and shall pay or deliver the same or any part thereof to the person or persons so losing and paying or delivering the same, shall be at liberty within three calendar months then next to sue for and recover the money or goods so lost and paid or delivered, or any part thereof, from the respective winner or winners thereof."

To win at any game by fair play more than 10*l.* from any one or more persons at any one time or sitting was forbidden. As it had thus become an offence to win more than 10*l.* at one time, it follows that the loser was *particeps criminis*, but the section last quoted enabled him, nevertheless, to recover his money. After this statute came into force, a person might at one sitting or time win up to the value of 10*l.* either by gaming or betting on the hands of the players, and recover by action, but the first section renders all securities for such transactions void; hence the curious result that whilst a legal obligation to pay 10*l.* might exist, yet any security, real or personal, or any conveyance executed in consideration of such obligation was void to all intents and purposes. The statute next orders that every person sued shall be compellable to answer upon oath any bill that shall be proffered against him for discovering the sum of money or other thing so won at play, and provides that on discovery and repayment he shall be acquitted, and discharged from any other punishment.

Under the limit the contract not avoided.

The statute also deals with fraudulent gaming, and enacts that if anyone "shall by any fraud or shift, cousenage, circumvention, deceipt, or unlawful device or ill practice whatsoever, in playing at or with cards, dice, or any of the games aforesaid," or by taking any part therein, obtain any sum or valuable thing, or " shall at any one time or sitting win of any one or more persons whatsoever above the sum or value of 10*l.*, that then every person so winning by such ill practice, and being convicted of any of the said offences, upon an indictment or information to be exhibited against him or them for that purpose, shall forfeit five times the value

Fraudulent gaming.

of the sum or sums of money or other thing so won as
aforesaid, and in case of such ill practice as aforesaid
shall be deemed infamous, and suffer such corporal
punishment as in cases of wilful perjury, and such
penalty to be recovered by such person or persons as
shall sue for the same by such action as aforesaid."

Living by gambling. The Act further states that divers lewd and dissolute
persons live by carrying on gaming, and to prevent this
the justices of the peace are authorized to have brought
before them every person whom they shall have just
cause to suspect to have no visible estate, and if such
person shall fail to make it appear that the principal
part of their expenses is not maintained by gambling,
the justices shall require of them sufficient securities for
their good behaviour for twelve months, and, in default
of their finding such securities, the justices are to
commit them to prison until they shall find such securities. And if the persons so finding securities shall,
during such time as they continue bound, at any one
time play or bet for any sum exceeding 20s., such play
shall be taken to be a breach of their behaviour, and
their recognizances shall be forfeited.

Quarrels at gaming, &c. The statute to prevent quarrelling enacts that if anyone shall assault or provoke anyone to fight on account
of money won at gaming or betting, such person, upon
being convicted, shall forfeit to the crown all his goods
and chattels and personal estate, and shall also suffer
imprisonment for two years without bail or mainprize.

Transactions within the two last-mentioned acts. It will have been noticed that the two statutes relate
solely to games, sports, and other pastimes. The earlier
statute makes an explicit enumeration of the games and
Games, sports, pastimes. sports concerning which it was passed—playing at or
with cards, dice, tables, tennis, bowls, skittles, shovel

board, or in any cock fightings, horse races, dog matches, foot races, or other pastime, game, or games whatsoever; and although the Statute of Anne only speaks of "any game whatsoever," it was expressed in its preamble to be an extension of the earlier statute, so there can be no doubt but that the subject matter of the latter Act is as inclusive as that of the earlier one. Thus, in *Goodburn* v. *Marley* (d), it was held that a horse race, though not explicitly mentioned in the Statute of Anne, came within its operation. In *Jeffreys* v. *Walker* (e), it was admitted that a match between certain persons who styled themselves "the County of Kent" against certain other persons who styled themselves "all England" at a certain game called cricket was within the statute. In the case of *Lynall* v. *Longbotham* (f), it was held that a foot race, even by one man running by himself against time in the way of play, was within the latter statute. For "there is no doubt that horse races are within the statute of Anne according to *Goodburn* v. *Marley* (d), and foot races must be also, for they are mentioned in 16 Car. II. c. 7, to which statute the later statute must relate." That horse races were within the statute of Anne is seen also by reference to *Clayton* v. *Jennings* (g), *Blaxton* v. *Pye* (h), *Brown* v. *Berkeley* (i), *Applegarth* v. *Colley* (k).

Only such bets as were made on the sides or hands Wagering on

(d) *Goodburn* v. *Marley*, 2 Strang. 1159.
(e) *Jeffreys* v. *Walker*, 1 Wils. 220.
(f) *Lynall* v. *Longbotham*, 2 Wils. 36.
(g) *Clayton* v. *Jennings*, 2 Bl. 706.
(h) *Blaxton* v. *Pye*, 2 Wils. 309.
(i) *Brown* v. *Berkeley*, 1 Cowp. 281.
(k) *Applegarth* v. *Colley*, 10 M. & W. 723; 12 L. J. Ex. 34; 7 Jur. 18.

E 2

the sides or hands, &c.

of such as do or shall play were effected by the statute. Thus in *Lynall* v. *Longbotham* (*l*), in defence to an action to recover money lost on a bet, it was declared that the money was lost by betting on the side of one J. C. at a certain game called a foot race; but the plaintiff failed on the ground that it was not stated in the decla-' ration, nor stated in the case, that J. C. was playing at a game called a foot race. Such a strict construction of the Act was necessitated by the fact that the statute was not remedial, but penal. But when there is play, then the bet, to be within the statutes, must be on the chance of the play, and not on anything collateral thereto, such as on the proper rules of the game. Thus, a bet for 100 guineas made by players at backgammon on a point as to the proper mode of playing the game was held to be enforceable (*m*). Again, in *Pugh* v. *Jenkins* (*n*), a wager pursuant to which the plaintiff was to pay the defendant 1*l*., or the defendant was to pay the plaintiff 50*l*., according to the success or failure of a certain horse in the Derby on the previous day, was enforced on the ground that it was a wager on the accuracy of information relating to the race, and not on the event of the game.

As to the limits.

When the game or wager was within the statute, the question of exceeding the statutory limit would next arise. Numerous cases were decided on the point as to what constituted one time or sitting (*o*), but under the

(*l*) *Lynall* v. *Longbotham*, 2 Wils. 36.

(*m*) *Pope* v. *St. Leger*, 1 Salk. 344; but cf. *Brown* v. *Leeson*, 2 H. Bl. 43.

(*n*) *Pugh* v. *Jenkins*, 1 Q. B. 631; 1 G. & D. 40; 5 Jur. 1082.

(*o*) *Edgebury* v. *Rosindale*, 2 Lev. 94; Vent. 253; *Hudson* v. *Malin*, 1 Freem. 432; 3 Keb. 671; *Hill* v. *Pheasant*, 2 Mod.

present state of the law these cases have no direct importance, though anyone curious to see how such a limitation works may consult them. It was not necessary for the money all to be lost to one man. The limit might be exceeded where more than the 100*l.* or the 10*l.* was lost to different people (*p*). In considering whether a wager exceeded the limit, it was sufficient, in order to maintain the affirmative, to prove that one party only stood thereunder to win or lose 10*l.* or more than that sum. Thus, in *Blaxton* v. *Pye* (*q*), the plaintiff sued the defendant for the sum of eight guineas, won on a wager by the plaintiff from the defendant; but seeing that if the defendant had won he would have been unable to recover the fourteen guineas to which amount he would then have been entitled, it was held that the plaintiff could not recover the eight. The same point was decided in the same way in the case of *Clayton* v. *Jennings* (*r*).

Where neither party to the wager stood to win or lose 10*l.*, or more than 10*l.*, the wager was enforceable, even though made on the hands or sides of persons playing at a game, sport, pastime, or exercise within the statute (*s*). *Wagers valid under the statute.*

There is a curious and, perhaps, intentional omission in the statute of Anne in relation to money knowingly lent or advanced for gaming or betting. The statute does not avoid the contract of loan, but it does avoid any and every security taken for the carrying out of *Money lent.*

541; 1 Freem. 200; *Danvers* v. *Thistlethwayte*, 1 Lev. 244; *Dickson* v. *Pawlet*, 1 Salk. 344; *Bones* v. *Booth*, 2 Bl. 1225.

(*p*) *Noell* v. *Reynolds*, 2 Show. 467.

(*q*) *Blaxton* v. *Pye*, 2 Wils. 309.

(*r*) *Clayton* v. *Jennings*, 2 Bl. 706.

(*s*) *M'Allester* v. *Haden*, 2 Camp. 438; *Bulling* v. *Frost*, 1 Esp. Cas. 235.

the obligation thereunder arising. In the case of *Barjeau* v. *Walmsley* (*t*), money lent for gaming without security was held to be recoverable as a loan. "The Parliament might think there would be no great harm in a parol contract where the credit was not like to run very high." In the case of *Robinson* v. *Bland* (*u*), the validity of the contract of loan and the invalidity of a bill of exchange given as security are strongly contrasted. The following were the facts:— The plaintiff lent Sir J. Bland the sum of 300*l.* at the time and place of play, and at the same time and place Sir J. Bland lost to the plaintiff a further sum of 372*l.* Thereupon Sir J. Bland drew a bill of exchange in favour of the plaintiff for 672*l.* It was held, first, that the bill of exchange was void, being indivisible, and in part to secure the payment of 372*l.* won at play; secondly, that, apart from the bill, the transaction was divisible, and that the money won was irrecoverable, but that the 300*l.* so lent as stated could be recovered. In neither of the last two cases was there any suggestion that the play was illegal, and the point does not seem to have been taken that the loans in question may have been tainted with the illegality arising from the winning or losing of more than 10*l.* at any game within the statute (*x*). However, in the case of *Young* v. *Moore* (*y*), where the plaintiff had won of the defendant the sum of 47*l.* at divers games of bragg and toss up, it was stated by the court that, "as the statute hath made

---

(*t*) *Barjeau* v. *Walmsley*, 2 Strang. 1248.

(*u*) *Robinson* v. *Bland*, 2 Burr. 1077. See also *Wettenhall* v. *Wood*, 1 Esp. 17.

(*x*) As to civil obligations connected with illegal transactions, see *post*, Chap. VI.

(*y*) *Young* v. *Moore*, 2 Wils. 67.

all securities for money won at play void, *à fortiori* all parol contracts of this sort are void." *Of this sort*, because on the affidavits it appeared that the lawful limit had been exceeded. In that case the contract itself was illegal.

If the money be lent for the purpose of paying a debt already incurred at gaming, but be not advanced at the time and place of such gaming, then such a loan does not come within the mischief of the words, "money knowingly lent or advanced for gaming or betting." Thus, in *Alcinbrook* v. *Hall* (*z*), the defendant lost a sum of money of more than 10*l.* on a bet on a horse race, and requested the plaintiff to pay the money for him. The plaintiff discharged the defendant's debt of honour, and subsequently upon an assumpsit recovered from the defendant the money so paid at his request (*a*). The decision in the case of *Ex parte Pyke* (*b*) demonstrates that a security taken for the money so advanced to or paid at the request of the loser would not have been within the Act.

Money lent to discharge a debt already incurred.

The policy of fixing a limit was affirmed in the statute of the 18th of Geo. II. c. 34, intituled, "An Act to explain, amend, and make more effectual the laws in being to prevent excessive and deceitful gaming . . . ." Under this statute, anyone who won or lost at play, or by betting, at any one time, the sum or value of 10*l.*, or within the space of twenty-four hours the sum or value of 20*l.*, was liable to indictment.

18 Geo. II. c. 34. Policy of fixing a limit affirmed.

(*z*) *Alcinbrook* v. *Hall*, 2 Wils. 309.

(*a*) See now Gaming Act, 1892, *post*, Chap. IX.

(*b*) *Ex parte Pyke*, 8 Ch. Div. 754; 47 L. J. Bk. 100; 38 L. T. 923; 26 W. R. 806.

But aban-
doned in 1845.

The policy of fixing a limit has been abandoned since 1845. The foregoing pages will exhibit that phase of the legislation. But their importance lies not only in that exhibition, but in the fact that on those statutes was based the subsequent Act of 5 & 6 Will. IV. c. 41, relating to securities. On the whole, it is found more convenient to treat of the law relating to securities in a separate chapter.

Section C.—*Horse Racing.*

Horse racing has been the subject of a long series of statutory restrictions, which now, however, have been entirely done away with. The only enactment affecting it at the present time is 42 & 43 Vict. c. 18, which requires that a licence shall be taken out to hold races in, and within a ten-mile radius of London.

History of the
statutes.

It will be remembered that section B. of this chapter, when dealing with the statute 16 Car. II. c. 7, showed that gaming on horse races was within the statute, and also within the restrictions of 9 Anne, c. 14. Neither of these statutes affected horse racing *per se*, or made it in any way illegal, their object being to prevent or curtail gambling. The result of the smallness of the 10*l.* limit imposed by the statute of Anne was that people, in order to keep themselves within the law, held numerous races for stakes below 10*l.*, with the further result of deteriorating the breed of horses, so that in 1740 the statute of 13 Geo. II. c. 19, was passed, which recites in the preamble as follows:—That the great number of horse races for small plates, prizes, or sums of money had contributed very much to the encouragement of idleness, to the impoverishment of many of the meaner sort of the subjects of the kingdom, and that

the breed of strong and useful horses had been much
prejudiced thereby. Sect. 1 enacts, that no one except
the true and *bonâ fide* owner shall enter, start, or run any
horse, mare, or gelding for any plate, prize, sum of
money, or other thing, and that no one shall enter more
than one horse, mare, or gelding for the same race, and
that if anyone not being the owner enters or runs a
horse he shall be liable to forfeit the horse or the value
thereof, and that anyone entering more than one horse
for the same race shall forfeit every horse other than
the first entered, or its or their value. Sect. 2 enacts,
that no race shall be run unless the full, real, and
intrinsic value of the prize shall be 50*l*. or upwards, and
imposes a penalty on anyone entering, starting, or
running any horse for a less sum, and further prohibits anyone from advertising, publishing, or pro-
claiming any race for a less sum than 50*l*., under a
penalty.

Section 3 directs that horses of five years old are to
carry ten stone weight; of six years old eleven stone;
and seven years old twelve stone; and horses carrying
less weight are to be forfeited, and the persons entering them are to pay a penalty. Every race must
be begun and ended in the same day. By section 4
an exception is made for matches held at Newmarket
and Blackhambleton, where the sum or value might be
less than 50*l*. The statute goes on to deal with the
application of the penalties, and makes provisions for
the horse coming in second to receive the entrance
money in a race for a plate or prize, and enacts that
gifts left for annual races are not to be altered. With
the one exception, that by 18 Geo. II. c. 34, s. 11, the
provisions of this statute with regard to the weights to
be carried by horses was repealed, it remained in force

till 1840, in which year 3 & 4 Vict. c. 5, was passed,
which repealed 13 Geo. II. c. 19, and removed the
restriction on horse-racing. In the case of *Evans* v.
Pratt (c), it was agreed between the plaintiff and defendant that they should each race a mare across a
country for four miles, and if the plaintiff's mare won
the defendant should pay the plaintiff 100*l.*, but if the
defendant's mare won the plaintiff should pay the defendant 25*l.*, and they appointed an umpire. The race
was run, and the umpire gave his decision in favour of
the plaintiff, but the defendant refused to pay the 100*l.*,
and on his behalf it was contended that the race was
not a *bonâ fide* horse race, run upon a race course, but
that it was a steeple-chase across country, and, as such
therefore, it did not come within the horse racing practised under and according to the statute, Maule, J., held
that 18 Geo. II. c. 34, relieved the parties not only
from the penalties imposed by 13 Geo. II. but also
from any illegality imposed by the former statutes . . .
and stated that the object of the legislature throughout these enactments has been to encourage the production of a strong and powerful breed of horses; and
that such a cross-country steeplechase as this was a race
calculated to further that object.

By 8 & 9 Vict. c. 109, s. 15, the Act of 16 Car. II.
c. 7, was repealed, and also so much of 9 Anne, c. 14,
as had not already been repealed by 5 & 6 Will. IV.
c. 41, and also as much of 18 Geo. II. c. 34, as related
to the Act of Anne.

The Act now in force, 42 & 43 Vict. c. 18.   In 1879, the 42 & 43 Vict. c. 18, was passed, which
is entitled an "Act for Licensing the Metropolitan

(c) *Evans* v. *Pratt*, 3 M. & Gr. 759; 4 Scott, N. R. 378; 1
D. N. S. 505; 6 Jur. 152.

Suburban Race Courses," which after reciting that annoyance and injury are caused by races being held in thickly populated places, defines a horse race as a competition of one horse against any other horse or against time, for any prize or for any bet to be made in respect of such horse, and at which more than twenty persons shall be present. This statute enacts that it shall be unlawful for any race to be held within a radius of ten miles from Charing Cross, unless in a place where a licence for horse racing has been obtained pursuant to the provisions of the Act. Such licence can be obtained from the local justices assembled at any Michaelmas Quarter Sessions of the peace. The justices are empowered at their discretion to grant or withhold the licence. When granted such licence is valid for twelve months dating from the 25th day of March next following the date of application.

As to licensing race courses within ten miles of Charing Cross.

Section 5 imposes a penalty of 10*l.* or an imprisonment not exceeding two months on any person who takes part in any horse race in any unlicensed place, and (section 6) everyone, who being the owner or lessee or in possession of any place allows racing without a licence is rendered guilty of a misdemeanor, and on conviction is punishable by a fine of not less than 5*l.* nor more than 25*l.*, or by imprisonment of not less than one nor more than three months. Horse races taking place in contravention of the provisions of this Act are to be deemed a nuisance. It will thus be seen that with the exception of the restrictions on holding races in and near London horseracing is, at the present time, a perfectly legal sport or pastime, and in no way restricted by any statute.

Section D.—*Cock Fighting and other Sports cruel to*
Animals.

The reader is referred to Brandt on Gaming, Chapters
XVII. and XVIII., for an historical account of the
various cruel sports and pastimes. These pastimes are
now under statutory prohibitions, and are condemned
by reason of their intrinsic cruelty.

It would appear that from time to time Royal Pro-
clamations denounced these exhibitions as " idle and
unlawful," " dishonest, trivial, and useless," and Lord
Ellenborough, in *Squiers* v. *Whisken* (d), described cock
fighting as " a barbarous diversion, which ought not to
be encouraged or sanctioned in a court of justice." But
the question of the illegality at common law of these
pastimes, or at least of cock fighting, would present
some difficulty if it were of sufficient importance to in-
vestigate. In the case of *R.* v. *Howel* (e), the defendant,
on an indictment at common law, was fined 12*l.* for
keeping a common cockpit for six days : the Court held
it an offence at common law to keep a cockpit, and
measured the penalty by the 33 Hen. VIII. c. 9.

In the case of *Squiers* v. *Whisken* (d), it was admitted
that there was no statutory prohibition in respect of
cock fighting, and none was enacted until shortly before
the commencement of the present reign.

The statute 5 & 6 Will. 4, by sect. 3, inflicted a
penalty not to exceed 5*l.* in all, or to be less than ten
shillings for each day, on any one who should keep or
use any place for the purpose of cock fighting and other
sports cruel to animals, and by the Metropolitan Police

(d) *Squiers* v. *Whisken*, 3 Camp. 140.
(e) *R.* v. *Howel*, 3 Keb. 465—510.

Act of 1839 (g), in addition to the above-mentioned penalty, a power to search suspected places was given to the police, and persons found therein were subjected to a fine of five shillings. By 12 & 13 Vict. c. 92, s. 3, the first-mentioned statute was repealed, and the penalty for keeping or using any place for the purpose of cock fighting was increased to 5l. for each day, and persons found encouraging, aiding, or assisting were likewise to be fined 5l.

(g) 2 & 3 Vict. c. 47, s. 47.

CHAPTER IV.

GAMES OF CHANCE—STATUTORY ENACTMENTS.

This chapter is concerned, almost exclusively, with lotteries, and with the long series of statutory enactments by which this species of gambling was gradually restricted. Other games of pure chance, as will hereafter be seen, were also dealt with incidentally in some of the Acts. The early history of the statutes is much involved in the fact that public lotteries were, until 1823, a recognised means of raising the revenue. No stronger economic condemnation of such a policy is to be found than the fact that it resulted in developing a public and widespread passion for that form of gambling. This evil existed as long as there were state lotteries, and the various statutes enacted for the purpose of abating the nuisance were found to be unsuccessful. Hence Blackstone was of opinion that the series of statutes exemplified the truth, "that the invention of sharpers is swifter than the punishments of the law, which only hunts them from one device to another." Lotteries may be said practically to have died with the abolition of the public lotteries, and from that time forward the repressive statutes have proved to be adequate.

1699.
The series of
Lottery Acts.
Prior to this date three kinds of lotteries had established themselves in the kingdom. (1.) The public lotteries, to which reference has already been made.

(2.) Lotteries held under patents or grants issued under the great seal of England. (3.) Lotteries held, both publicly and privately, without any authority whatever. An attempt was made to deal with the second and third of these three classes of evils by stat. 10 & 11 Will. III. c. 17, entitled " An Act for Suppressing Lotteries," the preamble of which sets out that such mischievous games had worked to the utter ruin and impoverishment of many families, and to the reproach of the English laws, so that " several evil-disposed persons had thereby most unjustly and fraudulently got to themselves great sums of money from children and servants and other unwary persons." It was, therefore, enacted that such lotteries under the colour of letters patent or grants or other lotteries are common and public nuisances, and that all grants, patents, and licences for such lotteries, or any other lottery, are void and against law. It was further made an offence for any person, either publicly or privately, to exercise, keep open, show, or expose to be played at, drawn at, or thrown at, any such lottery, either by dice, lots, cards, balls, or any other numbers or figures, or in any way whatsoever. The penalty for every such offence was fixed at 500*l.*, and everyone was forbidden to draw, throw, or play at any such lottery or any other lottery.

It would appear, however, that so far as the third class of lotteries was concerned, the statute was imperfectly operative, for we find it stated in a statute of 9 Anne, c. 6, that several persons had set up lotteries in imitation of the public lotteries, to the prejudice of the public and to the defrauding of her Majesty's subjects. By the 66th section of this statute the authorities were accordingly required to use their utmost endeavours to enforce the afore-mentioned Act, and it was further

1710.

enacted by the 67th section that it should be an offence
to set up, or by writing or printing to publish the setting
up of, any such unlawful lottery, with intent to have
such lottery drawn.

That these prohibitions were still evaded is shown by
1711. a statute of the following year (10 Anne, c. 26), which,
after reciting the two last-mentioned Acts, goes on to
state that many ill-disposed persons had set up offices
under the denomination of sales of gloves, fans, of cards,
of numbers, and of the Queen's picture, for the improvement of small sums of money, and that advertisements
thereof were daily published in the common printed
newspapers or otherwise. Any such formal disguise of
the real substance of the lottery was then rendered ineffectual by the 108th section of the statute, which
enacts that any person so guilty, or guilty of setting
up, &c., any like office or place under the pretence of
improving small sums of money, should forfeit for every
such offence the sum of 500l., and it was further made
an offence to publish by writing or printing any such
office or place.

1718. But the evasion of the statutes still continued. Thus,
in sect. 43 of 5 Geo. I. c. 10, it is stated that, notwithstanding previous enactments, several persons had
given public notice for taking subscriptions for the sale
of chances, or parts of chances, to arise in the tickets of
a public lottery, not being possessed of the tickets on
which such chances are proposed to be sold, and thereby
had erected another lottery, and had entered into an
undertaking resembling a lottery for their private benefit.
The section then lays down enactments for the suppression of such abuses.

It was not long, however, before it was discovered
that an office for the sale of houses, lands, advowsons,

presentations to livings, plate, jewels, ships, goods, and other things for the improvement of small sums of money, was not within the statute of 1711, and that, whilst the statute of 1718 undoubtedly prohibited the sale of chances on tickets in a public lottery, not actually in possession of the vendor, yet schemes or proposals for advancing small sums of money by several persons, amounting in the whole to large sums to be divided between them by chances of the prizes in a public lottery, could very easily be worked. Sect. 36 of statute 8 Geo. I. c. 2, was accordingly enacted to remedy these new evils.

1721.

Having, by the foregoing statute, endeavoured to suppress English lotteries, the legislature now found that, in order to elude these enactments, lotteries, or undertakings in the nature of lotteries, under the pretence of some grant or authority of foreign princes or states, were being carried on in this country. The statute 9 Geo. I. c. 19 was accordingly passed (a), whereby it was made an offence for any person, under the pretence aforesaid, to erect, set up, continue, or keep any lottery, or undertaking in the nature of a lottery, under any denomination whatsoever, or to make, print, or publish any proposal or scheme for such a transaction, or within the kingdom to sell or dispose of any ticket in any foreign lottery (b).

1722.

By this time it was evident that the statutes hitherto passed were inadequate for the attainment of their object. It was found that deceitful games and subscriptions were still daily carried on under the denomi-

(a) See also *MacNee* v. *Persian Investment Corporation*, 44 Ch. D. 306; 59 L. J. Ch. 695; 62 L. T. N. S. 894; 38 W. R. 59.

(b) See further, statute 6 Geo. II. c. 35 (1733).

F

nation of sales of houses, lands, advowsons, &c., and that proposals and schemes were published for the sale of such houses, &c., to be determined by raffles and mathematical machines, and by other indirect means, tending to evade the good and wholesome laws hereinbefore mentioned. Attention, again, was called to the games of ace of hearts, pharaoh, bassett, and hazard, whereby many people, ignorant of the disadvantages under which they played, had for many years lost their money. The evils complained of were accordingly dealt

1739.

with by statute 12 Geo. II. c. 28, by the 1st section of which it was made an offence for any person to set up, continue, or keep any office or place under the denomination of sales of houses, &c., by the way of chances as therein mentioned, or to print or advertise the proposals therein specified, or to deliver out tickets for the same, or for the sale of houses, &c., by any game, method, or device whatsoever depending upon, or to be determined by, any lot or drawing, whether it be out of a box, or wheel, or by cards or dice, or by any machine, engine, or device, of chance of any kind whatsoever.

By the 2nd section the games of ace of hearts, pharaoh, bassett, and hazard were declared to be games or lotteries by cards or dice within the intent and meaning of statutes 10 & 11 Will. III. c. 17, 9 Anne, c. 6, and 8 Geo. I. c. 2, and it was made an offence to set up or keep the said games.

By the 3rd section all persons who should be adventurers in any of the said games, lotteries, or sales were rendered liable to a penalty.

By the 4th section all such sales of houses, &c., as were thereinbefore prohibited were declared to be void to all intents and purposes whatsoever, and the houses,

&c., so exposed for sale were liable to be forfeited to such persons as should sue for the same.

By the 10th section an exception was made in favour of persons playing or gaming within any of the royal palaces where his Majesty, his heirs, and successors should then reside.

By the 11th section it was provided that the Act should not prejudice any estate in any lands, &c., which should be legally allotted by a partition by lots. Lands really held in joint ownership could, therefore, still be severed, and the respective shares determined by lot, scroll, chance, and allotment. The remaining sections of the statute were directed towards improving the methods for correcting offenders against the other Acts hereinbefore mentioned.

By section 13 of the statute 13 Geo. II. c. 19, the policy of the Act last mentioned was extended for the suppression of a game called passage, and of all other games then or afterwards to be invented, played with dice or dies, or with any other instrument, engine, or device in the nature of dice ; and punishments, similar to those in the last Act, were to be inflicted. Backgammon and other games played with the backgammon table were alone excepted. Subsequently, by statute 18 Geo. II. c. 34, the game called roulette or roly-poly was brought within the provisions of statute 12 Geo. II. c. 28.

In 1782 and 1787, statutes (c) were passed for licensing lottery house keepers, and for regulating the sale of tickets in the public lotteries, and for the suppression of adventurers in such lotteries by unlawful sales of tickets or chances of tickets, and for the further suppression of

Marginal notes: 1740. Passage. Dice. 1745. Roulette. 1782 and 1787.

(c) 22 Geo. III. c. 47 ; 27 Geo. III. c. 1.

the abuses arising from insurances for or against the drawing of such lotteries.

1802.

The next statute is, at the present day, the most important of the whole series. The statute 42 Geo. III. c. 119, intituled "An Act to repress certain games and lotteries not authorised by law," was directed against certain imitations of the public lotteries, which, under Little goes. the name of "little goes," had revived in a widespread manner those injuries against which the previous statutes had been passed. It was declared "that all such games and lotteries, called 'little goes,' shall, from and after the passing of this Act, be deemed and are hereby declared common and public nuisances," and any person keeping any office or place for the purpose of carrying on "little goes" was subjected to a penalty, and was to be deemed a rogue and vagabond. It was further made penal for anyone, under any pretence whatever, to promise to pay any sum, or to deliver any goods, or to do, or forbear doing, anything for the benefit of any person, either with or without consideration, in any contingency, in any "little go," or to publish any proposal for any such purpose.

1836.

Advertising foreign and other lotteries.

The attention of the legislature was next directed against "advertising foreign and other illegal lotteries," and in 1836 an Act was passed which prohibited the "printing or publishing any advertisement or other notice of any foreign lottery, or any lottery not authorized by Act of Parliament, or from advertising the sale of any ticket or chance in such lottery, or in any manner to advertise such lottery ticket or chance."

1823.

Abolition of public lotteries.

In the year 1823, public lotteries were abolished by the 19th section of the statute 4 Geo. IV. c. 60, and the only form of lottery since legalized by statute is

that connected with art unions. By the statute 9 & 10 1846.
Vict. c. 48, voluntary associations formed for the purpose
of distributing works of art by lot were legalized, provided that the incorporation of such association be
pursuant to a royal charter in that behalf obtained,
and that approval of the instrument whereunder the
association is incorporated, and of its rules and regulations, be obtained from the Privy Council.

Art Unions— Conditions of legality.

The statute relating to "little goes" is the one of
the widest extent, and many of the others which were
intimately connected with public lotteries are practically
obsolete. The first of the series might have been construed so as to have been very wide reaching, but the
subsequent statutes indicate that a narrower construction must have been placed on it. Sweepstakes, however, have been held to be within its terms, though such
a form of lottery is somewhat far removed from the
lotteries established pursuant to letters patent. In a
subsequent chapter the actual offences prescribed in
the Acts will be dissected. In the pages following the
cases cited will illustrate what transactions have been
held to be lotteries and what not.

Both Webster and Johnson, in their dictionaries, *Lottery defined.*
define a lottery "as a distribution of prizes by lot or
chance," and such definition has been held to be correct
for the purposes of construing the Lottery Acts (*e*).
The distribution of the prizes must not be determined
by judgment or skill, but by mere chance. Whilst the
chance may commonly be determined by the use of
dice, lots, cards, balls, or numbers or figures, yet it is
not essential to a lottery for any such physical means to

(*e*) *Taylor* v. *Smetten,* 11 Q. B. D. 207; 52 L. J. M. C. 101;
48 J. P. 36; *Barclay* v. *Pearson,* (1893) 2 Ch. 154; 62 L. J. Ch.
636; 68 L. T. 709; 42 W. R. 74; 3 R. 388.

be used; it suffices for the chance to be determined by mere arbitrary unfettered choice, exercised either before or after the lottery is opened to the adventurers (g).

Lotteries, two classes of. Lotteries so defined may for convenience be divided into two classes:—first, those where the adventurers create by their subscriptions the whole fund which, with or without deduction, is to be divided as prizes between them according to the determination of chance; secondly, those where the adventurers purchase the chances of prizes in a fund already put aside, or purported to be put aside, for the purpose of distribution by way of chance as prizes.

Sweepstakes. Allport v. Nutt. As touching the first class, the law has been discussed in the case of *Allport* v. *Nutt* (h). Here certain members subscribed 1l. each to the defendant, the secretary of their club, under the following rules; namely, that the subscriber whose name should be drawn out of a box next after the name drawn out of another box of the horse placed first in the race, should be entitled to receive from the defendant the sum of 100l. This transaction was held to be within the prohibition of the **Within 10 & 11 Will. III. c. 17; 42 Geo. III. c. 119.** Lottery Acts, 10 & 11 Will. III. c. 17, and 42 Geo. III. c. 119. And in another case, *Mearing* v. *Hillings* (i), where the plaintiff sought to recover the "sum of 13l. 6s. for money received by the defendant as treasurer of a club for the use of the plaintiff as the drawer of the second horse in the Derby Stakes," the Court arrived at the same conclusion. *Gatty* v. *Field* (k) is another

(g) *Barclay* v. *Pearson*, (1893) 2 Ch. 154; 62 L. J. Ch. 636; 68 L. T. 709; 42 W. R. 74; 3 R. 388.

(h) *Allport* v. *Nutt*, 1 C. B. 974; 3 D. & L. 233; 14 L. J. C. P. 272; 9 Jur. 900.

(i) *Mearing* v. *Hillings*, 14 M. & W. 711; 15 L. J. Ex. 168.

(k) *Gatty* v. *Field*, 9 Q. B. 431; 15 L. J. Q. B. 408; 10 Jur. 980.

very similar case. A number of 15s. subscriptions were deposited in the hands of a treasurer before the running of a horse race; the names of the subscribers were written on one set of cards, and the names of the horses on another, and each set was placed in a separate box. The cards were then drawn out alternately, as chance directed, and each subscriber was considered as holding the horse the name of which came out next before the drawing of his own name. The holders thereupon became entitled to prizes varying from 24*l.* downwards, according as the horses they held came in first, second, or later. This transaction was illegal.

In the more recent case of *Barclay* v. *Pearson* (*l*), the defendant inserted a notice in his paper, inviting the public to subscribe, in sums of 1s. each, to a fund which he undertook to divide equally amongst such of the contributors as should correctly guess a word which was omitted from a given sentence contained in his paper. He further stated that the missing word was in the hands of a chartered accountant, inclosed in a sealed envelope. It was not contended that the missing word was the most fitting wherewith to complete the sentence. Stirling, J., held that the competition constituted a lottery within the meaning of 42 Geo. III. c. 119; for the selection of the word was entirely a matter of chance. The fact that no physical lot, *ejusdem generis* with dice, balls, cards, numbers, or figures was used, was held to constitute a formal, and not a substantial, distinction : the arbitrary unfettered choice of the editor in selecting the word was an equivalent.

The second class of lotteries, where the adventurer

The missing word competition.

Barclay v. *Pearson.*

(*l*) *Barclay* v. *Pearson*, (1893) 2 Ch. 154; 62 L. J. Ch. 636; 68 L. T. 709; 42 W. R. 74; 3 R. 388.

purchases the chance of a prize in a fund already constituted, is illustrated in several cases. In *Morris* v. *Blackman* (*m*), the programme of an entertainment stated that at the conclusion " the proprietor would distribute amongst his audience a shower of gold and silver treasures on a scale utterly without parallel, besides a shower of smaller presents, all of which would be divided amongst the audience, and impartially given away." The public were admitted on purchasing tickets, which were not numbered, but the seats on which the audience sat were numbered, and at the conclusion of the entertainment the proprietor called out the number on a seat, and delivered one of the articles to the person occupying it, and in that way distributed all the articles amongst the audience. This scheme was also held to constitute a lottery within the meaning of 42 Geo. III. c. 119, s. 2 (*n*).

Eastern bazaar.

In another case, *Reg.* v. *Harris* (*o*), a watchmaker and hawker of watches announced that he would hold an " eastern bazaar," to be conducted according to art union principles, in which there were to be 5,000 tickets sold at 1s. each, and bonuses to the amount of 250l. were to be distributed, the chief ones ranging between 12l. and 2l., and others to consist of " geese, ducks, hares, rabbits, &c.," and so arranged that every subscriber obtained something. Everyone who paid 1s. obtained a ticket with a number on it, referring to a book from which the holder was informed of the bonus he had obtained. It was held by M. Smith, J., that, whether the full value of the 1s. was or was not received

(*m*) *Morris* v. *Blackman*, 2 H. & C. 912; 10 Jur. N. S. 520; 28 J. P. 199.

(*n*) See also *Roddy* v. *Stanley*, 5 Ir. Jur. 10.

(*o*) *Reg.* v. *Harris*, 10 Cox, C. C. 352.

by the subscribers, the case came within the mischief of the Acts, inasmuch as the subscribers were induced to part with their money in the hope of obtaining not only their alleged shilling's worth, but something of much greater value, the right to which was to be ascertained by chance.

In *Taylor* v. *Smetten* (*p*), the appellant had been convicted under the statute relating to little goes (*q*). He sold 1 lb. packets of tea for 2*s*. 6*d*. Each packet contained a coupon entitling the purchaser to some prize. The prizes were distributed according to the coupons; the tea was good, and was stated to be worth the money paid for it. The justices, inasmuch as each purchaser obtained a prize, with regard to which there was a chance or uncertainty, held the transaction to be a lottery. In the Divisional Court this decision was upheld on the grounds that the purchaser exercised no choice; what he obtained was the result of mere chance or accident. It was pointed out that if the coupon alone, sealed up, had been offered for sale, the purchaser taking his chance whether it represented a pen or a silver pencil case, or if a number written on a slip of paper were sold, entitling the purchaser to some article, the name of which was written against a corresponding number in an undisclosed list, no one could have doubted that these would have been lotteries. Hence it seemed utterly immaterial whether a specific article was or was not conjoined with the chance and as the subject-matter of the sale.

In the case of *Hunt* v. *Williams* (*r*), which was similar

Packets of tea plus prizes.

(*p*) *Taylor* v. *Smetten*, 11 Q. B. D. 207 ; 52 L. J. M. C. 101 ; 48 J. P. 36.

(*q*) 42 Geo. III. c. 119, s. 2.

(*r*) *Hunt* v. *Williams*, 52 J. P. 821.

THE LAW OF GAMBLING.

THE LAW OF GAMBLING.

on the facts to the last-mentioned case save in one respect, an attempt had been made to evade the Lottery Acts by non-advertising the existence of prizes. But it was held that the advertising was not of the essence, and that the transaction was none the less a lottery (s).

Schemes involving skill not lotteries. As distinguished from the cases in which the transactions have been held to be lotteries, there are others in which the contention has been unsuccessful. In *Caminada* v. *Hulton* (t), the transaction impeached arose out of the publication of a sporting newspaper at the price of 1d., on the last page of which was a coupon with the names of some six coming horse races; pecuniary prizes were offered to any purchaser who filled up one coupon with the names of six, five, or four winners, and returned the coupon to the office within a limited time under the conditions specified. It was held that there was no contrivance or device to obtain money by chance, or by anything analogous to chance, and that the transaction nowhere approached the description of a lottery. This case is distinguishable from *Barclay* v. *Pearson* in its essence, because in the latter case there was no room for the exercise of skill; it was chance only.

The case of *Caminada* v. *Hulton* was recently relied on in a summons against the proprietors of the paper called *Turf Life* (u). In that newspaper there was an advertisement of a coupon competition, a prize of 100*l.* being offered to the person who should place the first, second, third, and fourth horses in the Grand National. The conditions of the competition were set forth on the

(s) See also *Youdan* v. *Crookes*, 22 J. P. 287.

(t) *Caminada* v. *Hulton*, 60 L. J. M. C. 116; 64 L. T. N. S. 572; 39 W. R. 540; 55 J. P. 727.

(u) Mansion House, April, 1895.

coupons, of which there were twenty-five. The conditions were (*inter alia*) :—" 2. The No. 1 coupon in the above column can be used free of charge. This coupon can be filled up, cut out, and despatched to us, and will be accepted for competition without any fee or charge being sent with it. 3. If, however, the remaining twenty-four blank coupons are used, one penny stamp must be sent with each of these coupons so used. 4. The extra coupons are included in each issue for those who experience a difficulty in obtaining *Turf Life*. . . . 5. There is no limitation to the number of coupons to be sent in. 6. Predictions can also be made on plain paper on the same terms, but one free coupon must accompany the same, to show that the competitor is a subscriber to *Turf Life*. 7. There is no compulsion to use any more than the one free coupon if the competitor desires to confine himself to one attempt." This competition, being for the correct prediction of the first four horses in a given race, gave an opportunity for the contention that, as to the fourth horse, it was a question of chance and not of skill, as the fourth place was not ridden for on the merits. This contention succeeded in the first instance ; but, on a case stated, the Divisional Court reversed the decision, holding that a horse race was not a matter of chance, and that consequently there was no device or contrivance to obtain money by chance (*x*).

On the other hand, the distribution of the property may be by chance, and yet the transaction may not be a lottery ; for that which is distributed may not be of the nature of a prize. A well-established method at common law of dividing land amongst coparceners is

Division amongst coparceners.

described in Bacon's Abridgment, *sub tit.* Coparceners :—
"There is another manner of voluntary partition or
allotment, and that is when after partition each division
is written in a little scroll, and that is covered with wax
like a little ball, so as the scroll cannot be seen, and
then all the balls are put into a hat, to be kept in the
hands of an indifferent person, after which the eldest
daughter draws first, and then the rest according to their
seniority." It will be remembered that section 11 of
the statute 12 Geo. II. c. 28 (dealing, *inter alia*, with
lotteries under the guise of sales of lands, &c.), expressly preserved this mode of allotment or partition by
lots. Wherever persons are really and truly seised as
part owners, joint tenants, or tenants in common, of
any manors, honours, royalties, lands, tenements, advowsons, presentations, rents, services, and hereditaments,
they may still make partition by lot, notwithstanding
anything in the Act. The question whether a certain
transaction fell within the mischief of the Lottery Acts
or within the last-mentioned section was raised, though
in the result it became unnecessary to decide the point,
in the case of *O'Connor* v. *Bradshaw* (y). There a
company consisting of a large number of subscribers,
who contributed small sums of money, was formed for
the purpose of buying land, erecting dwelling-houses
thereon, and allotting the same to subscribers by ballot.
The company was illegal otherwise by virtue of some
of its operations infringing the Bank Acts. Baron
Parke, in his judgment, after pointing out that the
point was not necessary for decision, stated that he
could not bring himself to think the scheme illegal
within the Lottery Acts. His view, as suggested by a

(y) *O'Connor* v. *Bradshaw*, 5 Ex. 882; 20 L. J. Ex. 26.

remark in the course of the argument, was that members were co-owners and were legally determining their priorities; he put this case, "Suppose a number of persons were to buy a large collection of pictures, some of which far exceeded the others in value, might it not be determined who shall have the first choice?" But Pollock, C.B., thought it questionable whether land could be purchased with the object of dividing it under the section last mentioned. It is submitted that land could not be purchased for the purpose of and with the intent so to divide it; the owners would have become seised, but with an intent contrary to the statute. Again, with regard to the illustration of the pictures, if the transaction were a mere disguise to enable the adventurers to divide a fund of money subscribed by themselves unequally amongst themselves, then the disguise would clearly be ineffectual and the substance of the transaction would remain. It may be noticed that section 11 of the statute only refers to the partition of real property, and that the earlier statute dealing with the sales of fans, gloves, and other things, contains no such reservation (z). But this difference is not conclusive. In the case of *Sykes* v. *Beadon* (*a*), a "government securities trust," or combination of more than twenty persons, was formed on the principle of investing subscriptions of the members and dividing the capital fund and the profits among themselves by annual drawings by lot. The first question in the case, and the only one argued at the bar, was whether the combination in question was "an association for the acquisition of gain" within the meaning of section 4 of the

(z) 10 Anne, c. 26, s. 108.
(a) *Sykes* v. *Beadon*, 11 Ch. Div. 170; 48 L. J. Ch. 522; 27 W. R. 464; 40 L. T. 243.

THE LAW OF GAMBLING.

Companies Act, 1862. Jessel, M.R., held that it was. But its present importance arises from the fact that during the argument advanced to show that the association was not formed for the acquisition of gain within the meaning of the Companies Act, the Master of the Rolls expressed a doubt whether or not it was not within the prohibition of the Lottery Acts; and he distinguished building societies on the ground that they are loan societies, wherein it is a case of loans to be returned. In his judgment the Master of the Rolls said, " I do not intend to decide the point, as it was not argued; but stating my opinion as far as I ought to state it, this is a lottery, and is illegal under the Lottery Acts. The holders of certificates are persons who subscribe money to be invested in funds which are to be divided amongst them by lot, and divided unequally. . . . It depends on a chance which gets the greater or lesser advantage. It is, therefore, a subscription by a number of persons to a fund for the purpose of dividing that fund between them by chance and unequally. If that is not a lottery, then, at all events, to my mind it is very difficult to understand what a lottery is." Beyond doubt, if the matter had been argued, it would have been pressed on the learned judge that the subscriptions were made for the purpose of earning profits by the investments, though not within section 4 of the Companies Act, 1862, and that the subsequent and distinct transaction, the division by lot, was but ancillary to the main purpose of the scheme, and adopted merely because convenient. In the case of *Wallingford* v. *The Mutual Society* (b), it was held that the defendant society, which was constituted for

(b) *Wallingford* v. *The Mutual Society*, 5 App. Cas. 685; 50 L. J. Q. B. 49; 43 L. T. 258; 29 W. R. 81.

the purpose of accumulating capital by means of monthly subscriptions from its members, and for making advances thereout to the members in accordance in part with a process of periodical drawings, was not within the mischief of the Lottery Acts. The right to receive an advance was determined by lot, and, doubtless, was a right of some pecuniary value; yet Lord Selborne, after full argument and reference to the terms of the particular Lottery Acts stated, "One of those Acts plainly, on the face of its recitals (the enacting part not departing from those recitals), had reference to gambling transactions only; and in my judgment this was not a gambling transaction within the meaning of that Act. The other had reference to persons who kept lottery offices, at which the public were invited to pay for lottery tickets; and that Act could have no application to this case. No case, therefore, in my judgment, was made, worthy of a moment's consideration, in support of the contention that these were illegal transactions within the Lottery Acts." Another case, arising out of a trust for investment, with ancillary provisions for drawings by lot, is *Smith* v. *Anderson* (c), and no contention was advanced that the trust was illegal on account of the Lottery Acts, and the point was treated as precluded from argument by the case of *Wallingford* v. *The Mutual Society*.

(c) *Smith* v. *Anderson*, 15 Ch. Div. 247 ; 50 L. J. Ch. 47 ; 43 L. T. 336 ; 29 W. R. 22.

CHAPTER V.

PART I.

Gaming Securities under the Statutes 16 *Car. II. c.* 7,
9 *Anne, c.* 14.

In Chapter III., Section B., the scope of the above-
mentioned statutes of Charles and Anne was indicated,
but their effect on gaming securities was purposely
omitted, in order that such discussion might afford
a foundation for the examination of the statute of
Will. IV. and the present law.

Effect of the
statute of
Anne on
securities.

The statute of Anne rendered null and void for all
intents and purposes any note, bill, bond, judgment,
mortgage, or other security given in respect of money
won by gaming, or by betting on those who played, or
for money knowingly lent for such gaming or betting,
or lent at the time and place of such play to anyone so
gaming or betting.

Notes and
bills under
this statute.

The statute, in rendering such notes and bills null
and void to all intents and purposes, destroyed their
negotiability, and inflicted hardships on *bonâ fide* holders
for value. The lender or winner who became promisee
on the note, or the payee in whose favour the bill was
drawn, took the security for what it was worth; but a
third person, without notice of the origin, might, in the
ordinary course of commercial dealing, become an indorsee for value, and subsequently find that he could
not recover on such note or bill. The innocent indorsee

had only one remedy, and that was against his indorser on the indorsement, which is equivalent to an assertion of the validity of the security.

In the case of *Hussey* v. *Jacobs* (a), the plaintiff was the payee of a bill of exchange, of which the defendant was the acceptor; the bill was drawn by Lord Chandois in payment of 120 guineas lost by him to the plaintiff at gaming. In the argument for the plaintiff it was contended, that the defendant had undertaken to pay the sum in demand upon a subsequent contract made by himself, and that, therefore, his undertaking was neither within the intent nor the letter of the statute. But it was held that the defence was as available for the defendant as for Lord Chandois in an action brought by the plaintiff, who was privy to the first wrong, and a party to the illegal and tortuous winning; and Lord Holt, who decided the case, added that if the plaintiff had assigned the bill to a stranger *bonâ fide* upon good consideration, he had not been within the statute, for he was not privy to the tort, but an honest creditor, and to such a stranger the acceptor would be liable. According, then, to this *obiter dictum* of Lord Holt, the bill or note would be negotiable in spite of the statutes.

However, the exact point was raised in the case of *Bowyer* v. *Bampton* (b), and the dictum of Lord Holt was disapproved of and the contrary decided; in fact, Lee, C. J., said he had seen a report wherein notice was taken that all the learned part of the bar wondered at it. The plaintiff Bowyer was the indorsee of several promissory notes which had been given by the defendant Bampton to one J. C. for the repayment of money

Cases illustrating the foregoing.

Bowyer v. Bampton.

(a) *Hussey* v. *Jacobs*, 1 Comy. 4; 1 Salk. 344; 5 Mod. 170 (Cas. 85).

(b) *Bowyer* v. *Bampton*, Strang. 1155a.

G.   G

knowingly advanced to the defendant to game with at
dice, and which had been subsequently indorsed by
J. C. to the plaintiff for a full and valuable consideration, and without notice of the gaming. The Court
held that the plaintiff could not maintain his action
against the defendant on the notes; for if he could,
then the notes would be of some use to the lender,
seeing that he could therewith pay his own debts: the
Act would be evaded, as it is a matter of much difficulty
to prove that an indorsee had notice. It was pointed
out that, whilst the decision would involve an innocent
indorsee in some difficulty, yet the inconveniences would
not overbalance those on the other side; and, moreover,
the indorsee would not be left without remedy, for he
could sue the indorser on his indorsement. The position
of the innocent indorsee was in question in the case of
Lowe v. *Waller* (c), where the bills were usurious. Following *Bowyer* v. *Bampton*, it was held that the indorsee
could not maintain his action against the acceptor,
though, similarly there, the indorsee had a right of
action against his indorser. The case of *Robinson* v.
Bland (d) is another instance of the failure of a winner,
who became the drawer and the payee of a bill, to
recover from the loser, who was the acceptor, or, more
accurately, from the acceptor's personal representative.

Edwards v.
Dick.

In the case of *Edwards* v. *Dick* (e), the plaintiff, as
indorsee, brought an assumpsit against the defendant as
drawer and indorser of a bill of exchange. The bill was
drawn by the defendant upon and accepted by Lord R.
in discharge of a debt for money won at play, but the
plaintiff received it from the drawer in payment of a

(c) *Lowe* v. *Waller*, 2 Doug. 735.
(d) *Robinson* v. *Bland*, 2 Burr. 1077, and *ante*, p. 54.
(e) *Edwards* v. *Dick*, 4 B. & Ald. 212.

bond-fide debt. For the defendant it was argued that the bill was null and void, and that the position was the same as if no bill had ever existed. Bayley, J., said: " It would be most unjust to allow this defence to a defendant, who, having indorsed over, and thereby asserted the bill to be valid, afterwards, when called upon to pay it, says that it is invalid, and that in consequence of fraudulent conduct to which he himself has been a party." Thus the defendant could not escape his liability as indorser on the ground that he, the winner, was also the drawer. There are expressions in the judgments which indicate that *quâ* drawer he might have been successfully sued by a subsequent holder, even though, as drawer, he had no remedy or right against the loser, the acceptor of the bill.

In the later case of *Shilleto* v. *Theed* (*f*), where the defendant had lost a wager on the St. Leger, and had accepted a bill drawn on him by the winner, from whom, through a series of indorsements, it ultimately reached the plaintiff, it was scarcely contended that the plaintiff, claiming through the winner, could recover from the acceptor. But the contention was attempted that the horse race on which the bet was made, having been rendered valid by the statute 18 Geo. II. c. 34, the bet itself, as a collateral and incidental consequence, must be valid and create legal obligations. By the judgment it was decided that the legalizing of horse races did not interfere with the operation of the statute of Anne, and that the action on this bill against the acceptor could not be maintained. *Shilleto* v. *Theed.*

In *Boulton* v. *Coghlan* (*g*), the defendant accepted a *Boulton* v. *Coghlan.*

(*f*) *Shilleto* v. *Theed*, 7 Bing. 405.
(*g*) *Boulton* v. *Coghlan*, 1 Bing. N. C. 640; 1 Hodges, 145; 1 Scott, 588.

G 2

bill drawn on him for payment of losses at play, and
such bill was indorsed to one Knight. The defendant
: and Knight, before the bill matured, agreed to substi-
tute therefor a promissory note, which Knight subsequently indorsed to the plaintiff. The plaintiff sued
the defendant on this note. It was proved that the
note arose out of a gambling transaction ; but the defendant ultimately failed on the ground that he had not
pleaded the two agreements, and was unable to sub-
stantiate the plea as set up by him. The case does not
decide that he would have been liable if the two agreements had been duly pleaded. In the case of *Baker* v.
Williams (h), a bill was substituted for the original one ;
in *Graves* v. *Houlditch* (i), a second bill was substituted
for the first ; and in *Wynne* v. *Callander* (k), French
bills were substituted for the original English ones : in
each instance the substituted bill was held to be void.

A second security substituted for the first.

The judgments referred to in the statute were voluntary judgments given by the debtor to the creditor by
way of security, and did not include adverse judgments
obtained even in default of appearance, and even when
the plaintiff was the winner or lender (l).

Judgments within the statutes.

Bonds not being negotiable instruments, and being
at law unassignable, any assignee of the bond knew
that he was bound by the actual state of the indebtedness between the obligor and the obligee of the bond.
It was but a particular case in the state of such indebtedness that there should be no legal obligation
between the obligor and the obligee. A bond within
the statute was null and void in the hands of any

Bonds under the statutes.

- (h) *Baker* v. *Williams*, note to *Rawden* v. *Shadwell*, 1 Amb. 268.
(i) *Graves* v. *Houlditch*, 2 Price, 147.
- : (k) *Wynne* v. *Callander*, 1 Russ. 293.
(l) *Lane* v. *Chapman*, 11 A. & E. 966, 980.

assignee. In the case of *Bucknill* v. *Myler*, discussed at length in the judgment in the case of *Kenny* v. *Browne (m)*, the Lord Chancellor stated that a bond to secure the payment of 160*l*. won at billiards was grounded on an illicit contract, and that the obligee of the bond would, without hesitation, have been restrained from proceeding to levy the debt; so also would an assignee from the obligee. But the obligor of the bond would be estopped from denying the truth of any representation made by him to an intended assignee.

A legal mortgage consists of two elements: the one Mortgages. the unassignable covenant to pay the money secured; the other the legal estate, which was, of course, assignable at law. The question arose as to whether the unassignability of the covenant or the assignability of the estate determined the character of a mortgage as a transferable instrument. In *Matthews* v. *Wallwyn (n)*, it is stated in the judgment as follows :—" It is true there is a legal estate or term ; but it must be apparent upon the face of the title that it is not an absolute conveyance of the term or legal estate, but as a security for a debt, and the real transaction is an assignment of a debt from A. to B. ; that debt collaterally secured by a charge upon a real estate. The debt, therefore, is the principal thing ; and it is obvious that, if an action was brought upon the bond in the name of the mortgagee, as it must be, the mortgagor shall pay no more than what is really due upon the bond ; if an action of covenant was brought by the covenantee, the account must be settled in that action." The unassignability of the The assign-debt, as distinguished from the assignability of the legal mortgago is estate, is the dominant characteristic. governed by the debt.

(m) *Kenny* v. *Browne*, 3 Ridgway's Parl. Rep. 514.
(n) *Matthews* v. *Wallwyn*, 4 Ves. 118.

Effect of
9 Anne on
mortgages.

The statute of Anne rendered mortgages which were within its scope null and void; hence the mortgagee could take no benefit, although, as has been seen (*o*), the mortgagor was penalised by being divested of the pro- perty which he had attempted to mortgage. In *Baker* v. *Williams* (*p*), the defendant had won from the plain- tiff 161*l*. at hazard, and the plaintiff had given the defendant a promissory note for that amount. Subse- quently the defendant became dissatisfied with his se- curity, and in substitution therefor the plaintiff executed a mortgage of certain leasehold premises to secure to the defendant the sum of 126*l*., and gave him a promissory note for the balance. The defendant indorsed over the latter note to his brother, who had no knowledge of its origin. In the action the plaintiff sought to have the mortgaged leaseholds reconveyed to him, and the title deeds relating to same delivered up, and also to have the note cancelled and delivered up. He succeeded as to the note; but, whilst the mortgagee derived no benefit from the security, it was held that the plaintiff was not entitled to the reassignment, as under the statute his next-of-kin had become entitled thereto. Similarly, in *Fleetwood* v. *Jansen and Mennill* (*q*), where there had been a mortgage of freeholds, the heir-at-law had become entitled. Thus, then, such mortgages were, as between the mortgagor and the mortgagee, void *ab initio*, and, as the mortgagee acquired no right thereunder, he could assign no right to a third person. The position of the assignee of such a security is illustrated by the case of

---

(*o*) *Ante*, p. 48.

(*p*) *Baker* v. *Williams*, at the Rolls, 11 Geo. I.; see note to *Rawden* v. *Shadwell*, 1 Amb. 268.

(*q*) *Fleetwood* v. *Jansen*, 2 Atk. 467.

GAMING SECURITIES UNDER OLD STATUTES.   87

Parker v. *Clarke* (r).   The plaintiff had given a mort- *Parker* v.
gage to a person, who assigned it with notice to the *Clarke.*
defendant Clarke, by whom it was assigned, without
notice of any defect, to Phillips.   The plaintiff had
executed the mortgage without receiving any present
consideration, and in contemplation of a future consideration, which totally failed.   The Master of the Rolls
(Lord Romilly) held the deed to be void, being a mortgage deed for which no consideration was given.   As
against Clarke, who was the first assignee with notice,
the deed was cancelled.   With respect to Phillips, who
took without notice, the Master of the Rolls said: "I
am of opinion that he could only take what Clarke could
give him, and that he cannot stand in a better position
than Clarke himself.   Phillips, therefore, must deliver
up the deeds, and his only remedy will be against
Clarke."   Other instances where the position of a transferee, without notice and for value, of a void security
has been determined will be found in cases where there
has been personation and forgery (s).

The case of *Matthews* v. *Wallwyn* (cited *supra*) shows
that, where the mortgage security is a valid one, the
transferee, who in the absence of the mortgagor takes
a transfer, is bound by the actual state of the accounts
between the mortgagor and the mortgagee (t).   Hence
it follows that, as was stated in the same case, "persons
most conversant in conveyancing hold it extremely unfit

(r) *Parker* v. *Clarke*, 30 Bev. 54; 7 Jur. N. S. 1267; 9 W. R.
877.
(s) *Ogilvie* v. *Jeaffreson*, 2 Giff. 353; *In re Cooper, Cooper* v.
Vesey, 20 Ch. D. 611; 51 L. J. Ch. 862; 47 L. T. 89; 30 W. R.
648.
(t) See also *Williams* v. *Sorrell*, 4 Ves. 389; *Bradwell* v.
Catchpole, in note to *Walker* v. *Symonds*, 3 Sw. p. 1.

and very rash, and a very indifferent security, to take. an assignment without the privity of the mortgagor as to the sum really due . . . but no conveyancer of established practice would recommend it as a good title to take an assignment of a mortgage without making the. mortgagor a party and being satisfied that the money was really due." In those instances where the mortgagor was not a party to the transfer, a covenant was commonly taken from the transferor that the debt in question was justly due and owing.

The operation of the statute of Anne, in divesting the property from the mortgagor, has been entirely repealed (*u*), and is of interest now solely as a legal curiosity. But the foregoing paragraphs will exemplify the incidents of a null and void mortgage security. The same results apply to equitable charges, where there is no conveyance of the legal estate.

Estoppel, remedial action of. With regard to bonds and mortgages, the hardship which might be inflicted on innocent third persons was much diminished by the beneficial operation of the doctrine of estoppel. The obligor of a bond, who represents to an intended assignee that the money is due and justly owing, would not be allowed, as against such assignee, to perpetrate a gross fraud by subsequently setting up the statute, and denying the truth of his own representation. It would, however, seem that whilst the divesting operation of the statute of Anne was in force, the mortgagor could not raise an estoppel against his heir-at-law or next-of-kin; but such divesting operation having been abolished, a mortgagor can estop himself, even as the obligor of a bond, and it is in order to raise such estoppel that he is made a party to the transfer.

(*u*) 5 & 6 Will. IV. c. 41, s. 3.

In an old case, briefly reported (x), A. was justly
indebted to B. in the sum of 100l.; C. was, on a
gambling transaction, indebted to A. in the sum of
100l. By arrangement between A., B., and C., A. was
released by B., and C. was released by A., on C. giving
a bond for 100l. to B. B. did not know that C.'s indebtedness to A. arose out of a gambling transaction.
Subsequently C. endeavoured, as against B. in respect
of the bond, to set up the defence of gambling, but B.
recovered on the bond.

The ground of estoppel is clearly indicated in the
case of *Bucknell* v. *Myler* (y), the debtor prior to the
assignment of a bond and a judgment in answer to
the inquiries of the intended assignee, stated that the
debt was fair and the security safe, and by conduct
subsequent to the assignment he confirmed his earlier
representations; on those grounds the debtor failed
when he sought relief in a Court of Equity. Similarly
in *Davison* v. *Franklin* (z), in answer to inquiry of the
intended assignee, the debtor answered, "Yes, that is
my handwriting; I owe Mr. S. the money, and have no
objection to make to it; it will be paid when it is due,"
and he was in consequence deprived of the benefit of the
statute (a).

The cases show that the usual relief sought by a
person who had given a null and void security was
to apply for a declaration to that effect, and for an

Relief of the grantor of a null and void security.

(*x*) *Anonymous*, 2 Mod. 279 (Case 160); *Ellis* v. *Warner*, Cro.
Jac. 32, pl. 6, Yelverton, 47.

(*y*) Cited in *Kenny* v. *Browne*, 3 Ridgway's Par. Rep. 514.

(*z*) *Davison* v. *Franklin*, 1 B. & Ad. 142.

(*a*) *Hawker* v. *Hallewell*, 3 Sm. & G. 194; 2 Jur. N. S. 537,
affirmed on appeal 25 L. J. Ch. 558; 2 Jur. N. S. 794; *Mangles*
v. *Dixon*, 1 M. & G. 437; *Bickerton* v. *Walker*, 31 Ch. Div. 151; 55
L. J. Ch. 227; 53 L. T. 731; 34 W. R. 141.

order for cancellation. In those cases where payments had been made pursuant to the instrument, the Court would further order repayment of the moneys. Thus, in *Rawden* v. *Shadwell* (b), Lord Hardwicke held that the bond was void, and that no payment made thereunder could be supported. As long as statutes were in force for the protection of losers against winners, this equitable relief presented no difficulty.

PART II.

Gaming Securities under the Statute of Will. IV.

The statute of Will. IV., which forms the subject matter of this part of Chapter V., is the present law. It will be seen to be a modification of the previous statutes of Charles and Anne, and only to affect such securities as would have been by those statutes rendered null and void (c). Having regard to the subsequent passing of the Act, 8 & 9 Vict. c. 109, whereunder all wagering contracts are null and void (d), the curious result is produced that a debt under a void contract as distinguished from an illegal one may constitute an illegal consideration for a security given in respect of it.

The statute now in force. The statute, 5 & 6 Will. IV. c. 41, intituled "An Act to amend the Law relating to Securities given for considerations arising out of gaming, usurious, and The hardship to be remedied. certain other illegal transactions," after reciting the statutes of Charles and of Anne in its preamble stated

---

(b) *Rawden* v. *Shadwell*, 1 Amb. 268. See also *Turner* v. *Warren*, 2 Strang. 1079, and 1 Fonbl. Eq. bk. 1. ch. 4, sect. 6.

(c) *Ante*, Chap. III., pp. 46, 47.

(d) *Post*, Chap. VII.

that securities and instruments thereby made void were sometimes indorsed, transferred, assigned, or conveyed to purchasers or other persons for valuable consideration, without notice of the original consideration for which such securities and instruments were given, and the avoidance of such securities or instruments in the hands of such purchasers or other persons was often attended with great hardship and injustice, wherefore by way of remedy it enacted " That so much of the said Acts of 16 Car. II. and 9 Anne (*inter alia*) as enacts that any note, bill, or mortgage shall be absolutely void, shall be and the same is hereby repealed, but nevertheless every note, bill, or mortgage, which if this Act had not been passed would by virtue of the last several hereinbefore mentioned Acts, or any of them, have been absolutely void, shall be deemed and taken to have been made, drawn, accepted, given, or executed for an illegal consideration, and the said several acts shall have the same force and effect which they would respectively have had if instead of enacting that any such note, bill, or mortgage should be absolutely void, such Acts had respectively provided that every such note, bill, or mortgage should be deemed and taken to have been made, drawn, accepted, given, or executed for an illegal consideration. Provided always that nothing herein contained shall prejudice or affect any note, bill, or mortgage which would have been good and valid if this Act had not been passed."

Such securities no longer void,

but given for illegal consideration.

By section 2 it was enacted " That in case any person shall after the passing of this Act make, draw, give, or execute any note, bill, or mortgage for any consideration on account of which the same is by the hereinbefore recited Acts of 16 Car. II. and 9 Anne, . . . or by any one or more of such Acts declared to be void, and such

Relief to grantor of such securities

person shall actually pay to any indorsee, holder, or
assignee of such note, bill, or mortgage, the amount of
the money thereby secured or any part thereof, such
money so paid shall be deemed and taken to have been
paid for and on account of the person to whom such
note, bill, or mortgage was originally given upon such
illegal consideration as aforesaid, and shall be deemed
and taken to be a debt due and owing from such last
named person to the person who shall so have paid such
money, and shall accordingly be recoverable by action
at law in any of His Majesty's Courts of Record."

By section 3, the latter portion of the first section of
the statute of 9 Anne, whereunder the forfeiture of
lands attempted to be mortgaged was incurred, was
wholly repealed.

Operation of
the statute.
The operation of this statute in converting bills and
notes, which theretofore had been null and void, into
instruments given for an illegal consideration is a matter
which presents no difficulty; difficulties, however, will
be hereafter seen to arise from the inclusion of mortgages and the exclusion of bonds.

i. Notes and
bills.
As between the immediate parties to the note or bill,
who were the parties to or privy to the gaming transaction, a plea that the bill or note was given for an illegal
consideration is an answer to a claim on such instrument. The defendant who sets up the illegality must
discharge the onus of proof; similarly if the drawer of
the bill or the promissor seeks an injunction to restrain
the negotiation of the bill or note he must discharge the
same onus. If, however, the bill or note were assigned
to a third person for valuable consideration without
notice, the defence of illegality in the conception of the
bill or note would not prevail, nor could such a holder
be restrained by injunction.

GAMING SECURITIES UNDER WILL. IV.   93

The Bills of Exchange Act, 1882, has codified the The Bills of Exchange Act, 1882. law relating to this matter, and it will be convenient here to set forth the material sections of the Act.

By section 29.—(1.) A holder in due course is a holder who has taken a bill, complete and regular on the face of it under the following conditions; namely—

(a) That he became the holder of it before it was overdue, and without notice that it had been previously dishonoured, if such was the fact:

(b) That he took the bill in good faith and for value, and that at the time the bill was negotiated to him he had no notice of any defect in the title of the persons who negotiated it.

(2.) In particular the title of a person who negotiates a bill is defective within the meaning of this Act when he obtained the bill, or the acceptance thereof, by fraud, duress, or force and fear, or other unlawful means, or for an illegal consideration, or where he negotiates it in breach of faith, or under such circumstances as to amount to fraud.

(3.) A holder (whether for value or not), who derives his title to a bill through a holder in due course, and who is not himself a party to any fraud or irregularity affecting it, has all the rights of that holder in due course, as regards the acceptor and all parties to the bill prior to that holder.

By section 30.—(1.) Every party whose signature appears on a bill is *primâ facie* deemed to have become a party thereto for value.

(2.) Every holder of a bill is *primâ facie* deemed to be a holder in due course; but if in an action on a bill it is admitted or proved that the acceptance, issue, or subsequent negotiation of the bill is affected with fraud,

duress, or force and fear, or illegality, the burden of proof
is shifted, unless and until the holder proves that, subsequent to the alleged fraud or illegality, value has in
good faith been given for the bill.

By section 90, a thing is deemed to be done in good
faith in the meaning of this Act, when it is in fact done
honestly, whether it is done negligently or not.

It will be seen that in the Act "a holder in due
course" is the equivalent of a *bonâ fide* holder (e), and
that "any equity attaching" is a "defective title
within" the meaning of the Act.

In an action wherein the plaintiff seeks to restrain
the holder from negotiating a bill or note, or in an
action wherein the defendant seeks to escape liability
on the bill or note, the illegality must be specifically
pleaded (f), and must be proved by him who alleges
it. As soon as there is some evidence whereon the jury
may reasonably find that the bill is defective owing to
illegality, then under section 30, sub-section (2), the
onus is shifted, and the owner is put to the proof
that value has been given in good faith and without
notice of the illegality (g). If the plea of illegality be
not traversed, the illegality will be taken to be admitted (h), and the burden will then be thrown on the
admitting party of establishing that value was given
honestly. Prior to the Judicature Act and the Bills of
Exchange Act, it was held that an admission of the
illegality shifted the onus of proving consideration but

(e) See sects. 54, 55.

(f) R. S. C. Ord. XIX. r. 15. As to degree of particularity,
see *Boulton* v. *Coghlan*, 1 Bing. N. C. 640; 1 Hodges, 145; 1
Scott, 588.

(g) *Tatam* v. *Haslar*, 23 Q. B. D. 345; 58 L. J. Q. B. 432;
38 W. R. 109.

(h) R. S. C. Ord. XIX. r. 13.

.not the onus of proving the absence of notice (*i*) ; but it is submitted that at the present time the onus would be shifted both as to the consideration and as to. the honesty. With regard to the honesty, section 90 of Bills of Exchange Act has the effect of summarizing the authorities. A man may be grossly negligent, and by virtue of such neglect fail to make inquiries ; such negligence will be pertinent evidence of dishonesty though it may not amount to proof of notice (*k*). But directly it is shown that the party has wilfully shut his . eyes to obvious means of knowledge, then he will be placed in the same position as if he had made the reasonable inquiries (*l*). Apart from constructive notice it may in some cases be shown that a man had actual knowledge.

If A. draws a bill payable to himself on B. in dis- Sect. 29, charge of a gambling debt, and then assigns it to C., sub-sect. 3. Illustrated. with actual notice of the illegality, and then C. subsequently indorses to D., under (for example) such circumstances as would afflict D. with constructive notice of the illegality, and D. in turn indorse to E. under circumstances which make E. a holder in due course; then if E., whether or not for value, indorse the bill to F., who, whilst not a party to the actual illegality on which the note is based, has yet actual notice of that illegality, F. may, as claiming through E., recover as fully as E. could. If this were not so, E.'s power

(*i*) *Bingham* v. *Stanley*, 2 Q. B. 117 ; 1 G. & D. 237.

(*k*) *Goodman* v. *Harvey*, 4 Ad. & E. 870.

(*l*) *May* v. *Chapman*, 16 M. & W. 355 ; *Jones* v. *Gordon*, 2 App. Cas. 616 ; 47 L. J. Bk. 1 ; 37 L. T. 477 ; 26 W. R. 172 ; *Oakeley* v. *Ooddeen*, 2 F. & F. 656 ; 11 C. B. N. S. 805 ; *Jones* v. *Smith*, 1 Hare, 43 ; *Ware* v. *Egmont*, 4 De G. M. & G. 460 ; *A.-G.* v. *Stephens*, 6 De G. M. & G. 111 ; 19 J. P. 642 ; *Goodman* v. *Harvey*, 4 Ad. & El. 870.

of dealing with the bill would be limited by the illegality.

An illustration of what may amount to notice.

The case of *Lord Portarlington* v. *Soulby* (*m*) affords an example of the taint of illegality attaching to a holder. The plaintiff accepted the bill for 1,000*l*., drawn on him to secure the payment of money won at play. The bill was made payable to the keeper of a gaming house, by whom it was indorsed to one Brook, and by him to the defendants. The undervalue paid on the indorsement and the other circumstances of the assignment to the defendants must have raised suspicion, and should have led to inquiry. The plaintiff averred the illegality of the consideration. The defendants did not deny it, but endeavoured to rely on their own alleged ignorance, and their belief in the ignorance of their late partner, who carried out the transaction of the assignment from Brook. Although it was alleged that Brook was well aware of the illegality, yet the defendants produced no evidence from him to prove that he had not communicated that knowledge to them. The defendants admitted that they now knew that the drawer was the keeper of a gaming house, and that they had been in correspondence with him. On these grounds the plaintiff obtained the injunction sought by him.

Notice that the consideration at least in part was illegal.

In the case of *Hay* v. *Ayling* (*n*), the defendant, on a wager about a horse race, lost 100*l*. to one Arbuthnot, who, being indebted to the plaintiff in that amount, induced the defendant to accept a bill drawn by the plaintiff in his own favour for that amount. The bill was dishonoured. The plaintiff, at the defendant's re-

. (*m*) *Portarlington* v. *Soulby*, 3 M. & K. 104.
. (*n*) *Hay* v. *Ayling*, 16 Q. B. 423; *Boulton* v. *Coghlan*, and other cases there cited.

quest, gave further time, and received in lieu of the original bill two acceptances for 50*l.* each, which formed the subject of the. action. The plaintiff knew, when he received the substituted securities, that the defendant's original acceptance had been given for a gaming consideration. It was unanimously held that the gaming debt was, at all events, part of the consideration for the substituted bills, and that therefore the plaintiff, who took with notice, was unable to recover thereon.

 It has been decided in *Lynn* v. *Bell* (*o*), that cheques are within the operation of the statute. A cheque is in the nature of an inland bill of exchange (*p*). The term " bill of exchange " may, in a statute, include a cheque (*q*), and this particular statute was intended to operate on negotiable instruments. Hence the above decision follows. *Cheques are included.*

If mortgages were negotiable instruments, there would be no difficulty in their inclusion in section 1 of the statute. But, as was shown in Part I. of this chapter, mortgages are not negotiable. So far was this recognised that, prior to the Judicature Act, it was necessary for the transferor to give his transferee a power of attorney to enable him to sue for the debt; and again, having regard to the fact that the transferee was bound, in the absence of the mortgagor, by actual state of the account between the mortgagor and the transferor, it was suggested by Powell (*r*) that a note of hand would *ii. Mortgages.*

(*o*) *Lynn* v. *Bell*, 10 Ir. Rop. C. L. 487. ·

(*p*) *Robson* v. *Bennett*, 2 Taunt. 387; *Keene* v. *Beard*, 8 C. B. (N. S.) 372; 29 L. J. C. L. 287; 8 W. R. 469; 36 L. T. 240.

(*q*) *Eyre* v. *Waller*, 8 W. R. 450; 5 H. & N. 460; 29 L. J. Ex. 246, decided on 18 & 19 Vict. c. 67.

(*r*) Powell on Mortgages, 6th edit. p. 908a.

G.   II

be a valuable collateral security. In Coote on Mortgages (s) it is stated that the transferee, without notice
and for valuable consideration, is in no better position
than the mortgagee when the mortgage is absolutely
void from the beginning. An old case which presents
Newport's case doubted. some difficulty is *Newport's case* (t). The facts were,
that one Kendal created a mortgage, which, by divers
mesne assignments, was ultimately vested in Secretary
Coventry for a valuable consideration. Newport was
the executor of Secretary Coventry. Holt, C. J., held
that the mortgage was good between the parties, and,
being so, when the first mortgagee assigns for valuable
consideration, this is all one as if the first mortgage had
been upon a valuable consideration, for now the second
mortgagee (*scilicet*, the transferee) stands in his place.
The decision was that the fraud in the inception was
purged by the subsequent payment on the transfer.
But in an ordinary redemption or foreclosure action,
the account would have shown that nothing was due
and owing from the mortgagor to the mortgagee on the
security, and the transferee would, on the taking of
such account, have stood in the place of the mortgagee.
Such was the reasoning which led to the decision in
Parker v. Clarke. *Parker* v. *Clarke* (u), which, it is submitted, is correct,
and inconsistent with *Newport's case*. It will be re-
membered that it was Holt, C. J., who, in *Hussey* v.
Jacobs (x), erroneously decided that the transferee of a
void bill had a good cause of action against the acceptor.

(s) 5th edit. vol. 1, p. 724.
(t) *Newport's case*, Cas. t. Holt, 477; Skin. 423.
(u) See *ante*, p. 87.
(x) *Hussey* v. *Jacobs*, 1 Salk. 344; 5 Mod. 170 (cas. 85); 1
Com. 4. See *ante*, pp. 81 *et seq*.

A distinction has been drawn between the cases in which
the original mortgage was not void, but merely voidable; and it has been stated that in the latter case the
transferee for valuable consideration and without notice
acquires a valid security (y). In support of that proposition two cases are cited, *George* v. *Milbanke* (z) and
Earl of Aldborough v. *Trye* (a). In *George* v. *Milbanke*
an interest under a voluntary appointment had been
sold, and it was decided that the purchaser of this specific part of the estate had a better equity than the creditors of the appointor. In *Earl of Aldborough* v. *Trye*
the plaintiff had created an annuity and charged it on
his estates. If there was any consideration moving from
the annuitant to the grantor, it was in connection with
services rendered in the negotiation of certain advances.
The annuitant subsequently assigned the annuity to
a purchaser for valuable consideration. The Irish
Court had allowed the grantor of the annuity to set
aside the transaction on payment by him to the assignee
of the amount of the purchase-money actually paid by
the latter. These cases, it is submitted, do not support
the proposition cited above with regard to voidable
mortgages. Both the cases were cited in the argument in *Parker* v. *Clarke* (b). As the transfer of a mortgage depends upon the non-negotiable chose in action,
there arises the difficulty presented by the statute.

The title of the Act indicates that it is an amend- Effect of the
ment of the law relating to securities given for securities mortgages.

(y) Coote on Mortgages, 5th edit. vol. 1, p. 724.
(z) *George* v. *Milbanke*, 9 Ves. 190.
(a) *Earl of Aldborough* v. *Trye*, 7 Cl. & F. 436.
(b) *Parker* v. *Clarke*, 30 B. 54; 7 Jur. N. S. 1267; 9 W. R.
877.

H 2

Difficulty of determining.

arising out of illegal transactions, and the preamble specifically states the great hardship theretofore inflicted by the avoidance of the securities and instruments under the statute of Anne as against *bonâ fide* purchasers or other persons. The preamble is general, and has reference to any security and instrument within the statute of Anne, whether the same be negotiable or not. Section 1 of the Act deals with notes, bills, or mortgages. It has thus included one kind of unnegotiable instrument—the mortgages; but it has not included, expressly, at any rate, bonds and judgments. Pursuant to the section, such mortgages, instead of being absolutely void, are to be deemed to have been executed for an illegal consideration. By the second section, consequential relief is provided for the mortgagor, who shall pay money to an assignee, in respect of such payment, against the mortgagee. It is clear that the Act intended that those special classes of mortgages should be negotiable, and it is also reasonably clear that the Act intended to put such mortgages on the same footing as if the statute of Anne had not declared them void. The conclusion that the Act is based upon a misconception is difficult to avoid: for if a mortgage security is given for an illegal consideration, then, as between the mortgagor and the mortgagee, it is absolutely void, and no debt exists thereunder; hence, it must follow as a necessary consequence that no chose in action exists which can be transferred. There is no authority in point as to the rights of the transferee of such a mortgage. In Coote's Treatise on Mortgages (c), it is, however, stated that the preamble to the Act seems to warrant the assertion that such

(c) Coote on Mortgages, 5th edit. vol. 2, p. 976.

mortgages are no longer totally void, but can be enforced by a transferee for valuable consideration, and
without notice, and. by no other person. With great Conclusion
deference, the submission is here made that the statute, submitted.
by enacting that such mortgages shall be deemed to be
taken for an illegal consideration, has not had the
effect of rendering such instruments negotiable when,
ex natura, they are not.

The solution of the difficulty may be possibly found
in dealings with the estate. The mortgagee may sell
the estate to a purchaser for value without notice, and
in the conveyance may expressly grant in exercise of
the power of sale conferred by the Conveyancing and
Law of Property Act, 1881. It may be that the
purchaser would, under and by virtue of sect.' 22, sub-
sect. 2, obtain an indefeasible title, in spite of the fact
that no case had arisen for the exercise of the power.
But it is not so much with regard to mortgages by
deed that the difficulty would in practice arise, seeing
that the recitals would probably be sufficiently definite
to raise an estoppel (*d*) as against the mortgagor in
favour of the assignee or purchaser.

The preamble of the statute is large enough to in- iii. Bonds.
clude bonds, but the enacting part does not include
them. The difficulty lies in the explanation of the
inclusion of mortgages and the exclusion of bonds.
V.-C. Stuart, in the case of *Hawker* v. *Hallewell* (*e*), *Hawker* v.
said, " The statute, in its operative part, certainly only *Hallewell.*
extends to negotiable securities, but the recital of the
Act clearly includes bonds and securities of every kind.
The operative part of the Act is intended to give a

(*d*) See *ante*, pp. 88, 89.
(*e*) *Hawker* v. *Hallewell*, 3 Sm. & G. 194; 2 Jur. N. S. 537;
affirmed on appeal, 25 L. J. Ch. 558; 2 Jur. N. S. 794.

remedy in Courts of law to *bonâ fide* holders who could sue at law in their own names : but a bond can only be sued for in the name of the obligee at law, and the assignee cannot bring an action in his own name." The learned Vice-Chancellor then expresses an opinion that bonds were within the equity of the statute. He said, " Considering, therefore, that the case of the *bonâ fide* assignee of a bond without notice is clearly within the scope of the preamble, there are strong reasons for holding that he is within the equity of the Act. The recital of the Act, clearly embracing bonds as well as other securities, and the legislature seldom interfering to define or prescribe by express enactment the limits of the paramount jurisdiction of the Courts of equity, and the maxim that equity follows the law, are considerations which strongly support the application, by Courts of equity, of that same principle of natural justice in favour of the *bonâ fide* assignee of a bond for valuable consideration without notice, which this Act directs that courts of law shall apply to *bonâ fide* holders of bills of exchange under similar circumstances." Unfortunately, it was not necessary to dispose of the case on that ground. The Vice-Chancellor found as a fact that the onus of proving that the bond was to secure a gambling debt was not discharged, and even if it had been established, there was ground for setting up an estoppel. The facts were, that the plaintiff had given the bond to one Jenkins, by whom it was assigned to one Herbert, and by him to a certain bank, for value. In the bankruptcy of the plaintiff the bank sought to prove on the bond, but the plaintiff then for the first time alleged that the bond had arisen out of wagering transactions on horse races. The plaintiff alone gave evidence, and that not of a satisfactory character, in

support of his allegation. On appeal from the decision
of the Vice-Chancellor, his decision was upheld on the
ground that the allegation as to the origin of the bond
had not been established. Lords Justices Knight Bruce
and Turner apparently admit the validity of the plea
set up in opposition of the claim, but conclude that it
was not proved. Lord Justice Turner said, "The bank
had proved the execution of the bond, and that the
bond contained a recital that a debt was due from
Hawker, and the onus was therefore on him to show
that no debt was due from him to Jenkins, and that
what was referred to as a debt was in reality contracted
in a gambling transaction, and therefore nothing was
due on it." This case, then, is not an authority to
show that bonds are within the equity of the statute.
In an Irish case of *Lynn* v. *Bell* (*f*), there are *dicta*
which explain why bonds were excluded, namely, that
the securities in the operative part of the Act are those,
and those only (of the securities within the statute of
Anne), to which an indorsee or transferee for value
without notice, could acquire a title better than that
of the person from whom he took. "The scheme of
the Act depends upon the securities within it being of
that class." Thus the reason for the exclusion of bonds Bonds
and judgments is manifest, but the same reason would excluded.
have applied to the exclusion of mortgages.

The result of the exclusion of bonds from the statute Result as to
of Will. IV. is that, having thereby allowed the statute bonds.
of Anne to remain in force, as far as bonds were concerned, the subsequent Act of 8 & 9 Vict. c. 109, has
repealed that portion of the statute of Anne. The

(*f*) *Lynn* v. *Bell*, 10 Ir. Rep. C. L. 487.

wager is void under 8 & 9 Vict. c. 109, and a bond to secure a wagering debt is a voluntary security (g).

Procedure. Where there is a danger that a security, to which the taint of illegality attaches, may be assigned to the detriment of the maker, acceptor, or grantor, or persons interested in it, the present practice is to apply in the Chancery Division of the High Court of Justice for an injunction and other relief, such as the delivery up and cancellation of the security. The application for an injunction can be made *ex parte* on the strength of an affidavit, which must clearly show the illegality and the impending danger. The *ex parte* injunction will be until the next motion day, when the Court may restrain the defendant until the trial of the action or further order, and may direct the deposit of the security into Court (h). Under the old procedure this kind of case usually came before the Court of Chancery upon an application to restrain proceedings at law upon the instrument. However, by the Judicature Act, 1873, s. 24 (5), this jurisdiction has been abolished; any equitable defence which would have supported an injunction against the prosecution of an action at law may be relied upon by way of defence in whatever Division of the High Court of Justice the action may have been brought.

Sect. 2 of 5 & 6 Will. IV. c. 41. The second section of the Act of Will. IV. is complementary to the first. A. loses ——l. to B. at gaming, and gives a bill, note, or mortgage to B. as security. B., in consideration of ——l. paid to him by C., assigns the security to C. Subsequently C. enforces payment of

(g) *Bubb* v. *Yelverton*, L. R. 9 Eq. 471; 39 L. J. Ch. 428; 22 L. T. 258; 18 W. R. 512 (this point was argued but not decided).
(h) Forms of Order, Seton, p. 616, and the cases there cited.

the ——*l.* so secured from A. Then the second section
enables A. to recover from B. the amount, ——*l.*,
which he has paid to C. In the case of *Lynn* v. *Bell*(*i*),
the plaintiff lost to the defendant, on bets on three horse
races, sums which he paid by three cheques in form as
follows:—"To the Ulster Banking Company. Pay
Mr. R. Bell or bearer ——*l.*, which charge to the
account of James Lynn." The first and second cheques
were indorsed by Bell to third persons *bonâ fide* holders
for value, who cashed them; the last was indorsed by
Bell alone, and was cashed by a person who received it
from him in payment of losses on betting transactions.
Lynn thereupon brought his action to recover the
amount of the cheques. It was held that payment by
the bankers was payment by Lynn within the statute,
and that he was entitled to recover. The statute was
not intended to alter the rights and liabilities of the
parties, *inter se*, by whom and to whom such securities
were given. However, where A., the loser, draws on
B. in favour of C., who indorses to D., and then D.
recovers from B. the amount of the bill, A. cannot
under the statute sustain an action against the payee,
C., in virtue of B.'s payment; the payment must be by
the loser himself. Again, in the same case, the defendant counterclaimed as against the plaintiff in respect
of a cheque for 18*l.*, drawn by a third person, and
indorsed by the defendant to the plaintiff for payment
of a bet; but the counterclaim failed in so far as the
payment sought to be recovered was not made by the
defendant himself, who had merely given the third
person credit for the 18*l.* In the case of *Gilpin* v.
Clutterbuck (*k*), the plaintiff had lost 1,000*l.* at one

(*i*) *Lynn* v. *Bell*, 10 Ir. Rep. C. L. 487.
(*k*) *Gilpin* v. *Clutterbuck*, 13 L. T. 71, 159.

sitting to the defendant, at cards, and had accepted bills for the amount. The defendant indorsed one of the bills to a third person, who in an action recovered the debt and costs from the plaintiff. The plaintiff thereupon successfully sued the defendant to recoup him the amount which he had thus been compelled to pay to the indorsee.

A particular instance under the second section.

There is one particular instance of the operation of the section which merits notice. A. gives B. a security for the repayment of money knowingly advanced by B. to A. (say ——*l.*) for the purpose of gaming, or lent at the time and place of the gaming to A., a player. B. assigns the security to C. for ——*l.* C. enforces the security against A., and thereby compels A. to repay the money advanced by B. to him. Can A. now sue B. for the recovery of the ——*l.* so paid by A. to C. in respect of the assigned security? If yes, then B. first lends A. ——*l.*, and then, because he takes a security for the payment of the money so lent and assigns the same, he has again to pay A. a further sum of ——*l.* In the result, he is compelled to lose the amount he actually advanced to A. in the first instance.

CHAPTER VI.

CIVIL OBLIGATIONS ARISING OUT OF ILLEGAL
TRANSACTIONS.

IN Chapters III. and IV. the sphere of the illegal transactions with which this book is concerned was indicated by an examination of the various statutes, containing implied or expressed prohibitions; and in the last chapter the enactments relating to certain classes of securities deemed to be given for an illegal consideration have been examined. It now remains to discuss generally the effect of illegality on transactions in a nearer or in a more remote degree connected therewith.

It is a well-recognized general rule that no right of General rule. action arises out of an illegal transaction: *Ex turpi causa non oritur actio.* The civil law was emphatic: " Rei turpis nullum mandatum est: et ideo hac actione non agitur. Illud quoque mandatum non est obligatorium, quod contra bonos mores est. Veluti si Titius de furto, aut de damno faciendo, aut de injuria facienda, tibi mandet; licet enim pœnam istius facti nomine præstitem non tamen ullam habes adversus Titium actionem. Pacta quæ contra leges constitutionesque vel contra bonos mores fiunt, nullum vim habere, indubitati juris est "(a). In the well-known case of *Collins* v. *Blantern* (b), Wilmot, C. J., said: " This is a contract

(a) Dig. Lib. 17, t. 1, l. 6, sect. 3; Instit. Lib. 3, tit. 26, sect. 7.

(b) *Collins* v. *Blantern,* 2 Wils. 341, 347.

to tempt a man to transgress the law, to do that which is injurious to the community : it is void by the common law: and the reason why the common law says such contracts are void, is for the public good. *You shall not stipulate for iniquity.* All writers upon our law agree in this, no polluted hand shall touch the pure fountains of justice. Whoever is a party to an unlawful contract, if he hath once paid the money stipulated to be paid in pursuance thereof, he shall not have the help of the Court to fetch it back again, you shall have no right of action when you come into a Court of Justice in this unclean manner to recover it back. *Procul, O! procul este profani.*"

What is a *turpis causa.* The rule embraces equally transactions which are *mala in se*, intrinsically immoral, and those which are *mala prohibita*, as contrary to statutory provisions. A distinction, the tendency of which was to consider acts *mala prohibita* less illegal than those *mala in se*, was, however, taken between the two classes in (1767) *Faikney* v. *Reynous* (c), and (1789) *Petrie* v. *Hannay* (d); but such distinction has long since, by a series of cases, been declared unsound (e). In *Bartlett* v. *Vinor* (f), Holt, C. J., said: "Every contract made for or about any matter or thing which is prohibited and made unlawful by statute is a void contract, though the statute does not mention that it shall be so, but only inflicts a penalty on the offender, because a penalty

(c) *Faikney* v. *Reynous,* 4 Burr. 2070.

(d) *Petrie* v. *Hannay,* 3 T. R. 418.

(e) *Steers* v. *Lashley,* 6 T. R. 61; *Mitchell* v. *Cockburn,* 2 H. Bl. 380; *Brown* v. *Turner,* 7 T. R. 630; 2 Esp. 631; *Aubert* v. *Maze,* 2 B. & P. 371; *Webb* v. *Brooke,* 3 Taunt. 6; *Langton* v. *Hughes,* 1 M. & S. 593; *Ex parte Bell,* 1 M. & S. 751; *Cannan* v. *Bryce,* 3 B. & Ald. 179; *Ex parte Mather,* 3 Ves. 373.

(f) *Bartlett* v. *Vinor,* Carth. 251.

implies a prohibition, though there are no prohibitory words in the statute." The principle of the general rule is thoroughly sound; but its application is frequently difficult, for it is not easy to determine how far the taint of illegality extends (g).

Thus, in *Faikney* v. *Reynous* (h), the plaintiff and one Richardson were jointly concerned in certain illegal transactions, and the plaintiff in execution thereof paid a large sum of money on behalf of himself and Richardson. Subsequently, by way of security for the repayment by Richardson to the plaintiff of the former's share in the latter's disbursements, the defendant gave the plaintiff a bond, on which the action was founded. In the action, the plaintiff was met with the defence of the illegality of the original transactions, hence arose the question whether the taint therefrom extended to the bond. Lord Mansfield distinguished the bond from one given in payment by the plaintiff and Richardson to the other parties to the illegal transaction, and held the bond to be valid. Again, in *Petrie* v. *Hannay* (i), the plaintiff and defendant jointly engaged in illegal (j) stock-jobbing transactions, and incurred losses, and employed a broker to pay the difference, and the plaintiff repaid the broker the whole amount with the privity and consent of the defendant, it was held that the fact that the original transaction was illegal did not vitiate the subsequent payment by the plaintiff and prevent him from recovering from the defendant in an action for money paid to his use. But Lord Eldon, in *Aubert*

(g) *Armstrong* v. *Toler*, 11 Wheat. 258.
(h) *Faikney* v. *Reynous*, 4 Burr. 2070.
(i) *Petrie* v. *Hannay*, 3 T. R. 418.
(j) Barnard's Act, 7 Geo. II. c. 8.

v. *Maze* (*k*), stated that if the principle of the two foregoing cases was to be supported the Act of Parliament
would be of very little use. Both cases are now overruled in England. For instance, a broker paid money
in respect of illegal stock-jobbing transactions, and in
consideration of such payment drew a bill on his principal. But the bill was held to be drawn for an illegal
consideration, and consequently would not support an
action by the broker or by his assignee who took with
notice (*l*). In illegal partnerships, one partner cannot
recover his share of the profits from the others, nor can
he make the others recoup him their shares of the
losses (*m*).

Fisher v.
Bridges.

The important case of *Fisher* v. *Bridges* (*n*) affords
another illustration of the difficulty of the application
of the general rule. The plaintiff agreed to sell a
parcel of land to the defendant for a sum of money,
" to the intent and in order and for the purpose, as the
plaintiff at the time of the agreement for sale well
knew, that the land should be sold by lottery, contrary
to the statute." In pursuance of such agreement the

(*k*) *Aubert* v. *Maze*, 2 Bos. & P. 371.

(*l*) *Steers* v. *Lashley*, 6 T. R. 61 ; *Brown* v. *Turner*, 7 T. R.
630 ; 2 Esp. 631.

(*m*) *Sullivan* v. *Greaves*, Park on Insurance, 8 ; *Mitchell* v.
Cockburn, 2 H. Bl. 380 ; *Booth* v. *Hodgson*, 6 T. R. 405.

(*n*) *Fisher* v. *Bridges*, 2 E. & B. 118, in the Queen's Bench
3 E. & B. 642 ; 2 C. L. R. 928 ; 2 L. J. Q. B. 165 ; 1 Jur. N. S.
157 (in error in Exch. Chamber) ; followed in *Hilton* v. *Eckersley*,
6 E. & B. 47, 66 ; 25 L. J. Q. B. 199 ; 2 Jur. N. S. 587 ; *Geere*
v. *Mare*, 2 H. & C. 339 ; 33 L. J. Ex. 50 ; 8 L. T. N. S. 463.
The connexion too remote, see *A.-G.* v. *Hollingsworth*, 2 H. & N.
416 ; 27 L. J. Ex. 102 ; *Flight* v. *Reed*, 1 H. & C. 703 ; 9 Jur.
N. S. 1016 ; 32 L. J. Ex. 265 ; 12 W. R. 53 ; cf. *Payne* v. *Mayor
of Brecon*, 3 H. & N. 572 ; 27 L. J. Ex. 495.

plaintiff conveyed the land to the defendant. The defendant paid a part of the consideration money, but, by way of security for the payment of the residue, gave the plaintiff a bond. In the action the plaintiff sought to enforce the bond, and the defendant pleaded the above facts as showing illegality. The issue was whether or not the bond could be treated as so severed from the illegal sale as to be valid. The Court of Queen's Bench held that the bond was good, or, rather, that the plea in defence was bad; for, as Erle, J., said, " that whatever is entirely posterior to the illegal act may be supported as not being tainted with the illegality;" and in the original illegal agreement there was no stipulation for the giving of such a deed of covenant, and the deed was not executed in contemplation or in furtherance of the illegal contract. The Court of Exchequer Chamber, however, came to the contrary conclusion, saying that " It is clear that the covenant was given for payment of the purchase money. It springs from and is the creature of the illegal agreement, and as the law would not enforce the original illegal contract, so neither will it allow the parties to enforce a security for the purchase money, which, by the original bargain, was tainted with illegality." The cases on bonds given in consideration of past cohabitation were considered in the course of the case, and in the Exchequer Chamber it was pointed out that if an agreement had been made to pay a sum of money in consideration of future cohabitation, and after cohabitation, the money being unpaid, a bond had been given to secure that money, then such a bond could not, under the circumstances, be enforced.

Exception has been taken to the decision of the Court of Exchequer Chamber on the ground that to hold a contract void because it was to pay a sum of money tainted with illegality is vague and dangerous as a precedent, and liable to degenerate into the mere private discretion of the majority of the Court (o). But it is submitted that there was a very substantial connection between the bond in question and the illegal transaction, and that the decision of the Court of Queen's Bench is open to the objection which Lord Eldon took with regard to *Faikney* v. *Reynous*, that it would impair seriously the operation of the statute.

Illegality
relating back.

Sometimes a contract may be tainted with the illegality of a subsequent transaction. For instance, at a time when brewers were prohibited from using certain drugs (p), but before druggists had been by statute prohibited (q) from selling such drugs to brewers (q), it was held that a druggist could not recover the price of drugs sold by him to a brewer, knowing that the drugs were to be used in the brewery (r). That case led to the decision of *Cannan* v. *Bryce* (s), where, on behalf of the plaintiff, it was contended that the loan of money there in question had been made for the express purpose of enabling a third person to pay differences on illegal stock-jobbing transactions, and that the loan was itself illegal, and that consequently any security given for its repayment must be void. On the behalf of the defendant it was advanced that he was not a party to the illegal transaction, and that the loan was not illegal, and that the securities were therefore available in law. Abbot, C. J., said: "The statute has absolutely pro-

---

(o) *Collins* v. *Blantern*, 2 Wils. 341; Smith's Leading Cases, 9th ed. vol. 1, pp. 423, 424.

(p) 42 Geo. III.

(q) 51 Geo. III.

(r) *Langton* v. *Hughes*, 1 M. & S. 593.

(s) *Cannan* v. *Bryce*, 3 B. & Ald. 179.

·hibited the payment of money for compounding differences, it is impossible to say that the making such payment is not an unlawful act ; and if it be unlawful in one man to pay, how can it be lawful for another man to furnish him with the means of payment ? I am speaking of a case where the means were furnished with full knowledge of the object, and for the express purpose of accomplishing that object." In *M'Kinnell* v. *Robinson (t)*, the plaintiff sued for money lent and found to be due on account stated ; the defendant pleaded that the money was lent in a common gambling room, for the purpose of illegal gaming by the defendant at hazard. It was, in the result, held that the principle of *Cannan* v. *Bryce* applied : and that the plaintiff could not recover.

Similarly, where rooms were knowingly let for an illegal purpose, the rent could not be recovered (*u*). The rooms in question were not merely knowingly let to a prostitute, but were let for the purpose of prostitution. In the case of *Cowan* v. *Milbourn (v)*, the defendant agreed to let rooms to the plaintiff, and afterwards discovered that the same were intended to be used for the delivery of blasphemous lectures ; he thereupon declined to carry out the contract. It was held against the plaintiff, that his intended illegal user deprived him of any right of action on the contract, which did not bind the defendant, though, at the time of contracting, he was ignorant of the plaintiff's unlawful purpose. These two cases would be in point, for example, with regard to the letting of rooms for purposes unlawful,

Knowledge of purpose.

(t) *M'Kinnell* v. *Robinson*, 3 M. & W. 434.

(u) *Jennings* v. *Throgmorton*, R. & M. 251 ; *Girardy* v. *Richardson*, 1 Esp. 13 ; *Lloyd* v. *Johnson*, 1 B. & P. 340 ; see also *Bowry* v. *Bennet*, 1 Camp. 348.

(v) *Cowan* v. *Milbourn*, L. R. 2 Ex. 230 ; 36 L. J. Ex. 124 ; 16 L. T. 290 ; 15 W. R. 750.

and prohibited by the Lottery Acts, or Gaming or Betting House Acts.

Chattels supplied in furtherance of illegal purpose.

Again, where goods are knowingly sold for an illegal purpose, the contract cannot be enforced or sued on. In the case of *Pearce* v. *Brookes* (*w*), the point was raised with regard to the sale of a brougham. The defendant pleaded that she, to the knowledge of the plaintiff, was a prostitute, and that the supposed agreement was made for the supply of a brougham to be used by her as such prostitute, and to assist her in her immoral vocation, as the plaintiff well knew. The jury found, first, that the defendant did hire the brougham for the purposes of her prostitution; and, secondly, that the plaintiff knew the purposes for which she hired it. Pollock, C. B., on the authority of *Cannan* v. *Bryce*, *M'Kinnell* v. *Robinson*, said it was settled law "that any person who contributes to the performance of an illegal act, by supplying a thing with the knowledge that it is going to be used for that purpose, cannot recover the price of the thing so supplied." Bramwell, B., in the same case pointed out that "it need not be a part of the bargain that the subject of the contract should be used unlawfully, but that it is enough if it is handed over for the purpose that the borrower should so apply it." But, for instance, if money or goods be handed over, with a knowledge that the same may or may not be used for an illegal purpose, the lender or the vendor may recover. Thus, in *Bagot* v. *Arnott* (*x*), the money was advanced for the purpose of obtaining a security for a pre-existing debt, with knowledge that it might be used to enable a criminal to escape; nevertheless the lender recovered his loan.

(*w*) *Pearce* v. *Brookes*, L. R. 1 Ex. 213; 35 L. J. Ex. 134; 12 Jur. N. S. 342; 14 L. T. 288; 14 W. R. 614.

(*x*) *Bagot* v. *Arnott*, I. R. 2 C. L. 1.

So, also, remuneration for work and labour done to effectuate an illegal purpose cannot be recovered. In *Bensley* v. *Bignold* (*y*), the printer failed to recover for printing a pamphlet, or for the paper on which it was printed. Abbott, C. J., said:—"I am of opinion that a party cannot be permitted to sue either for work and labour done, or for materials provided, where the whole combined forms one entire subject-matter made in direct violation of the provisions of an Act of Parliament." This case would apply, for example, to the printing of advertisements or betting lists, within the prohibition of the Betting House Acts (*z*). Similarly where the transaction is *malum in se*. A question may arise as to whether the work and labour was done for an improper purpose: for instance, washing clothes and gentlemen's nightcaps for a prostitute; the Court may decline to inquire which of the articles were used for an improper purpose, and which not (*a*).

Work and labour.

Where a part of the consideration of a contract is illegal, the whole contract is vitiated; for the illegal consideration affects the whole contract. For instance, if a sum of money be advanced partly for the purpose of playing at hazard, and partly for some innocent purpose, then any security given to secure the advance would be wholly tainted with the illegality of the part of the consideration (*b*).

If one of the considerations of the contract illegal, whole promise is void.

The defence of illegality should, pursuant to the Rules of the Supreme Court, be pleaded by stating the facts

Pleading illegality.

(*y*) *Bensley* v. *Bignold*, 5 B. & Ald. 335.
(*z*) See *post*, Chap. XIII.
(*a*) *Lloyd* v. *Johnson*, 1 B. & P. 340.
(*b*) *Featherstone* v. *Hutchinson*, Cro. Eliz. 199; *Waite* v. *Jones*, 1 Bing. N. C. 656; 1 Scott, 730; *Shackell* v. *Rosier*, 2 Bing. N. C. 646; *Howden* v. *Haigh*, 11 A. & E. 1033; 3 P. & D. 661; *Lound* v. *Grimwade*, 39 Ch. D. 605; 57 L. J. Ch. 725; 59 L. T. 168. See, as to illegal conditions of bonds, Smith's L. C. vol. 1, pp. 416, 417.

I 2

which show its existence (*c*). In the case of *Potts* v. *Sparrow* (*d*), it was stated by Tindal, C. J., that " he had never heard that if the defendant omits to avail himself of the plea, that the Court is to go on and discover it for him. There are many cases in which the claim in respect of services performed or goods delivered would be plainly illegal, and as such would impose on the defendant the necessity of pleading the illegality, although no express contract would be proved at the trial." Again, in *Varney* v. *Hickman* (*e*), where the plaintiff brought an action of debt for money had and received, and the defendant merely pleaded that he was never indebted, instead of stating facts showing that the transaction was a wager on a trotting match, Maule, J., said that the scope of the new rules is to restrain the defendant from proving, under the general traverse, affirmative matter which goes to impeach the legality of the contract declared on without interfering with its existence in point of fact. But the Court, in spite of the omission to plead the illegality, may take cognizance of it, and refuse to entertain the action (*f*).

Right of rescission whilst illegal contract executory.

    The previous part of this chapter has exemplified the general rule. There is, however, a well-established right which enables a party to an illegal contract to rescind the contract, and to claim consequential relief on that

(*c*) R. S. C. Ord. XIX. r. 15.

(*d*) *Potts* v. *Sparrow*, 1 Bing. N. C. 594.

(*e*) *Varney* v. *Hickman*, 5 C. B. 271 ; 5 D. & L. 364 ; 17 L. J. C. P. 102.

(*f*) *Begbie* v. *Phosphate Sewage Co.*, 1 Q. B. D. 679 ;˙ 35 L. T. 350 ; 25 W. R. 85 (C. A.), affirming, L. R. 10 Q. B. 491 ; 44 L. J. Q. B. 233 ; 33 L. T. 470 ; 24 W. R. 115 ; *Scott* v. *Brown, Dœring, MacNab & Co., Slaughter and May* v. *Brown, Dœring, MacNab & Co.*, (1892) 2 Q. B. 724 ; 4 R. 42 ; 61 L. J. Q. B. 738 ; 67 L. T. 782 ; 41 W. R. 116 ; 57 J. P. 213.

footing. The following authorities will show when that right exists and when it ceases.

In 1780, in the case of *Lowry* v. *Bourdieu* (*g*), Buller, *Restitutio in* J., stated—"There is a sound distinction between con- *integrum.* tracts executed and executory, and if an action is brought with a view to rescind a contract, you must do it whilst the contract continues executory and then it can only be done on terms of restoring the other party to his original situation." The contract, in that case, was an illegal insurance in the nature of a hedging bet. Again, in *Tappenden* v. *Randall* (*h*), after the money had been paid over, and before the event had happened, the plaintiff, having demanded his money back, was allowed to recover. So, in *Aubert* v. *Walsh* (*i*), where money had been deposited upon a then illegal wager on a future event, the plaintiff was allowed to recover it back before the happening of the event. Lord Mansfield stated that the demand of the money back before the day rescinded the contract, and that as the contract was illegal, the plaintiff was allowed so to rescind it. Neither in *Tappenden* v. *Randall*, nor in *Aubert* v. *Walsh*, nor in *Busk* v. *Walsh*, was there a suggestion that the defendant could not be put back into his original situation. The principle was enunciated by Mellish, L. J., in the case of *Taylor* v. *Bowers* (*j*)— "If money is paid or goods delivered for an illegal purpose, the person who has delivered the goods or paid the money, may recover them back before the illegal purpose is carried out; but if he waits till the illegal

(*g*) *Lowry* v. *Bourdieu*, 2 Doug. 468.

(*h*) *Tappenden* v. *Randall*, 2 B. & P. 467.

(*i*) *Aubert* v. *Walsh*, 3 Taunt. 277; *Busk* v. *Walsh*, 4 Taunt. 290.

(*j*) *Taylor* v. *Bowers*, 1 Q. B. D. 291; 45 L. J. Q. B. 163; 34 L. T. 263; 24 W. R. 499.

purpose is carried out, or if he seeks to enforce the illegal
transaction, in neither case can he maintain his action."
In *Wilson* v. *Strugnell* (k) the principle is stated in similar terms.   In the case of *Herman* v. *Jeuchner* (l), in the
Court of Appeal, Baggallay, L. J., after allowing that
when the illegal purpose had not been effected the
money deposited might be recovered back, added, "but,
on the other hand, I am hardly prepared to say that,
in order to prevent a plaintiff from succeeding who sues
to recover back money deposited in furtherance of an
illegal purpose, the illegal object itself must be fully
carried out."   In the recent case of *Kearley* v. *Thomson* (m), Lord Justice Fry, delivering judgment on
behalf of Lord Chief Justice Coleridge and the Master
of the Rolls, stated the general rule, and examined the
several exceptions or apparent exceptions thereto.   He
cited the passage quoted above from the case of *Taylor*
v. *Bowers*, and added—" It is remarkable that this proposition is, as I believe, to be found in no earlier case
than *Taylor* v. *Bowers*, which occurred in 1867. . . . .
I cannot help saying that I think the extent of the
application of that principle, and even the principle
itself, may at some time hereafter, require consideration, if not in this Court, yet in a higher tribunal."
It is, however, submitted that, having regard to authorities prior to 1867, the principle is well established,

(k) *Wilson* v. *Strugnell*, 7 Q. B. D. 548; 50 L. J. M. C. 145;
45 L. T. 218; 45 J. P. 831; 14 Cox, C. C. 624; see also *Bone* v.
Eckless, 5 H. & N. 925; 29 L. J. Ex. 438; *Symes* v. *Hughes*,
L. R. 9 Eq. 475; 39 L. J. Ch. 304; 22 L. T. 462.

(l) *Herman* v. *Jeuchner*, 15 Q. B. D. 561; 54 L. J. Q. B. 340;
53 L. T. 94; 33 W. R. 606; 49 J. P. 502 (C. A.), reversing 1 C.
& E. 364.

(m) *Kearley* v. *Thomson*, 24 Q. B. D. 742; 59 L. J. Q. B.
288; 63 L. T. 150; 38 W. R. 614.

though the extent of its application is not strictly definite. The case of *Kearley* v. *Thomson* is an express decision that when the illegal contract has been partly carried into effect and partly remains unperformed, that money paid thereunder to the other party cannot be recovered. This illustration was given:—Suppose a payment of 100*l.* by A. to B., on a contract that the latter shall murder C. and D. He has murdered C. but not D. Can the money be recovered back? It cannot. But if that illustration be tested by the principle as enunciated by Buller, J., in *Lowry* v. *Bourdieu*, the same result is arrived at, because B. cannot be restored to his original position. Further illustrations of the power to rescind an illegal contract will be hereafter given in considering the position of agents in illegal transactions (*n*).

The next exception to the general rule arises where the illegal transaction has been completed, but the parties thereto have respectively occupied the positions of oppressor and oppressed. The cases on this subject are mostly derived from illegal transactions in connection with financial embarrassments, or in cases of extortion by duress (*o*); but it is not without application to gambling transactions. Thus, in the case of *Thistlewood* v. *Cracroft* (*p*), where the defendant had won money of the plaintiff at play at hazard, the plaintiff would have

Oppressor and oppressed.

(*n*) *Post,* pp. 127 *et seq.*

(*o*) In connection with bankruptcy: *Smith* v. *Bromley,* 2 Doug. 695; *Smith* v. *Cuff,* 6 M. & S. 160; *Wilson* v. *Ray,* 10 Ad. & El. 82; 3 Jur. 384; 2 P. & D. 253; in connection with penal actions: *Williams* v. *Hedley,* 8 East, 378; *Unwin* v. *Leaper,* 1 M. & Gr. 747; 1 Drink. 3; 4 Jur. 1037; in connection with colourable legal process: *Cardaval* v. *Collins,* 4 Ad. & El. 858. See also *Goodall* v. *Lowndes,* 6 Q. B. 464; 9 Jur. 177.

(*p*) *Thistlewood* v. *Cracroft,* 1 M. & S. 500.

been allowed to recover the money so won, if he could have shown any traces of foul play, so as to form a shade of delinquency between himself and the defendant, by making it a case of oppression or fraud on one. The Court would then have eagerly interfered in order to administer relief.

Where the *delictum* is not *par*. Sometimes a statute renders a transaction illegal, but the object of the statute is to protect one class of persons from another class. The two classes with reference to such a transaction do not stand *in pari delicto*, and therefore an exception, whereunder the protected are allowed to sue, is engrafted on the general rule. This is the case with regard to the Lottery Acts. Speaking particularly with reference to the statute 14 Geo. III. c. 76, De Grey, C. J., said : " The statute is made to protect the ignorant and deluded multitude, who, in hopes of gain and prizes, and not conversant in calculations, are drawn in by the office keepers " (*q*). In the case of *Jaques* v. *Golightly* the plaintiff had insured lottery tickets in various manners at the defendant's office. He paid 64*l*. in premiums. Upon some chances he was a winner; on others a loser. The balance due to him was 90*l*., which sum the defendant refused to pay, alleging that the insuring was illegal ; but he none the less insisted on retaining the premiums. On behalf of the defendant it was contended that the plaintiff was *particeps criminis*. But that contention failed, because the statute did not render the contract on the part of the insured more than void, and therefore, having advanced his premium without any consideration, he was entitled to recover it back. Mr. Justice Blackstone contrasted the Act in question with Barnard's Act (*r*),

(*q*) *Jaques* v. *Golightly*, 2 Bl. 1073.
(*r*) 7 Geo. II. c. 8, Chap. X.

whereunder both parties to a forbidden stock-jobbing transaction were made criminal and subject to penalties. There was in that Act a provision which gave the loser a right to an indemnity against the penalties if he sued and recovered back the money lost; but in order to enable him so to sue, it was, under the circumstances, necessary to insert in the Act an express power to maintain the action. The case of *Jaques* v. *Withy* (*s*) is similar. The principle was concisely stated by Lord Mansfield in the case of *Browning* v. *Morris* (*t*) : "Where contracts are prohibited by positive statutes for the sake of protecting one set of men from another set of men, the one being likely to be imposed upon by the other, then the parties are not *in pari delicto*, and in furtherance of these statutes the person injured after the transaction is finished and completed may bring his action and defeat the contract." So, again, in that case the plaintiff was allowed to recover, as distinguished from his winnings, moneys actually paid by him to the office keeper of the lottery. In the recent case of *Barclay* v. *Pearson* (*u*), Mr. Justice Stirling held that the competitors in the missing word competition form a class protected by the statute, and that, in the absence of special circumstances, each unsuccessful competitor is entitled, notwithstanding that the competition is finished and the prize winners ascertained, to bring an action at law for the recovery of what was paid by him to the defendant, and none the less so because the fund had been distributed.

Apart from questions of oppression or of statutory protection, the true test for determining whether or not

Test of par delictum.

(*s*) *Jaques* v. *Withy*, 1 H. Bl. 65.

(*t*) *Browning* v. *Morris*, 2 Cowp. 790.

(*u*) *Barclay* v. *Pearson*, (1893) 2 Ch. 154; 62 L. J. Ch. 636; 68 L. T. 709; 42 W. R. 74; 3 R. 388, and *ante*, p. 71.

the plaintiff and defendant are *in pari delicto* is stated to be, whether the plaintiff can make out his case otherwise than through the medium of, and by the aid of the illegal transaction to which he was himself a party. Thus, in *Simpson* v. *Bloss* (v), the plaintiff sued the defendant for money lent. It appeared that at Epsom, in 1813, the plaintiff made a ten guinea bet with Captain Bograve. The defendant advised him to increase the bet to twenty-five guineas, and assumed a part of it to the amount of ten guineas. The horse, backed by the plaintiff and defendant, won. The plaintiff, at the request of the defendant, immediately paid him his share of the winnings, which, it was expected, would be paid at Tattersall's on the following Monday. But, in the meantime, Captain Bograve died insolvent, and the bet was never paid. The plaintiff brought this action to recover back the sum of ten guineas which he had so advanced, and he contended that the payment was on a condition which had failed. But it was decided that the plaintiff could not recover, because it was impossible to prove failure of the condition, which was that Bograve should make good the plaintiff's advance to the defendant by paying the whole amount of the bet to the plaintiff, without going into the illegal contract (w), in which all parties were equally concerned. In the course of the judgment it was pointed out that the case was on all fours with the illegal insurance case, *Ex parte Bell* (x).

(v) *Simpson* v. *Bloss*, 7 Taunt. 246.

(w) Then illegal on account of the amount of the bet, see p. 55, *ante*.

(x) *Ex parte Bell*, 1 M. & S. 751. See also *Fivaz* v. *Nicholls*, 2 C. B. 501; 15 L. J. C. P. 125; *Begbie* v. *Phosphate Sewage Company*, 1 Q. B. 679; 35 L. T. 350; 25 W. R. 85 (C. A.), affirming L. R. 10 Q. B. 491; 44 L. J. Q. B. 233; 33 L. T. 470; 24 W. R. 115.

The case of *Taylor* v. *Chester* (*y*) affords another instance of the application of this test. The plaintiff declared on the bailment of the half of a 50*l.* Bank of England note to the defendant, to be redelivered on request, alleging a refusal by the defendant to redeliver such half note. The second count was for detinue of the same half note. The defendant, after traversing the delivery and detention of the note, and to the second count denying that it was the property of the plaintiff, pleaded separately and specially to both counts, to the effect, that the half note in question had been deposited by the plaintiff with the defendant by way of pledge, to secure the repayment of money due and money then advanced by the defendant to the plaintiff and then due. The plaintiff joined issue on the defendant's pleas, and specially replied with regard to the alleged debt, that under the circumstances stated therein, the loan was knowingly made for an illegal purpose. The plaintiff, in order then to meet the plea of a valid pledge, was obliged to advance the illegality in his special replication; he could, therefore, only recover through the medium and by the aid of the illegal transaction to which he was himself a party. Under such circumstances, the maxim *in pari delicto potior est conditio possidentis* was decisive of the case.

The subject of agency in relation to the illegal trans- Agency. actions with which this book is concerned, is mostly important in connection with that class of agents who are stakeholders; but the rights and obligations of agents generally are material, and therefore will be briefly indicated.

If an agent is employed to negotiate an illegal Agent not liable for

(*y*) *Taylor* v. *Chester*, L. R. 4 Q. B. 309; 38 L. J. Q. B. 225; 21 L. T. 359; 17 W. R. 94.

contract for his principal, the principal cannot recover by action for a breach of contract. Thus, in the case of *Webster* v. *De Tastet* (z), where a sailor on board a ship was to receive slaves in lieu of wages, and employed an agent to insure them, it was held that as the slaves were not the subject of a legal insurance, the plaintiff could not recover against his agent for negligence in not procuring such an insurance. The ille-

gality, however, must be clearly shown (a). Again, an agent cannot recover from his principal commission for work done where the transaction is illegal. In the case of *Josephs* v. *Pebrer* (b), the plaintiff claimed his commission for purchasing shares in an illegal association. As the plaintiff claimed remuneration in respect of services rendered for an illegal purpose, it was held that he could not maintain his action. But in *Lyne* v. *Siesfeld* (c), which was a similar action for money paid, and for commission, part of the transactions were lawful and part unlawful, Pollock, C.B., said, "The causes of action to which the pleas are pleaded are founded on distinct considerations, to show that part is illegal does not afford an answer to the whole," and the plaintiff was allowed to recover.

Again, neither principal nor agent can recover from each other money that has been advanced for an illegal purpose. In *Bayntun* v. *Cattle* (d), the plaintiff had been a candidate for parliament, and the defendant had acted as his agent. The plaintiff, in the course of his candidature, had paid to the defendant considerable sums of money for the purposes of the election. In this action,

(z) *Webster* v. *De Tastet*, 7 T. R. 157.
(a) *Catlin* v. *Bell*, 4 Camp. 183.
(b) *Josephs* v. *Pebrer*, 3 B. & C. 639; 5 D. & R. 542; 1 C. & P. 341 and 507.
(c) *Lyne* v. *Siesfeld*, 1 H. & N. 278.
(d) *Bayntun* v. *Cattle*, 1 M. & R. 265.

he sought to recover a balance from his agent. In support of his action he put in evidence an account rendered to him by the defendant; this account showed that the defendant's disbursements exceeded his receipts, thereupon the plaintiff sought to falsify it. The jury found as a fact, that the defendant had no moneys of the plaintiff then in his hands; then arose the further question, whether the defendant could, as against the plaintiff, rely on the illegal disbursements; if the defendant could prove that the plaintiff had knowledge of the illegality of the payments at the time they were made, or subsequently assented thereto, then the plaintiff was bound thereby. Alderson, J., said, "Did the plaintiff know of, and authorize these illegal payments? If he did not, he has a right to recover the amount in this action, for if a person entrusts money to an agent to be by him laid out in legal disbursements, but the agent chooses to lay out part of the money in disbursements which are not legal, he cannot claim credit for those disbursements when he comes to settle with his employer."

The same rule applies where an agent without authority advances money to pay an illegal debt; money so advanced cannot be recovered (e).

But if an agent has received money from a third party to be paid over to his principal, he cannot retain it on the ground that the money is the result of an illegal transaction between his principal and the third party. Thus, in *Tenant* v. *Elliott* (f), the defendant, as a broker, effected a policy of assurance on behalf of

Money received by agent to the use of his principal may be recovered by principal.

(e) *Amory* v. *Meryweather,* 2 B. & C. 573; *Steers* v. *Lashley* 6 T. R. 61.

(f) *Tenant* v. *Elliott,* 1 B. & P. 3; approved in *Thomson* v. *Thomson,* 7 Ves. 470.

the plaintiff. The policy was illegal, but the underwriters nevertheless made a payment thereunder to the defendant on behalf of the plaintiff. The defendant, without any intimation from the underwriters, refused to pay this money over to the plaintiff, who then brought his action on account of such refusal. It was argued for the defendant, that as the plaintiff could not have succeeded in an action against the underwriters, he could not recover against the defendant. But it was held by Buller, J., that the illegality having been waived by the underwriter paying over the money for the use of the plaintiff, the defendant was not entitled to retain it.

The case of *Farmer* v. *Russell* (g), is another authority on the same point. It is now well established that if A., in pursuance of an illegal transaction between himself and B., makes a payment to B.'s agent, B. may recover from the agent, for as between them the receipt of the money is upon a legal transaction.

The money must be actually received, and to the use of the principal. There must, however, have been an actual receipt of the money by the agent. Thus, an account stated wherein the agent is credited with the amounts, will not support the action of the principal. If the transaction were not illegal, it might be otherwise (h). Again, not only must there be an actual receipt, but the money so received must have been paid to the use of the plaintiff. For example, A. contracts with B. that in consideration of B.'s starting an illegal lottery, A. will pay him 100*l.*; B. sets up the illegal lottery, A. then pays the money to C. saying that it is the stipulated reward for setting up the lottery, but directs C. to distribute it amongst the losers in the lottery, and C. so

(g) *Farmer* v. *Russell*, 1 B. & P. 296.
(h) *Edgar* v. *Fowler*, 3 East, 222.

applies it. B. could not maintain an action against C. to recover the amount (i).

But if the agent is *particeps criminis*, the principal cannot recover from him. In pursuance of a fraud in the guise of a scheme for establishing a colony on the coast of Honduras, the agent, who was a party to the fraud, negotiated a loan for the principal, but only paid over a portion of the money which he had received on behalf of his principal in respect of the loan. The bubble subsequently burst, and the principal then brought an action to recover the residue of the money in the hands of his agent, but it was held that as the agent was *particeps criminis*, the action could not be maintained (j).

Two or more people agree to carry through a given transaction, the event of which is uncertain, and they further deposit money or other valuable things in the hands of an outsider, to be held by him and disposed of by him according as the event shall result in the one way or the other : such a person is a stakeholder (k). It now remains to consider the stakeholder's position, where the event to be decided, depends on and arises out of an illegal transaction.

The law has gone far in allowing a party to an illegal transaction to rescind the contract, and to revoke the stakeholder's authority to pay over the money according to the original illegal agreement. True though it may be, that the actual placing of the money in the hands of the stakeholder for the illegal purpose, is a part execution of such purpose, and the possession of

Marginal notes:

Where agent is *particeps criminis*.

Stakeholders.

Principal's power of rescission.

(i) *Nicholson* v. *Gooch*, 5 E. & B. 999; 25 L. J. Q. B. 137; 2 Jur. N. S. 303.

(j) *Bousfield* v. *Wilson*, 16 M. & W. 185; 16 L. J. Ex. 44; *M'Gregor* v. *Lowe*, 1 R. & M. 57; 1 C. & P. 200.

(k) See *post*, p. 189.

the stakeholder is a direct result of the agreement to execute such purpose, yet such part performance does not destroy the principal's power of rescission. But further, where the deposit of the stakes has been followed by the determination of the event, the principal can rescind, even at such a late stage, the agent's authority to pay over the stakes, and can recover his own deposit ; and should the stakeholder pay over after receiving notice not to do so, he will be liable to repay the objector's deposit. The power to rescind exists until the event has been determined, and the stakes paid over.

In *Cotton* v. *Thurland* (*l*), the plaintiff deposited fifteen guineas with the defendant as the plaintiff's share of a stake to be dealt with according to the event of a boxing match between the plaintiff and another. The battle was fought, but a dispute arose, and the defendant was warned not to pay the money over until the parties met and the matter was decided. The defendant claimed to hold the money until the event was decided. But it was held that there was neither equity nor conscience on the part of the defendant, for if the contract were illegal between the parties to the wager, yet as long as the money remained in his hands he was answerable to some one for it, and in the absence of a decision of the event, he was under an obligation to restore one half of the money to each party.

In *Smith* v. *Bickmore* (*m*), which was another case of a stakeholder at a boxing match, the jury found as a fact that the battle had been decided, and the defendant, the stakeholder, obtained a verdict. But subsequently a new trial was ordered on the ground that the plaintiff, by reason of his demand for the return of his deposit

(*l*) *Cotton* v. *Thurland*, 5 T. R. 405.
(*m*) *Smith* v. *Bickmore*, 4 Taunt. 474.

before payment over, was entitled to recover back that sum. On the facts, the case was distinguished from those actions wherein one of the parties to a wager sues another party thereto; as where the assured sues the underwriter for the return of premiums paid in respect of illegal insurances. These cases were followed in *Bate* v. *Cartwright* (*n*), which arose out of a foot-race, then illegal on account of the amount of the stakes. Again, in *Hudson* v. *Terrill* (*o*), the defendant stake-holder paid over the whole stake after he had received notice from the plaintiff not to pay over his deposit: the defendant was ordered to repay. Again, in the recent case of *Barclay* v. *Pearson* (*p*), one of the competitors in the lottery, was held entitled to recover back the shilling which he had deposited with the defendant stakeholder, before the latter had distributed the stakes to the winners. Mr. Justice Stirling, in that case, pointed out the distinction which exists between such cases where a stakeholder is concerned, and other cases where there is no stakeholder, as in *Kearley* v. *Thomson* (*q*).

These cases of rescission, where a stakeholder is concerned, show how far the Court will interfere to frustrate an illegal transaction, and may not be without importance in relation to the doctrine of *Lowry* v. *Bourdieu*, and the cases following it, such as *Taylor* v. *Bowers* (*r*).

Every partnership, which has for its object something the attainment of which is contrary to law, is an illegal Illegal partnerships.

(*n*) *Bate* v. *Cartwright*, 7 Price, 540.

(*o*) *Hudson* v. *Terrill*, 1 Cr. & M. 797; see also *Robinson* v. *Mearns*, 6 D. & R. 26; *Hastelow* v. *Jackson*, 8 B. & C. 221.

(*p*) *Barclay* v. *Pearson*, (1893) 2 Ch. p. 168.

(*q*) *Kearley* v. *Thomson*, 24 Q. B. D. 742; 59 L. J. Q. B. 288; 63 L. T. 150; 38 W. R. 614; *ante*, p. 118.

(*r*) *Ante*, p. 117.

G.   K

partnership; it will suffice if the object be one forbidden by statute and not otherwise illegal. For example, a partnership in an adventure of setting up a lottery, or of keeping a common gaming house, or a betting house, or using a place for cock fighting or dog fighting, or for holding a horse race contrary to the Racecourse Licensing Act, 1879, would be illegal, and the contract to form such a partnership would be illegal (s). Therefore, under the general rule, the contract would be unenforceable either at law or at equity; the illegal association might enter into transactions which in themselves were legal, and in respect of such collateral legal transactions the members of the illegal firm might be sued. But if the plaintiff could be proved to have been aware of all the facts, which show that his demand arises out of a transaction tainted with the illegality of the partnership, he could not succeed (t).

Illegality destroys the rights of partners *inter se.* But the effect of the illegality in the constitution of the firm is most strikingly illustrated by the destruction of the usual rights of the partners *inter se.* The members have no rights of contribution or of apportionment in respect of the partnership dealings and transactions; one member may have paid all the losses, but he can obtain no contribution (u); one member may have received profits, but the others cannot obtain shares (v), not even where there is an express covenant to pay such shares (w), or where the amount has been

---

(s) *Duvergier* v. *Fellowes*, 5 Bing. 248; 10 B. & C. 826; 1 Cl. & F. 39.

(t) *In re South Wales Atlantic Steamship Company*, 2 Ch. Div. 763; 46 L. J. Ch. 177; 35 L. T. 294.

(u) *Mitchell* v. *Cockburn*, 2 H. Black. 380.

(v) *Booth* v. *Hodgson*, 6 T. R. 405.

(w) *Lees* v. *Smith*, 7 T. R. 338.

determined by an arbitrator (x). As the late Master of the Rolls said in the case of *Sykes* v. *Beadon* (y), "I think the principle is clear that you cannot directly enforce an illegal contract, and you cannot ask the Court to assist you in carrying it out. You cannot enforce it indirectly, that is, by claiming damages or compensation for the breach of it, or contribution from the persons making the profits realized from it " (z).

It would follow that an action for an account, brought by one partner against the others, would not be maintainable in respect of the partnership dealings and transactions. The case of *Knowles* v. *Houghton* (a), arising out of an illegal insurance business, is a decision in point.

The case of *Sharp* v. *Taylor* (b) is of importance in regard to the foregoing principles. Sharp and Taylor, subjects of this country, purchased an American-built ship on a joint speculation, with a view of employing her in the trade between the two countries until they could sell her at a profit, and for that purpose they caused her to be registered in America in the name of Robertson, an American. Subsequently Robertson stated that he should be obliged to assume the whole *bonâ fide* ownership of the vessel. From the facts

Sharp v. *Taylor.*

(x) *Aubert* v. *Maze*, 2 Bos. & Pul. 371 ; the cases of *Petrie* v. *Hannay*, 3 T. R. 418 ; *Faikney* v. *Reynous*, 4 Burr. 2070, are overruled. See also *De Begnis* v. *Armistead*, 10 Bing. 107.

(y) *Sykes* v. *Beadon*, 11 Ch. Div. 170 ; 48 L. J. Ch. 522 ; 40 L. T. 243 ; 27 W. R. 404.

(z) See also *Holman* v. *Johnson*, 1 Cowp. 341 ; *Cousins* v. *Smith*, 13 Ves. 542 ; *Thomson* v. *Thomson*, 7 Ves. 470.

(a) *Knowles* v. *Houghton*, 11 Ves. 168, overrules *Watts* v. *Brooks*, 3 Ves. 612 ; see further *Armstrong* v. *Armstrong*, 3 M. & K. 45 ; *Harvey* v. *Collett*, 15 Sim. 332.

(b) *Sharp* v. *Taylor*, 2 Phil. 801.

appearing in the report, it seems that Sharp was willing
to surrender his interest in the ship to Robertson on
terms. In Lord Cottenham's judgment it is stated, that
Robertson's desire to become the actual owner as well
as the registered owner, was for the purpose of further-
ing a scheme between himself and Taylor, with the
object of excluding Sharp. But the Lord Chancellor
did not consider that part of the case material in considering the question between Sharp and Taylor. Sharp
alleged and proved that Taylor had attempted to exclude
him from his share of the speculation, and he required
an account and payment of his share of the realised
profits. Lord Cottenham was of opinion, that it was
immaterial whether the sums received arose from freight
or other profits due to Taylor and the plaintiff as owners
of the ship, or from payments made or allowed by
Robertson on account of the ship, of which he was the
real owner. Hence the question of ownership was
not determined. But this point is important, because
if Robertson was the real owner, then there was no
illegality in the transactions; for " the importation of the
goods in a ship American built, and not professing to
have any English registry, would not be illegal, and
the American owner might assign the freight to anyone " (c). In the absence of proof of illegality, the
presumption is against its existence. Hence the *ratio
decidendi* of this case, it is submitted, does not involve
any principle touching illegal partnerships. The Lord
Chancellor's judgment then contains, as stated by
Jessel, M. R., in *Sykes* v. *Beadon* (d), *obiter dicta*, which
as such are important. The defendant had set up the
illegality of the adventure in answer to the plaintiff's
bill: the Lord Chancellor said, " But the answer to the

(c) *Sharp* v. *Taylor*, 2 Phil. at p. 818.
(d) *Sykes* v. *Beadon*, 11 Ch. Div. at p. 196.

objection appears to me to be this, that the plaintiff does
not ask to enforce any agreement adverse to the provisions of the Act of Parliament. He is not seeking
compensation and payment for an illegal voyage: that
matter was disposed of when Taylor received the money;
and the plaintiff is now only seeking for payment of his
share of the realised profits. The violation of law suggested was not any fraud upon the revenue, or omission
to pay what might be due; but, at most, an invasion of
a parliamentary provision, supposed to be beneficial to
the shipowners of this country; an evil, if any, which
must remain the same, whether the freight be divided
between Sharp and Taylor, according to their shares, or
remain altogether in the hands of Taylor. As between
these two, can this supposed evasion of the law be set
up as a defence by one against the otherwise clear title
of the other? In this particular suit, can the one
tenant in common dispute the title common to both?
Can one of two partners possess himself of the property
of the firm, and be permitted to retain it, if he can show
that, in realising it, some provision in some Act of Parliament has been violated or neglected? Can one of
two partners, in any import trade, defeat the other, by
showing that there was some irregularity in passing the
goods through the custom house? *The answer to this,
as to the former case, will be, that the transaction alleged to
be illegal is completed and closed, and will not be in any
manner affected by what the Court is asked to do, as between
the parties.* Do the authorities negative this view of the
case? The difference between enforcing illegal contracts and asserting title to money which has arisen
from them is distinctly taken in *Tenant* v. *Elliott* (e) and

---

(e) *Tenant* v. *Elliott*, 1 Bos. & Pul. 3.

Farmer v. *Russell* (*f*), and recognised and approved by
Sir William Grant in *Thomson* v. *Thomson* (*g*). But the
alleged illegality in this case was not in the freight
being paid to English subjects claiming as owners of
the ship, as in *Campbell* v. *Innes*" (*h*). The Lord Chancellor, in pointing out that the evil, if any, would remain
the same whether the freight was divided between
Sharp and Taylor, or remain in the hands of Taylor,
obviously was not advancing a consideration applicable
to illegal transactions (*i*). With regard to the passage
in italics, it may be mentioned that *Mitchell* v. *Cockburn*,
Booth v. *Hodgson*, *Lees* v. *Smith*, *Aubert* v. *Maze* (*k*)
were not cited in the argument. The cases of *Tenant* v.
Elliott and *Farmer* v. *Russell*, it will be remembered, were
decided on the grounds that the third person, the defendant, was not *particeps criminis* (*l*), as it is submitted
the partners would have been had the transaction been
illegal. The above-quoted *dicta* were dissented from by
Jessel, M. R., in the case of *Sykes* v. *Beadon* (*i*) :—" I
must say, speaking with some hesitation, as I always
do, when differing from any judgment of Lord Cottenham's, that that reasoning, to my mind, is inconclusive
and unsatisfactory. The notion that because a transaction which is illegal is closed, that therefore a court of
equity is to interfere in dividing the proceeds of the
illegal transaction, is not only opposed to principle, but
to authority—to authority in the well-known case of the

(*f*) *Farmer* v. *Russell*, 1 Bos. & Pul. 296.

(*g*) *Thomson* v. *Thomson*, 7 Ves. 470.

(*h*) *Campbell* v. *Innes*, 4 B. & Ald. 426.

(*i*) See *Sykes* v. *Beadon*, 11 Ch. Div. at p. 195.

(*k*) *Ante*, p. 130, cited with approval in *Mortimer* v. *M'Calln*,
9 M. & W. 636; 4 Jur. 172.

(*l*) *Ante*, pp. 125 *et seq.*

highwaymen (*m*), where a robbery had been committed,
and one of the highwaymen unsuccessfully sued the
other for a division of the proceeds of the robbery."
Subsequently the learned judge states, that he was satisfied that no bill could be maintained by one partner in
a gaming house against another, for accounts on the
footing that the gaming house had been closed.

The case of *Sharp* v. *Taylor* was referred to with
approval in *Beeston* v. *Beeston* (*n*); but in the latter
case the transactions were not illegal (*o*).

When a partner in an illegal partnership dies, and
his personal representative obtains possession of his
assets, the latter cannot, as against the beneficiaries,
refuse to account on the ground of the illegality of the
transactions in which the deceased was concerned (*p*).
The personal representative cannot do so even when he
happens to have been a co-partner in the illegal partnership (*p*); though, if no account had been settled, as
such partner he might decline to account (*q*). — *Personal representative of deceased partner.*

The position of illegal trusts is similar in a Court
of equity to that of illegal partnerships: the Court
declines to enforce them. In *Ottley* v. *Browne* (*q*) there
was a secret trust of an illegal nature, which the Court
declined to enforce (*r*). — *Illegal trusts.*

(*m*) *Everet* v. *Williams*, Lindley on Partnership, 6th edit.
p. 101.

(*n*) *Beeston* v. *Beeston*, 1 Ex. Div. 13; 33 L. T. N. S. 700; 45
L. J. Ex. 230; 24 W. R. 96. See judgment of Amphlett, B.

(*o*) See also *Bridger* v. *Savage*, 15 Q. B. D. 363; 54 L. J.
Q. B. 464; 53 L. T. 129; 33 W. R. 891; 49 J. P. 725.

(*p*) *Joy* v. *Campbell*, 1 Sch. & Lef. 328.

(*q*) *Ottley* v. *Browne*, 1 Ball & Beat. 360.

(*r*) See also *Thomson* v. *Thomson*, 7 Ves. 470, and *Barclay* v.
Pearson, (1893) 2 Ch. Div. at p. 170.

CHAPTER VII.

AN ACT TO AMEND THE LAW CONCERNING GAMES AND
WAGERS (8 & 9 VICT. C. 109).

THE title to this chapter, is the title of the most important Act, which came into operation on the 8th August, 1845, whereunder the attitude of the law towards wagers in general, and games of skill and play for excessive amounts, was altered into what it remains substantially at the present day, subject, however, to the Gaming Act, 1892.

The preamble of the Act recites, that the laws theretofore made in restraint of unlawful games had been found of no avail to prevent the mischiefs which happen therefrom, and also apply to sundry games of skill from which the like mischiefs could not arise. It is therefore enacted "that so much of the statute intituled 'The Bill for maintaining Artillery and the debarring of unlawful games' (33 Hen. VIII. c. 9), whereby any game of mere skill, such as bowling, coyting, cloyshcayles, half-bowl, tennis, or the like, is declared an unlawful game, or which enacts any penalty for playing at any such game of skill as aforesaid, or which enacts any penalty for lacking bows and arrows, or for not making and continuing butts, or which regulates the making, selling, or using of bows and arrows, and also so much of the said Act as requires the mayors, sheriffs, bailiffs, constables, and other head officers within every city, borough, and town within this realm

Partial repeal of 33 Hen. VIII. c. 9.

to make search weekly, or at the furthest once a month, in all places where houses, alleys, plays, or places of dicing, carding, or gaming shall be suspected to be had, kept, and maintained, shall be repealed, and also so much of the said Act as makes it lawful for every master to license his or their servants, and for every nobleman and other having manors, lands, tenements, and other yearly profits for term of life, in his own right or in his wife's right, to the yearly value of 100*l.* or above, to command, appoint, or license, by his or their discretion, his or their servants or family of his or their house or houses to play at cards, dice, or tables, or any unlawful game as therein more fully set forth, shall be repealed; and that no such commandment, appointment, or licence, shall avail any person, to exempt him from the danger or penalty, of playing at any unlawful game, or in any common gaming house."

To legalise to all persons and at all times mere games of skill, but to preserve untouched and undiminished all the penalties which under the old statute then attached to the playing of unlawful games anywhere, or playing at all games, whether lawful or unlawful, in a common gaming house, and to deprive every person of the power to license such playing or gaming, was the intention of the legislature as is clearly and explicitly stated. *Intention to legalise all games of mere skill.*

The second section deals with the question of what evidence is required to prove that a house is a common gaming house: "in default of other evidence proving any house or place to be a common gaming house, it shall be sufficient, in support of the allegation in any indictment or information that any house or place is a common gaming house, to prove that such house or place is kept or used for playing therein at any unlaw- *Sect. 2. Evidence of a common gaming house.*

ful game, and that a bank is kept there by one or more
of the players exclusively of the others, or that the
chances of any game played therein are not alike
favourable to all the players, including among the
players the banker or other person by whom the game
is managed, or against whom the other players stake,
play, or bet; and every such house or place shall be
deemed a common gaming house such as is contrary to
law and forbidden to be kept by 33 Hen. VIII."

This matter will be pursued in Part II. of this book,
when treating of criminal processes. The foregoing
citation will suffice to show, that whilst the undesirable
restrictions of 33 Hen. VIII. on games of mere skill
were abolished, yet the law was strengthened for the
suppression of other games, by striking at common
gaming houses. The next seven sections made further
reference to the suppression of gaming houses (a).
Sections 10 to 14 (both inclusive) regulate licences for
keeping public billiard tables, bagatelle boards, or instruments used in any game of the like kind, but,
subject to such regulations, in no way affected the
legality of the games (b).

Partial repeal of 16 Car. II. c. 7, and 9 Anne, c. 14, and 18 Geo. II. c. 34.

By section 15, it was enacted "that the statute intituled 'An Act against deceitful, disorderly, and excessive Gaming' (16 Car. II. c. 7), and so much of the
statute intituled 'An Act for the better preventing of
Excessive and Deceitful Gaming' (9 Anne, c. 14) as
was not altered by the statute intituled 'An Act to
amend the Law relating to Securities given for Considerations arising out of gaming, usurious, and certain
other illegal transactions' (5 & 6 Will. IV. c. 41), and

(a) For sects. 3 to 9, both inclusive, see *post*, Chap. XII.
(b) See *post*, Chap. XIV.; *Parsons* v. *Alexander*, 5 E. & B. 263;
24 L. J. Q. B. 277; 1 Jur. N. S. 660.

so much of the statute intituled 'An Act to explain, amend, and make more effectual the Laws in being to prevent excessive and deceitful Gaming, and to restrain and prevent the excessive increase of Horse Races' (18 Geo. II. c. 34), as relates to the said Act of Queen Anne, or as renders any person liable to be indicted and punished for winning or losing, at play or betting, at any one time, the sum or value of ten pounds, or within the space of twenty-four hours the sum or value of twenty pounds, shall be repealed . . . ."

This section, therefore, removes the restrictions on *Removal of limit restrictions.* excessive play or wagering imposed by 16 Car. II. c. 7, 9 Anne, c. 14, 18 Geo. II. c. 34, and the restrictions on horse racing in the last-mentioned Act. It leaves the operation of 5 & 6 Will. IV. c. 41, untouched, and, therefore, the law with regard to securities remains as explained in Chapter V. But with regard to deceitful and fraudulent gaming or wagering, by section 17, a person guilty of such misconduct was declared to commit the offence of obtaining money by false pretences.

However, the Act did not revert to the common law *Sect. 18.* with regard to games and betting on the sides or hands of the players for ready money, for by the 18th section it was enacted :—

" That all contracts or agreements, whether by parole *Wagers void.* or in writing, by way of gaming or wagering, shall be null and void; and that no suit shall be brought or maintained in any Court of Law or Equity for recovering any sum of money or valuable thing alleged to be won upon any wager, or which shall have been deposited in the hands of any person to abide the event on which any wager shall have been made : Provided always, that this enactment shall not be deemed to apply to any subscription or contribution, or agreement to subscribe or contribute, for or towards any plate, prize, or sum of money to be awarded to the winner or winners of any lawful game, sport, pastime, or exercise."

The remaining sections of the Act do not bear on

Construction of sect. 18.

any question of construction of the 18th section, and do not call for further notice at this point. The 18th section splits into two portions, first the enacting part,

Varney v. *Hickman*.

and secondly the proviso. In the case of *Varney* v. *Hickman* (c), the enacting portion was critically and grammatically examined :—"The first part enacts 'that all contracts or agreements, whether by parole or in writing, by way of gaming and wagering, shall be null and void.' It then goes on to enact, 'and that no suit shall be brought or maintained in any Court of Law or Equity, for recovering any sum of money or valuable thing alleged to be won upon any wager, or which shall have been deposited in the hands of any person to abide the event on which any wager shall have been made.' Now the first branch of this section declares the contract to be null and void; the second prevents the winner from bringing an action to recover the amount of his bet from the loser; and the third prevents the winner from suing the stakeholder. It certainly is true that the second branch is involved in the first; that is to say, that if the section had stopped at the end of the first branch, it would have followed that no action could be brought to enforce a contract so declared to be void. But I apprehend there is nothing unusual in an Act of Parliament stating a legal consequence in that way. Then, the third branch, it is said, will be idle and insensible unless there be given to it the further effect of prohibiting the parties from recover-

(c) *Varney* v. *Hickman*, 5 C. B. 271 ; 5 D. & L. 364 ; 17 L. J. C. P. 102.

ing their deposits from the stakeholder upon a repudiation of the illegal contract. It is true that that would
be giving to that clause a more extended construction
than that which treats it as a mere statement of the
legal consequence resulting from the first branch. But
I think if the second branch of the clause be looked at,
it is more consistent with the whole, to treat the third
as an exposition only, of the first; the second branch,
as before observed, merely prohibiting the winner from
suing the loser for the sum won, and the third applying
to the case of an action brought by the winner against
the stakeholder for the whole sum deposited with him.
Although, perhaps, the third clause might have been
omitted as well as the second, the second being inserted,
the third became necessary also." In the case of *Diggle*
v. *Higgs* (d), Bramwell, L.J., said, "the clause of
section 18, 'that no suit shall be brought for recovering money won upon a wager,' is unnecessary, and
might have been left out of the statute; it seems to me
to be wholly superfluous."

The title of the Act refers to "games and wagers," Ambit of
and the preamble refers to the restraints on unlawful sect. 18.
gaming, and the previous sections dealt with gaming.
Section 18 deals with *all* contracts by way of gaming
and wagering. The general tenour of the Act would
have led one to expect that section 18, following the
then repealed statutes of Charles and Anne, would have
related solely to wagers connected with games, sports,
and pastimes, yet no such restriction is expressed, and
there is no implication of an intention so to limit the
beneficial operation of the Act. Thus it follows that

(d) *Diggle* v. *Higgs*, 2 Ex. Div. 422; 46 L. J. Ex. 721; 37 L.
T. 27; 25 W. R. 777 (C. A.), reversing 25 W. R. 607.

the difference transactions, which in Chapter I. were shown to be wagers, are within the statute (e). Any contract which is a wagering one is within the Act.

The common law whereunder wagers generally were enforceable has thus been altered, simply by making wagers not illegal, but unenforceable. With regard to the effect of the Act on those wagers which, at common law, were unenforceable, it is at least questionable whether it has made any alteration. Such wagers as were unenforceable at common law, may have been so either because they were void or were illegal. Certainly the term illegal is frequently applied to the exceptional wagers at common law as will have been seen in Chapter II. But it must be admitted, that in the old cases the use of the term illegal is not accurately contrasted with that of void (f), the reason being either that the contrast was unknown, or, being known, did not affect the result of the actions commonly brought on wagers by one party thereto against the other. The wagers were not illegal in the sense of being *mala prohibita* and of involving the sanction of a penalty. But many of the wagers were, from their circumstances and subject-matter, *mala per se*, and as such were illegal. In *Da Costa* v. *Jones* (g), Lord Mansfield gave various instances of the exceptional wagers, with regard to which he

(Side note: Effect of, on the common law — i. On valid wagers; ii. On invalid wagers.)

(e) *Grizewood* v. *Blane*, 11 C. B. 526; 12 L. J. C. P. 46; *Barry* v. *Croskey*, 2 J. & H. 1; *Cooper* v. *Neil*, W. N. (1878) 128, and the other cases cited in Chap. I. at pp. 11—20.

(f) See, for example, the citation from *Collins* v. *Blantern*, *ante*, p. 107. In the *Mogul Steamship Company* v. *M'Gregor, Gow & Co.*, 23 Q. B. D. at p. 605, Esher, M.R., in his dissentient judgment, said of an agreement: "The only reasons that it can be held void, is because it is illegal."

(g) *Da Costa* v. *Jones*, 2 Cowp. 729.

vigorously states, "You offend; you misbehave by
laying such a wager." It must be open to serious
question, whether section 18 of the Act was intended to
make such wagers as were illegal at common law merely
void and null. There is, however, a decision in point.
In the case of *Fitch* v. *Jones* (*h*), a promissory note had *Fitch* v. *Jones.*
been given to secure a wager on the amount of the hop
duties, and formed the basis of the action between the
plaintiff as indorsee, and the defendant as maker. It
became necessary to decide whether the note had been
given for an illegal consideration, or for a merely void
consideration, equivalent in law to no consideration at
all. In *Atherfold* v. *Beard* (*i*), a similar wager had been
held to be contrary to public policy, on the ground that
it was improper to discuss matters of revenue in any
place other than Parliament, and would be productive
of public inconvenience. Campbell, C. J., delivering
judgment in *Fitch* v. *Jones*, said : " The note was given
to secure payment of a wagering contract, which, even
before 8 & 9 Vict. c. 109, the law would not enforce ;
but it was not illegal. There is no penalty attached to
such a wager ; it is not in violation of any statute nor
of the common law, but is simply void, so that the consideration was not an illegal consideration, but equivalent in law to no consideration at all. Though it is said,
in *Atherfold* v. *Beard* (*i*), that a wager as to the amount
of the hop duty is contrary to public policy, it is not
there meant that it is punishable, but merely that it was
an idle wager on a matter in which the parties had no
concern, and the discussion of which might prejudice
others, like the wager on the sex of the Chevalier

(*h*) *Fitch* v. *Jones* 5 E. & B. 238 ; 24 L. J. Q. B. 293 ; 1 Jur.
N. S. 854.
(*i*) *Atherfold* v. *Beard*, 2 T. R. 610.

D'Eon, and therefore was a wager not enforceable by
law, though not a breach of any law." Erle, J., also
said : " I think the defendant might, without violating
any law, make a wager. If he lost, he might, without
violating any law, pay what he had lost, or give a note
for the amount."

But, on turning to the judgment in *Atherfold* v.
Beard, it is found that Ashurst, J., with the assent of
the other judges, explicitly stated that wagers which
tend to introduce indecent discussion are illegal, and he
spoke of that particular wager as being "in itself
illegal," and further added that no admission of the
defendant that he had lost the wager could make " that
legal which is in its nature illegal." In *Jones* v. *Randall* (*j*), Lord Mansfield stated that the wager there in
question was not against any positive law, and that no
case could be found to show its illegality. " But it is
argued, and rightly, that notwithstanding it is not prohibited by any positive law, nor adjudged illegal by any
precedents, yet it may be decided to be so on principles."
Such a principle would be that contracts contrary to
morality are illegal. An examination of the old cases
suggests the conclusion, that the learned judges had not
present to their minds the distinction between an illegal
and a void contract. A contract was void because it
was illegal ; a contract was valid because it was not
illegal. The existence of a *tertium quid* between an
illegal and a valid contract is not clearly (if at all)
recognized.

Submission as
to effect of
sect. 18 on
wagers illegal
at common
law.

However, it is submitted that certain wagers were
at common law illegal so far that a promissory note,
given by way of payment thereunder, would be tainted

(*j*) *Jones* v. *Randall*, 1 Cowp. 37 ; Lofft, 383, 428.

with illegality. Further, with submission, the conclusion
is put forward that section 18 of the Act has not destroyed the taint of illegality which the common law
attached to such wagering contracts. Should this point
come before the courts for decision, reliance as against
the submission here made will probably be placed on a
dictum of Cairns, L. C., in the case of *Diggle* v. *Higgs*,
where, speaking of the first part of the section, he de-
scribes it as one " which applies to all contracts, lawful
and unlawful, by way of gaming and wagering" (*k*); and
also on that of the Privy Council in the case of *Trimble*
v. *Hill* (*l*), where it is stated, " This enactment annuls all
contracts by way of gaming and wagering, thus abolish-
ing the distinction between legal and illegal wagers,
which had frequently raised vexed questions for the
consideration of the courts." But those statements must
be read with regard to the circumstances of the particular cases, and it does not appear that the effect of
section 18 on wagering contracts illegal at common law
was directly in controversy.

The proviso contemplates the recovery of something, a   The proviso.
subscription or contribution, by the winner or winners
of a lawful game, sport, pastime, or exercise. The first
question is, who is the winner? The competition will
be conducted on the terms agreed upon between the
parties thereto. The whole agreement must be considered, both as directly expressed and as incorporating
rules—it may be the Jockey Club rules of racing, or
the rules of boat racing, or other rules, according to the
subject-matter, as agreed upon by the parties. The
parties are bound by the whole of the rules or regulations which constitute their agreement. The terms of

(*k*) *Diggle* v. *Higgs*, 2 Ex. Div. at p. 427.
(*l*) *Trimble* v. *Hill*, L. R. 5 App. Cas. at p. 344.

the agreement are open to alteration by the consent of all parties: but short of that, there will be difficulty in showing a binding waiver of any of the rules and regulations.

Thus, in *Weller* v. *Deakin* (*m*), it was one of the conditions that the horses should have been "regularly hunted" with certain hounds. The plaintiff endeavoured to set up a waiver of that condition. He had remarked to the defendant, the clerk of the course, before the race, that "he hoped he was satisfied about the mare's hunting," and that the defendant had replied—" Quite so: you run your mare, we have arranged that." But it was held that "It must be shown that the clerk of the course had authority from the other subscribers to waive the conditions of the race. There was a printed proposal to run horses on certain terms; what the clerk said, after this was published, cannot have the effect of waiving any of those terms, without all the other subscribers have agreed to it." In *Marryat* v. *Broderick* (*n*), a race had been run under an agreement that two named persons should act as stewards: neither were present at the race, but one sent a deputy. It was held that there could be no valid arbitration without both stewards concurring, and that no agreement had been proved that the parties had agreed to submit to the sole decision of the one steward who sent a deputy; but that clear proof would be required, that the disputing parties, and probably also the clerk of the course, had submitted to his authority. In the case of *Dines* v. *Wolfe* (*o*), the agreement contained (*inter alia*) the following stipulations:—

(*m*) *Weller* v. *Deakin*, 2 C. & P. 618.

(*n*) *Marryat* v. *Broderick*, 2 M. & W. 369; 1 Jur. 242.

(*o*) *Dines* v. *Wolfe*, L. R. 2 P. C. 288; 5 Moore, P. C. C. N. S. 382; 20 L. T. 251.

The match to be run under the Australian Jockey Club Rules, and under the auspices of that Club, and the defendant to act as stakeholder. It was a common, though not proved to be an inflexible rule of the Australian Jockey Club, that their treasurer should act as stakeholder. Prior to the race, all the persons other than the plaintiff were agreeable that the money should be deposited with the treasurer, but the plaintiff would not consent. After the event, the plaintiff contended that the race was not run under the agreement. But it was held against him, that, if under the agreement the money ought to have been deposited with the treasurer, he could not take advantage of his own non-compliance with the rules to demand his money back; or, that, if under the agreement he had appointed the defendant stakeholder, and thereby expressly excluded the rules of the Jockey Club, there had been no breach of the actual agreement. In the case of *Evans* v. *Summers* (*p*), an objection was taken to the plaintiff's horse; but, under the conditions, the plaintiff might have said that the objection was out of time. He did not. Subsequently, after the committee had decided against him, he tried to take the objection; Blackburn, J., "thought, on the whole, that the rule as to time was for the benefit of the person objected to, and which he might, if he thought proper, waive, and having waived he could not now set it up."

If the agreement between the parties be sued on, it will, of course, require to be stamped before being admitted as evidence (*q*).

In anticipation of disputes arising as to who is the Disputes as to winner.

(*p*) *Evans* v. *Summers*, 35 J. P. 761.
(*q*) *Evans* v. *Pratt*, 3 M. & G. 759; 4 Scott, N. R. 378; 1 D. N. S. 505; 6 Jur. 152.

winner the agreements provide, as a general rule, a
machinery for the summary determination of such
questions. The parties agree to be bound by such determination. Take, for instance, a horse race. The race
is started according to the agreement, the judge decides
the order of passing the winning-post, and there having
thus been a race, the jurisdiction of the stewards or
the referee, as agreed, to settle all disputes arises. Assuming the officials have, as agreed, exercised their
respective jurisdictions, there will be no possibility of
disputing their decisions.

But questions have been brought before the Courts as
to whether the jurisdiction has been exercised, or, if
exercised, whether properly exercised. In the above-
metioned case of *Marryat* v. *Broderick*, the two
stewards had not acted, and, under the circumstances,
the decision of the one was not binding. In the case of
Brown v. *Overbury* (*r*), certain persons had subscribed to
a steeplechase; the defendant was the treasurer of the
race, and the plaintiff sought to recover from him 26*l*.,
being the amount of the stakes which he alleged had
been won by his horse. According to the articles of
agreement, any dispute as to the race was to be decided
by the award of four stewards. A dispute arose. Two
stewards were in favour of holding the plaintiff's horse
the winner, and two in favour of another horse. The
plaintiff contended that he was entitled to have the
question settled by a jury. Alderson, B., said, "Every
contract must be determined according to the circumstances. This is one of racing, and the universal practice has been, that, in order to ascertain who is to have
the stakes, it must first be determined who is the winner,
not in the opinion of the jury, but of the persons ap-

(*r*) *Brown* v. *Overbury*, 11 Ex. 715; 25 L. J. Ex. 169.

pointed to decide it, namely, the judges or the stewards
. . . . In this case the stewards have come to no decision,
but it may be that they will when they meet again. . . . .
Further he (the plaintiff) is not entitled to get back his
contribution, . . . for he has not shown that he is unable
to get a decision from the stewards." Martin, B., states
that a decision of the stewards, even though erroneous
but not fraudulent, would bind the parties, and prevent
any question being submitted to a jury. In *Ellis* v.
Hopper (s), the plaintiff had alleged that his horse was
winner because the defendant's had "crossed" another
horse. It had been provided that all disputes should
be settled by the stewards. There were four stewards,
a majority of whom decided for the plaintiff; but one
of the majority had made a bet against the defendant's
horse. It was contended that this fact invalidated the
decision on the ground of interest in one of several arbitrators. It was held on the interpleader issue, that the
stewards were not judges of Courts of law, nor even
arbitrators in the strict legal sense, and the decision
was upheld. Again, in *Parr* v. *Winteringham* (t), following the last case, it was held that the stewards are
not in the position of arbitrators between the persons
who have horses in the race. "They are functionaries
of a very peculiar nature with peculiar powers." As
long as their opinion has been fairly and honestly given,
it is enough, whether that opinion was severally or
jointly given, and the decision of the majority prevailed
over that of the minority.

In the case of *Benbow* v. *Jones* (u), the steward being

Stewards are not arbitrators in the strict legal sense.

(s) *Ellis* v. *Hopper*, 28 L. J. Ex. 1; 3 H. & N. 766; 4 Jur. N.
S. 1025; 7 W. R. 15.

(t) *Parr* v. *Winteringham*, 28 L. J. Q. B. 123; 1 El. & El. 394;
5 Jur. N. S. 787; 7 W. R. 288.

(u) *Benbow* v. *Jones*, 14 M. & W. 193; 14 L. J. Ex. 257.

empowered to decide all disputes, intimated, before the race, to the plaintiff, who had entered his horse for a steeplechase, that his intended rider, W., was a "professional jockey," and that his riding would disqualify the horse. However, W. rode the horse, and came in first. But the steward the next day directed the stakes to be paid to the owner of the horse second past the post. The plaintiff contended that the decision was informal and irregular, being pronounced before the race was run, and that W. was not a professional jockey. Alderson, B., said, "It would be very strange to say that it is to be held that all proceedings before the stewards of races are to be according to the strict rules of law; that there is to be a point regularly raised before him, and parties heard upon it—I suppose by counsel—and a formal decision on the hearing. It would next be said that the evidence must be given on oath. The truth is, that the parties mean that the matter shall be subject to the decision of the steward; and that if he decides in fact, that shall be final." Again, in *Smith* v. *Littledale* (v), where the stewards had decided that a horse had not been hunted in a genuine and *bonâ fide* manner, it was held that, under the conditions giving final power to decide disputes, they "were absolute judges of fact and law."

Stewards must observe the conditions.

In the case of *Newcomen* v. *Lynch* (w), which was an interpleader issue, arising out of a dispute on a race held under the Irish National Hunt Steeplechase and Irish Turf Club Rules, for prizes, including a plate of 250*l.*, "weight for age—four, 12 st.; five, 12 st. 10 lb.; six and aged, 13 st.," the question was raised whether

(v) *Smith* v. *Littledale*, 15 W. R. 69.
(w) *Newcomen* v. *Lynch*, Ir. R. 9 C. L. 1, affirmed on appeal, Ir. R. 10 C. L. 248.

or not the stewards had waived a condition about "wrong nominations." The defendant's horse was entered as "aged :" he came in first, and the plaintiff objected that he was entered under a false description. The material rules were the following: "The decision of the stewards shall be final in everything connected with steeplechasing, and there is no appeal whatever to a Court of law." "The age of the horse must be mentioned when horses of different ages are admitted." "If any horse be entered by a false description, he shall be disqualified." The fact was, that the defendant's horse was six years : the stewards held that the weights being the same for six years and for aged, the horse was not disqualified. In the Queen's Bench the majority of the judges held that the stewards were not authorized to decide, after a race was run, that the non-observance of some of the rules according to which the race was agreed to be run was immaterial, and on that ground to award the stakes to the party who had violated the rules. On appeal in the Exchequer Chamber, the validity of that principle was admitted; but the judges differed from the Court below as to its application to the facts ; the stewards had not set aside or dispensed with any rule, they had construed the rule about naming the age, in connection with that about false description. In a matter of interpretation their decision was binding.

In *Carr* v. *Martinson* (x), it was decided that the judge's jurisdiction did not arise until the race had been run. The plaintiff and one Horner entered into a specific agreement to run one horse against another on a specified day, W. Cottingham to be the starter, and another named person the judge. The starter did not appear

Conditions precedent to jurisdiction.

(x) *Carr* v. *Martinson*, 1 El. & El. 456; 28 L. J. Q. B. 126; 5 Jur. N. S. 788; 7 W. R. 293.

on the ground, and Horner refused to run the race, but the plaintiff's horse walked over the course and was declared by the judge to be the winner. The plaintiff demanded the stakes from the defendant, who was the stakeholder. Lord Campbell, C.J., said, "If the plaintiff's horse had been started by the starter appointed, and had trotted over the course, and had been declared by the judge to be the winner, that judgment would have been final : but I think his power to act as judge never arose, in consequence of the race never having been run. It was made a condition precedent to the running of the race, that W. Cottingham should be the starter, and therefore as that condition was not performed, the judge had no power to give any decision upon the matter." It was held further, that on demand, the plaintiff was entitled to have his own contribution to the stakes returned.

Sadler v. *Smith.*

A somewhat similar point arose in the case of *Sadler* v. *Smith* (y). The plaintiff deposited a stake with the defendant with a view to a race between the plaintiff and one Kelley, upon the terms " that the race was to be a rightaway sculler's race, and the decision of the referee to be final." In such a race it was the practice for the men to start themselves, but in the event of the men not starting through default of either or both, the referee was entitled to interfere. Sadler at the time appointed made default in starting; Kelley complained to the referee: the referee gave an order that Kelley should inform the plaintiff that if he did not start Kelley was to row over the course without him. Kelley alone rowed over the course, and the referee, without communication with or inquiry of the

(y) *Sadler* v. *Smith*, L. R. 4 Q. B. 214; 38 L. J. Q. B. 91; 19 L. T. 779; 17 W. R. 371; affirmed on appeal, L. R. 5 Q. B. 40; 39 L. J. Q. B. 17; 21 L. T. 502; 18 W. R, 148.

plaintiff, awarded the stakes to Kelley. The plaintiff
sued the defendant for money received to the use of the
plaintiff. Cockburn, C.J., left the following questions
to the jury :—1. Did Sadler intend to start? *A.* He did.
2. Had the referee, by actual observation or otherwise,
the means of knowing whether Sadler intended to start
or not? *A.* He had not. 3. The order of the referee
being, if Sadler would not start, Kelley should row over
the course, and that this should be communicated to
Sadler; was it so communicated? *A.* No. 4. Was a
fair opportunity afforded to Sadler to start? *A.* No.
The Chief Justice directed a verdict for the plaintiff,
giving the defendant leave to move to enter a nonsuit
or a verdict for the defendant, on the ground that the
referee's decision was, for the purposes of the action,
final. A rule was accordingly obtained; but it was
decided that the referee's order for a start was conditional on its communication to Sadler, and without
such communication there was no start, and therefore
no race, and consequently no jurisdiction for the referee to award the stakes. On appeal, this decision
was upheld. Willes, J., said : " I am clearly of opinion,
that even if the referee had had insufficient means of
determining whether Kelley had communicated the
order to start to the plaintiff, yet, provided he had
decided that a communication was made, although, in
fact, it was not made, his decision would have been
conclusive and final; but it appears to me that he took
no steps to ascertain whether Kelley had communicated
his order to the plaintiff. He ought not, without ascertaining that cardinal fact, to have ordered the stakes
to be paid over to Kelley." Thus, according to this
judgment, the referee has jurisdiction to decide the
existence or non-existence of that which was a con-

dition precedent to his jurisdiction. This decision shows that the stakeholder should be extremely careful to be satisfied that there has been a due determination by the competent authority before he pays over the stakes.

Determination by the Courts. When the agreement does not provide for the settlement of disputes, or where the machinery provided proves absolutely incompetent, the Courts, with the assistance of jury, will decide the disputes and determine the winner. On questions of construction of ambiguous terms in the written agreement, parol evidence will be admitted. The following terms have Technical racing terms. been the subject of judicial decision :—" Entrance money" (z), "added money" (a), "regularly hunted" (b), " across country " (c), " trotting match " (d), " gentleman rider " (e), " Play or Pay," i. e., " P. P. " (f). In *Daintree* v. *Hutchinson*, which involved the construction of the words following : " the said match to be run on Wednesday during the Newmarket February Meeting, 1841. P. P."—the Court received evidence to show that the Newmarket meetings were meetings of a coursing club, and of the practice as to the dates of the meeting, and held that, according to its true construction, the meeting was in the nature of a moveable feast, not fixed definitely for a particular day, but dependent in some degree on circumstances.

(z) *Dowson* v. *Scriven*, 1 H. Bl. 219.
(a) *Applegarth* v. *Colley*, 10 M. & W. 723; 12 L. J. Ex. 34; 7 Jur. 18.
(b) *Weller* v. *Deakin*, 2 C. & P. 618.
(c) *Evans* v. *Pratt*, 3 M. & Gr. 759; 4 Scott, N. R. 378; 1 D. N. S. 505; 6 Jur. 152.
(d) *Robson* v. *Hall*, Peake, 172.
(e) *Walmsley* v. *Matthews*, 3 M. & Gr. 133; 3 Scott, N. R. 584; 5 Jur. 508.
(f) *Daintree* v. *Hutchinson*, 10 M. & W. 85; 6 Jur. 39.

In the case of *Crofton* v. *Colgan* (*g*) a contention that in   Winners. a given race there could only be one winner within the meaning of the proviso was disallowed, and it was held that there was nothing in the clause requiring that the entire sum subscribed should be awarded to the first horse, or to prevent the Court from considering both the first and second horses winners, each entitled to a portion of the sum subscribed. But in *Batson* v. *New-man* (*h*), which arose out of a trotting match against time, Mellish, L. J., asked, "How could there be a 'winner' here? Does not the word import competition between two or more?" and in his judgment he said : "There can only be a winner when two or more persons are to compete in doing something." In that case the loser was the loser of a wager, and there was no loser of a race. In the case of *Irwin* v. *Osborne and others* (*i*), the defendants had no proprietary interest in the horse which they nominated to run against the plaintiff's horse. If the defendants had won, it would have been on account of their good fortune in naming the successful horse, and "the contract would have depended on that accidental circumstance, and not on the running of the race." The defendants, therefore, could not be winners within the meaning of the pro-viso. This decision would prevent breeders recovering the breeders' stakes in an action at law.

The proviso states that the enactment does not apply   What the to any subscription or contribution, or agreement to   winner may subscribe or contribute, for or towards any plate, prize,   recover. or sum of money to be awarded to . . . . Having determined the winner, the second question is what

(*g*) *Crofton* v. *Colgan*, 10 Ir. C. L. R. 133.
(*h*) *Batson* v. *Newman*, 1 C. P. D. 573; 25 W. R. 85.
(*i*) *Irwin* v. *Osborne*, 5 Ir. C. L. R. 404.

Plate.

may he recover under this proviso. The term "plate," under the Rules of Racing, is a prize in money not made up by the subscriptions of the competitors. It thus differs essentially from the stake or prize contributed by the competitors themselves, for, *quoad* their own contributions, they are entering into a wager; but with regard to the plate or added money, the givers of that are not parties to the wager, they must lose their contributions, and do not take any chance of winning from the competitors. Hence, this distinction with regard to "added money" was observed in the case of *Applegarth* v. *Colley* (k). But the term "prize" has no such definite meaning, and is as general as "sum of money."

This proviso was first construed in the case of *Batty* v. *Marriott* (l), which has since been overruled. In that case two persons agreed to run a foot-race, and each of them deposited 10*l.* with a third person on condition that the whole 20*l.* should be paid over to the winner. The loser sought to recover his deposit. For the loser it was contended that the race was illegal, and not legalized by the proviso, and that therefore the loser could rescind the contract and demand his deposit. For the defendant it was contended that the contract was legal, and fell within the proviso. To maintain that position reference was made to a distinction taken in *Connor* v. *Quick* (m) between running a horse for 50*l.*, which was lawful, and betting on the side of the horse, which was not, and the case of *Evans*

(k) *Applegarth* v. *Colley*, 10 M. & W. 723; 12 L. J. Ex. 34; 7 Jur. 18.

(l) *Batty* v. *Marriott*, 5 C. B. 818; 17 L. J. C. P. 215; 12 Jur. 462.

(m) Referred to in *Clayton* v. *Jennings*, 2 Bl. 706.

v. *Pratt* (*n*) was relied on. In *Evans* v. *Pratt* the competition was a steeplechase, the owners backing their
horses in named sums. The whole of the question discussed in that case was the legality of a steeplechase,
being a match of over 50*l*., and turned on the effect of
18 Geo. II. c. 34, after the repeal of 13 Geo. II. c. 19
by 3 & 4 Vict. c. 5. It was not suggested that the
match amounted to a wager, and *quâ* wager was illegal
under 9 Anne, c. 14. It was contended that such
matches were legal, and differed from collateral wagers,
and that such being the law prior to 8 & 9 Vict. c. 109,
this statute intended, by the operation of the proviso,
to maintain the distinction. The judges in *Batty* v.
Marriott considered, that the proviso was inserted out
of regard to horse racing and such like lawful sports.
Wilde, C. J., said:—" The race, not being an illegal
game, and the money having been subscribed by these
two persons, the question is, whether the case falls
within the enacting part or the proviso. There may
possibly be a difference when the money is not placed
in the hands of a stakeholder. The difficulty is in
saying when two persons—and only two—mutually
agree to put down a stake, the whole of which is to be
paid over to the winner, in what respect that differs
from a wager. . . . . Here two sums of 10*l*. each
have been deposited by two persons to abide the event
of a lawful race, the whole to be awarded to the
winner. The case is clearly one which falls within the
proviso, and the Court can only deal with the precise
words before them." Coltman, J., having pointed out
the anomaly that the contract should be valid, and yet
any security given for the amount illegal, said :—" The

(*n*) *Evans* v. *Pratt*, 3 M. & Gr. 759 ; 4 Scott, N. R. 378 ; 1 D.
N. S. 505; 6 Jur. 152.

proviso evidently contemplated the case of a sweepstakes where several persons subscribe to a stake or fund, the whole of which becomes, under certain regulations, the property of the winner. It does not define the number of the subscribers or contributors; it seems to me to make no difference whether the number be two or fifty." Cresswell, J., agreed, and in the course of his judgment said:—"It might have been different if contributions to a *plate* only had been mentioned; but the words are plate, prize, or *sum of money*." It follows from this decision that such contracts are valid, and that the winner can sue for the whole stakes, and that the parties have no more power to rescind such a contract than any other valid contract.

The test suggested is that there must have been an actual deposit. But that overlooks the words, "agree to subscribe or contribute." The decision makes an indefinite inroad into the enacting part of the section. An examination of the authorities discloses no case in which the winner has recovered the whole stakes, and only one in which one of the parties has been denied a power to rescind, as would have existed had the contract been void.

In *Parsons* v. *Alexander* (o), Campbell, C. J., said: "But for *Batty* v. *Marriott*, I should have said that proviso was confined to cases in which persons contributed to a plate or something analogous to a plate." Coleridge, J., said: "I should have thought it was confined to cases in which a prize is made up by subscriptions; but there is certainly nothing in the words to prevent some of the subscribers from playing." Crompton, J., also expressed difficulty with regard to

(o) *Parsons* v. *Alexander*, 5 E. & B. 263; 24 L. J. Q. B. 277; 1 Jur. N. S. 660.

Batty v. *Marriott.* On the facts, *Parsons* v. *Alexander* was distinguishable from *Batty* v. *Marriott,* seeing that there was no actual deposit or holding forth as having in effect contributed, and it therefore became unnecessary to dissent from that case. The construction suggested is a subscription or contribution to a plate, or something *ejusdem generis* (that is to say), "added money."

Again, in *Brown* v. *Overbury* (*p*), there was a dispute as to who was the winner of a steeplechase, and as the plaintiff, under the conditions of the race, was unable to prove that he was the winner, it became unnecessary to decide whether or not, if he had been the winner, he could have recovered the stakes. But the winner was held not to be entitled to rescind until he could show that performance of the contract was impossible. So far the case is a decision following *Batty* v. *Marriott.*

In the case of *Irwin* v. *Osborne and others* (*q*), where the plaintiff had agreed with the three defendants that a match should be made between a mare, the property of M., and a mare the property of the plaintiff, and that the party nominating the winner should receive from the others 100*l.*, it was held that there was no subscription, no contribution, and no deposit. The action was, in fact, brought by the plaintiff to recover 100*l.*, which was the penalty agreed to be paid by anyone making default in causing the mare nominated by him to run. The penalty was, in effect, damages for breach of a wagering contract which fell within the first part of section 18. In the case of *Crofton* v. *Colgan* (*r*), the claim arose out of the sale of a horse for a fixed sum

(*p*) *Brown* v. *Overbury,* 11 Ex. 715; 25 L. J. Ex. 169.
(*q*) *Irwin* v. *Osborne,* 5 Ir. C. L. R. 404.
(*r*) *Crofton* v. *Colgan,* 10 Ir. C. L. R. 133.

of money plus a share of the horse's winnings. The horse won a race in relation to which five persons had subscribed 3*l.* each on their respective horses, and the stewards added 30*l.*, making "the whole plate" 45*l.* The horse won, and the defendant received the winnings, but he contested the plaintiff's right to recover a share. The case presents two difficulties : first, no distinction seems to have been drawn between the 30*l.* added money, and the 15*l.* subscribed by the competitors ; secondly, even on the assumption that the money received by the defendant could not have been recovered by him at law, it does not follow that a legal obligation would not exist as between the plaintiff and the defendant on their contract of sale and purchase. In the case the 45*l.* is treated as constituting "the whole plate," and to be within the proviso of this section. A curious contention was advanced on behalf of the defendant, namely, that the winnings in question did not fall within the proviso, because the whole plate did not in its entirety fall to the first horse, owing to the fact that there was a second prize. The Court held that such fact did not suffice to take the transaction outside the proviso, whereunder it was not necessary that the winner should receive every sixpence of the sum subscribed.

The next case is that of *Dines* v. *Wolfe* (*s*), which has been cited, *supra*, as an authority with regard to waiver of conditions. The dispute arose out of an alleged disqualification of the winner of a match between two horses, which respectively had been backed to the amount of 500*l.* The plaintiff's horse lost, and the plaintiff then, relying on the alleged disqualification, claimed the whole stake (1,000*l.*). The stewards of the

(*s*) *Dines* v. *Wolfe*, L. R. 2 P. C. 280 ; 5 Moore, P. C. C. N. S. 382 ; 20 L. T. 251.

Australian Jockey Club decided against the plaintiff, who thereupon brought his action against the stakeholder to recover the 1,000*l.* The jury returned a special verdict, awarding the plaintiff 500*l.* ; subsequently a rule absolute for a new trial was obtained, and the plaintiff appealed. On his behalf, in the Privy Council, it was sought to uphold the verdict of the jury. But it was held that the plaintiff was bound by the decision of the stewards on the alleged disqualification, and, further, that, as the race had been duly run, he could not recover his stakes back again. The judgment then contains the following *dictum* :—"And he (the plaintiff) could not be entitled to recover the whole of the stakes without a decision in his favour as to the age of Traveller (the winning horse), which he has failed to obtain." This *dictum*, it must be admitted, approximates to a decision that if he had succeeded he would have been entitled to recover the whole. So far as it goes, it supports *Batty* v. *Marriott* (*u*).

However, the later case of *Diggle* v. *Higgs* (*t*) is the authority which overrules *Batty* v. *Marriott* (*u*). The plaintiff Diggle and one Simmonite agreed to a walking-match, and each deposited the sum of 200*l.* with the defendant, as stakeholder. The walking-match took place, and the referee decided in favour of Simmonite. Before the defendant paid over the stakes to the winner, the plaintiff demanded a return of the sum of 200*l.* deposited by him with the defendant. Subsequently the defendant, pursuant to the referee's decision, paid the whole 400*l.* to Simmonite. Judgment was entered for the defendant, pursuant to *Batty* v. *Marriott.* On

Diggle v. *Higgs.*

(*t*) *Diggle* v. *Higgs*, 2 Ex. Div. 422 ; 46 L. T. Ex. 721 ; 37 L. T. 27 ; 25 W. R. 777 (C. A.), reversing, 25 W. R. 607.

(*u*) *Batty* v. *Marriott*, 5 C. B. 818 ; 17 L. J. C. P. 215 ; 12 Jur. 462.

appeal, it was contended for the plaintiff that, as he had demanded the sum deposited by him with the stake-holder before it was paid over, but after the event had happened, he could recover it back; and that the agreement between the parties was a wager, whereunder one bet the other that he would beat him in a walking-match and therefore was not within the proviso; and that *Batty* v. *Marriott* had been disapproved in *Batson* v. *Newman* (*u*). On behalf of the defendant, it was urged that it was not a wager, but a subscription towards a sum of money to be awarded to the winner of a lawful game. Lord Chancellor Cairns, in his judgment, decided that the transaction was a wager, and continued: Now, upon that, what is the true construction of sect. 18 of 8 & 9 Vict. c. 109 ? Is a contract of this kind excepted by the proviso? We start with this, that the contract was clearly a wager, and was within the first part of the section. That section says, all contracts and agreements, whether by parol or in writing, by way of gaming and wagering shall be null and void: and then there is a proviso which follows upon an intervening sentence, in these words: "And no suit shall be brought or maintained in any Court of law or equity for recovering any sum of money or valuable thing alleged to have been won upon any wager, or which shall have been deposited in the hands of any person to abide the event on which any wager shall have been made." Then comes the proviso on which this question mainly rests: "Provided always, that this enactment shall not be deemed to apply to any subscription or contribution or agreement to subscribe or contribute for or towards any plate, prize, or sum of money to be awarded to the

(*u*) *Batson* v. *Newman*, 1 C. P. D. 573; 25 W. R. 85.

winner or winners of any lawful game, sport, pastime,
or exercise." It it clear that there may be scores of
forms of "subscriptions, or contributions" towards a
plate or prize without there being any wager, and I
cannot read this proviso, which has a natural and intelligible meaning, in a different way, and one which
would have the effect of neutralising the enactment.
The legislature, I think, never intended to say that
there should be no action brought to recover a sum of
money which shall have been deposited in the hands of
any person to abide the event on which any wager shall
have been made, and yet, that if the wager is in the
form of a subscription or contribution, the winner may
recover it. I read the proviso thus—Provided that so
long as there is a subscription, which is not a wager, the
second part of the section shall not apply to it. . . .
I think the Court (in *Batty* v. *Marriott*) overlooked the
first part of the section which applies to all contracts,
lawful or unlawful, by way of gaming and wagering.
. . . . I cannot follow that case. " I therefore think
that, although there was a deposit of money, the contract in this case was a wager, and that all the consequences which are imposed by sect. 18 on contracts by
way of wagering follow." Cockburn, C. J., and Bramwell, L. J., concurred. In the case of *Trimble* v. *Hill* (*x*),
in the Privy Council, the case of *Diggle* v. *Higgs* was
followed, and was held to have " decided the vexed
question of the construction of a not very intelligible
enactment." On the footing of this decision, it is submitted, that the proviso is superfluous and unnecessary.

(*x*) *Trimble* v. *Hill*, 5 App. Cas. 342 ; 49 L. J. P. C. 49 ; 42
L. T. 103 ; 28 W. R. 479.

Without it, the winner of a lawful game could have recovered " added money ;" for, as between the winner and the subscriber or contributor of the " added money" there is a valid contract. Sect. 18, as thus construed, must be taken to have afforded an example of the danger of superfluous words in a statute.

Proviso limited to lawful games. The proviso is limited to contributions or subscriptions to *lawful* games, sports, pastimes, or exercises. In order to determine whether a given transaction is lawful within the meaning of this proviso, reference must be made to the statutes which have modified the common law. In the case of *Jenks* v. *Turpin* (y), Hawkins, J., summarizes the *unlawful* games as " ace of hearts, pharaoh, basset, hazard, passage, roulet, every game of dice, except backgammon, and every game of cards which is not a game of *mere* skill; and, I incline to add, any other game of mere chance." Of course, this enumeration includes lotteries. With regard to pastimes which, on the ground of cruelty to animals, have been rendered illegal, the reader is referred to Section D. of Chapter III. Generally, the statement of Best, J., in *R.* v. *Rogier* (z), is important—" It is quite clear that any practice that has a tendency to injure public morals is a common law offence. No game is unlawful in itself; but every game may be rendered so by playing at it for an excessive stake; for it is the amount played for and not the name or nature of the game which is the essence of it, and which constitutes an offence in the eyes of the law " (a).

(y) *Jenks* v. *Turpin*, 13 Q. B. D. at p. 524.
(z) *R.* v. *Rogier*, 2 D. & R. at p. 435.
(a) Cited with approval by Smith, J., in *Jenks* v. *Turpin*, but see Chap. II., p. 38, for wagers for excessive amounts at common law.

CHAPTER VIII.

OBLIGATIONS ARISING OUT OF VOID TRANSACTIONS.

WHEN two persons enter into a contract which is null Between and void, no legal obligation is thereby created as principals. between them; the mutual promises to pay are un-enforceable. But the loser, if he desires, may lawfully pay, and such payment, being in the eyes of law for no consideration, is a voluntary payment (a). In the case of *Hill* v. *Fox* (b), the question was raised as to whether the plaintiff had endeavoured to obtain a legal obliga-tion by means of a colourable evasion of the statute. The plaintiff had won a considerable sum of money from the defendant by certain contracts by way of wagering on horse races. The defendant was unable to pay; he applied to the plaintiff for a loan of 2,000*l.* The defendant alleged that the plaintiff lent him the money on condition that he (the defendant) should pay the plaintiff thereout the moneys owing in respect of the bets on horse races; the plaintiff denied that there was any such condition, although he admitted that he expected to be paid out of such moneys, and, as a fact, was so paid. The loan was secured by a mortgage of certain policies of assurance and by a covenant to pay.

(a) *Fitch* v. *Jones*, 5 E. & B. 238; 24 L. J. Q. B. 293; 1 Jur. N. S. 854.

(b) *Hill* v. *Fox*, 4 H. & N. 359.

The plaintiff brought his action on the covenant. Erle, C. J. (and he was affirmed on appeal), told the jury that the defendant's allegation would invalidate the security, but, in the absence of such stipulation or agreement, the deed would be valid. If the defendant was correct, it was a mortgage given for an illegal consideration (c) in substance, whatever it may have been in form.

Payment by a third person. If a principal in a wagering contract can lawfully pay, it would follow that he can request a third person to pay on his behalf, and thereby create, as between himself and such third person, a binding obligation to repay the moneys so paid at his request. Until the Gaming Law Amendment Act, 1892, came into operation, such was the law (d). In *Rosewarne* v. *Billing* (e), Erle, C. J., said : " I am clearly of opinion that if a man loses a wager, and gets another to pay the money for him, an action lies for the recovery of the money so paid." This doctrine, when applied to agents, as will be seen hereafter, had far-reaching effects, and led to the passage, after the decision of the well-known case of *Read* v. *Anderson* (f), of the Act of 1892.

Payment by a personal representative. As it was lawful for a principal to pay moneys so lost, there arose the question whether or not, after the death of a principal, his personal representative could make such payments, and charge the same against the

(c) Chap. V., Part II.

(d) 20th May, 1892. See *post*, Chap. IX.

(e) *Rosewarne* v. *Billing*, 15 C. B. (N. S.) 316; 33 L. J. C. P. 55; 10 Jur. N. S. 496; 9 L. T. 441; 12 W. R. 104; see also *Jessop* v. *Lutwyche*, 10 Exch. 614; 3 C. L. R. 359; 24 L. J. Ex. 65; *Knight* v. *Cambers*, 15 C. B. 562; 3 C. L. R. 565; 24 L. J. C. P. 121; 1 Jur. N. S. 525.

(f) *Read* v. *Anderson*, 10 Q. B. D. 100; 13 Q. B. D. 779; 52 L. J. Q. B. 214; 48 L. T. 74; 31 W. R. 453; 47 J. P. 311.

estate of the testator or intestate. In the case of
Manning v. *Purcell* (g), the testator, whose administratrix *cum testamento annexo* the plaintiff was, had kept
a betting office, and had been in the habit of taking and
giving the odds against horses entered for particular
races, and, on these occasions, had received deposits
from the persons making the bets, and had given them
tickets, which entitled them, in the event of their being
winners, to the return of such deposits, together with
payment to them of the amount payable in respect of
the bets. According to the custom adopted in betting
on horse races, the death of either party before the race
vacates the bet. At the time of the testator's death,
many persons held tickets given by him to secure deposits for bets that had been made by them upon the
terms above mentioned. Some of the bets so secured,
having been determined against the testator, were then
actually payable. These the administratrix had paid,
returning at the same time the corresponding deposits.
The residue of such bets were still pending at the testator's death, the events upon which they depended not
having then happened. The administratrix had returned the deposits upon these. The Lord Justice
Knight Bruce said : "As to bets not decided in his
lifetime, we are of opinion that those payments ought
to be allowed as against the general estate ; but as to
payments in respect of bets decided in the testator's
lifetime, there appears to us neither justification, nor
what in the court can be considered as an excuse, for
making the payments, however proper, and in a sense

(g) *Manning* v. *Purcell*, 7 De G. M. & G. 55 ; 24 L. J. Ch.
522 ; before Vice-Chancellor Stuart, 2 S. & G. 284.

laudable on the part of the lady, the feeling under which they may have been made." Lord Justice Turner said : " I am of opinion, as to payments of the first class (*i. e.*, bets decided before the death of the testator), that, having regard to the provisions of the statute, they could not have been recovered from the testator in his lifetime, and that, therefore, the payments by the administratrix in respect of these can be regarded only as voluntary payments, and not as valid as against the estate. But, with regard to the payments in respect of bets left undecided at the testator's death, I think the case stands very differently. The deposits upon them had been received, indeed, by the testator upon an *illegal* contract ; but it was, I think, within the powers of the administratrix to determine such *illegal* contract, and I take it that, in making these payments, she must be considered as having done so, and that these payments must, therefore, be allowed against the estate." This case, then, is an express decision that a personal representative, in his representative capacity, cannot make payments of moneys so lost on wagers. The effect of an express direction and power so to pay has not been decided ; it would appear to justify the payment.

Securities for payment.

There is, as has been shown, nothing unlawful or illegal in making a payment pursuant to a void wager. But securities for such payments are frequently, though not always, subject to statutory enactment. In Chapter V. there is an account of the securities which are within the statutes of Charles and Anne, and in the Part II. of the same chapter the effect of the statute of 5 & 6 Will. IV. c. 41 is examined. The statute 8 & 9 Vict. c. 109 leaves the operation of that statute unaffected. Securities which are within that statute are given for an illegal consideration, though the contract in respect of and incident to which the security has been given is merely void. This anomaly does not arise where the security is not comprised within the operation of 5 & 6 Will. IV. c. 41. Thus, the case of *Fitch* v. *Jones* (*g*), which was discussed in the last chapter with regard to another point, is an authority to show that a bill of exchange not comprised within 5 & 6 Will. IV. c. 41, though given in respect of a wagering debt, is given for that which in law is equivalent to no consideration. It was held that a merely void consideration would not throw on the indorsee the onus of proving that he was a *bona fide* holder for value.

In the case of *Strachan* v. *Universal Stock Exchange* (*h*), the plaintiff deposited certain shares with the defendants by way of "cover" as regards certain transactions which the plaintiff was about to carry on with the defendants. The jury said that the transactions in question were wagering contracts in spite of their form. Hence, Cave, J., held that the plaintiff was entitled to the relief which he sought, namely, the recovery of the shares or their value. In the Court of Appeal that judgment was upheld. Rigby, L. J., was inclined to call the claim one of redemption. He said :—" Here is a man who claims to be a mortgagee. Directly the transactions are held to be gaming transactions, it follows as a matter of course that his claim in respect

Mortgage by deposit in respect of difference transactions. Right of mortgagor.

(*g*) *Fitch* v. *Jones*, 5 E. & B. 238 ; 24 L. J. Q. B. 293 ; 1 Jur. N. S. 854.

(*h*) *Strachan* v. *Universal Stock Exchange*, (1895) 2 Q. B. 329 ; 43 W. R. 611.

of them fails ; and where from the nature of the transaction itself nothing can be due on the mortgage, the
mortgagee must deliver up the security." An order for
the delivery up of the security or payment of the value
could in such a case, where nothing is due, be made
either at law or in equity.

Payment by wager.

Where one person is legally indebted to another, that
indebtedness cannot be discharged by a wager, say,
tossing for "double or quits." If the creditor sued for
the double sum he could only do so by setting up the
wagering contract. If he, having lost the wager,
sued for the original amount, the defendant would
be compelled to set up the wagering contract which
the Court would not enforce. This point came before
the Courts in the case of *Wilson* v. *Cole* (i). The
defendant was under a binding contract to take a
lease of the plaintiff's house. The defendant offered
the plaintiff 50*l.* to be discharged from his contract,
but the plaintiff refused. Subsequently the plaintiff
agreed to rescind the contract for a payment of 50*l.*
by the defendant, together with a further payment of
25*l.* by the defendant if the plaintiff should win on the
toss of a coin. The defendant won the toss. The
plaintiff sued for the 50*l.* The Court held that the
agreement was severable, and consisted of two parts :
first, that in any event the agreement should be rescinded for 50*l.* ; secondly, the contingency as to the
further payment of 25*l.*, which was a wagering element.
The plaintiff was held entitled to recover the 50*l.* ; but
secus if the whole contract had been a wager.

(i) *Wilson* v. *Cole*, 36 L. T. N. S. 703; cf. *Rourke* v. *Short*, 5
E. & B. 904; 25 L. J. Q. B. 196; 2 Jur. N. S. 352; *Crofton* v.
Colgan, 10 Ir. C. L. R. 133; see Chap. I.

With wagering contracts which are null and void, and whereunder no obligation is created *inter partes*, it may seem immaterial whether the contract be purported to be rescinded or not. But the importance of rescission arises in connection with contracts collateral to the wager; and in two instances: first, where a deposit is made by the one principal with the other— by the client with the bookmaker; secondly, where a third person is employed as agent. In this paragraph the first instance will be dealt with. The question, then, is whether the one principal who has made a deposit with the other to abide a contingency, can before the determination of the wager demand back his deposit, or if the wager be determined in his favour sue for the return of his deposit. There are two principles of law: (a) a voluntary payment cannot be recovered by the payer; (b) a voluntary bailment can be revoked. The question, so far as there is a question, is, which principle applies to the facts. On the one hand, if the transaction were an out-and-out payment of money in consideration of a promise in a certain uncertain event to repay a larger sum, the consideration for such payment would in law be no consideration, and the payment would be a voluntary one. On the other hand, if the intention of the parties was merely to secure a future payment, then the transfer of the money or other valuable chattel would be pursuant, as is suggested by term "deposit," to some contract of bailment, either a *depositum*, with an obligation on the depositary to hold the specific coins or chattel, or a *commodatum*, whereunder he might use the specific coins. The obligation of the bailee would be to retain the specific coins or chattels until the happening of a

Power to rescind where no agent employed. Voluntary payments or deposits.

If deposits, obligations and rights stated.

definite uncertain event, and then, according as that event happened in the one way or the other, either to return to the bailor, or to hold for his (the bailee's) own benefit absolutely. Where there is a power of user, and no duty on the bailee with regard to the specific coins, the obligation in the event of his losing the wager would be to repay to the bailor an equal sum of money. Until that event happens which ends the bailment by converting the bailee into the owner, or which releases him from his obligation to repay, the bailment can be revoked by the bailor, and on the footing of such revocation the repayment of the deposit obtained. Thus, not only could the depositor demand the return prior to the determination of the wager, but after the determination in his favour he could sue for the same repayment (i).

Manning v. Purcell.

The point was involved in the above-mentioned case of *Manning* v. *Purcell* (j): the case was a decision on the question of whether a personal representative could charge against the estate certain payments made by her; and is subject to the observation that, though a personal representative be allowed payments actually made, it does not follow that the creditor could have compelled payment, for instance, debts barred by the Statute of Limitations. The personal representative made three payments: first, she paid the amounts won on bets lost by the testator in his lifetime; secondly, she repaid the deposits made in respect of the bets so lost; thirdly, she repaid the deposits on bets which had not been decided in the tes-

(i) See *post*, pp. 190 *et seq.*
(j) *Manning* v. *Purcell*, 7 De G. M. & G. 55; 24 L. J. Ch. 522; 2 S. & G. 284.

tator's lifetime. She was disallowed the first; not allowed the second; and allowed the third. On the principles of the valid though gratuitous bailment, the third was a proper payment; but the difficulty arises in the disallowance of the second. The event which alone entitled the testator to hold such deposits absolutely for his own benefit, or which released him from an obligation to repay, had not and could not happen; the administratrix in making such payment was discharging, it is submitted, a legal obligation of the testator's estate. The Court spoke of the wager as illegal; but neither before the Vice-Chancellor nor in the Court above, was any suggestion made that the contract was not valid otherwise than under sect. 18 of 8 & 9 Vict. c. 109, though the facts are suggestive of a business illegal under the Betting House Act. If the Court had adopted the construction of that section, which was accepted in the case of *Beyer* v. *Adams* (k), since overruled, the probability is that the third payments would have been disallowed. The decision as it stands admits the existence of the bailment, but erroneously denies an obligation arising therefrom (l).

In the later case of *Reggio* v. *Stevens* (m), the plaintiff *Reggio* v. *Stevens*. had purported to employ the defendants, who were outside brokers, to buy and sell stocks and shares for him. The plaintiff sued for a balance of his account, and for the sum of 40l. deposited by him by way of cover. The defendants pleaded that the transactions were mere wagers. The jury were not satisfied as to the plaintiff's intention, and found that the transactions were not dif-

(k) *Beyer* v. *Adams*, 26 L. J. Ch. 841; 3 Jur. N. S. 709; 5 W. R. 795.

(l) See p. 186.

(m) *Reggio* v. *Stevens*, 4 T. L. R. 326.

ference transactions. The defendants applied to set
aside the verdict. The Court were of opinion that the
transactions were mere wagers, and that the balance of
the account in the plaintiff's favour represented winnings,
which he could not recover; but the plaintiff was held
entitled to recover his deposit. In the course of the
argument *Manning* v. *Purcell* was cited, and Baron
Huddleston remarked, "That case shows that before the
event the money can be recovered." In the judgment
of Baron Huddleston it was stated that, as to the 40*l.*
deposited as "cover," "that is, a certain sum deposited
to cover possible losses and to protect the agents in that
event, though it had been deposited for the purpose of
entering into illegal transactions, the party paying it
might revoke his authority and demand its return."
Manisty, J., said that "the plaintiff was entitled to
recover back the 40*l.*, because he was entitled to say he
would gamble no more." It is curious that in this case,
as in *Manning* v. *Purcell*, the transactions should have
been called illegal. The decision is based on the fact
that, in the view of the learned judges, the defendants
were principals in wagering transactions, and as such,
principals could not be sued for the winnings, but in
the other of their dual capacities, namely, as bailees,
they were liable for the deposits.

In *Strachan* v. *The Universal Stock Exchange* (*n*), one
principal to a wager deposited certain shares with the
other principal. The Court of Appeal held that the
depositor could nullify the deposit at any time before
the realization of the security. Smith, L. J., stated
that the defendants were none the less stakeholders
because they were also co-wagerers. Obviously the de-

(n) See *ante*, p. 169.

fendants, if money instead of shares had been the subject of the deposit, would equally have held such money *quâ* stakeholders.

Hence it follows that such deposits are not voluntary payments, but are made under a gratuitous, and therefore revocable, bailment; and the authorities, cited *post* (*o*), as to the right of rescission, where a third person intervenes as stakeholder, are in point. The Gaming Act, 1892, will hereafter be seen not to have annulled this right of recovery.

When it is desired to rely on the defence that the contract is void under the statute 8 & 9 Vict. c. 109, the facts which show it to be must be pleaded, as in the defence of illegality (*p*).

Where the agency is a lawful one, the contract of employment involves the usual rights, on the one hand, of the principal against the agent to recover damages for breach of the contract (*q*); on the other hand, of the agent as against the principal to recover his commission, to be reimbursed his advances and expenses, and to be indemnified against damages flowing naturally from the agency (*r*). Such contract of agency may be revoked by the act of the parties or by operation of law. In the former case, where the agent has part performed his contract, the question arises as to whether the principal can revoke the authority, either in whole or as to the part which remains unexecuted; when the authority is not severable, and damage would arise to the agent on account of the execution of the authority *pro tanto*, there the principal will not be allowed to revoke the

Pleading.

Agency generally.

(*o*) See *post*, pp. 190 *et seq.*
(*p*) *Ante*, p. 115.
(*q*) Story on Agency, 7th edit. sect. 222.
(*r*) Story on Agency, 7th edit. sects. 335, 341.

unexecuted part, or at least, not without indemnifying the agent. Again, when the power is coupled with an interest, then, unless there is an express stipulation that the contract shall be revocable, it is, from its own nature, in contemplation of law, irrevocable, whether it is expressed to be so on the face of the instrument creating the authority or not. In the latter case, revocation by operation of law depends on the principle that the derivative authority expires with the original authority from which it proceeds: thus death or bankruptcy of the principal would terminate the agent's authority (s).

Application of foregoing principles.

The application of the foregoing principles to the positions of principal and agent, with regard to contracts null and void under 8 & 9 Vict. c. 109, will now be considered. It will be convenient to discuss the law as it was prior to the Gaming Act, 1892, which operates on such transactions as were entered into subsequently to the 20th May, 1892, with a view also to demonstrate the changes introduced by the last-mentioned Act.

The principal cannot recover against his agent for breach of contract to make a wager.

The right of the principal to recover against his agent damages for breach of contract by the defendant, in not making wagers on his behalf, was before the Courts in the case of *Cohen* v. *Kittell* (t). This claim for damages was advanced as an alternative to a claim for money had and received by the defendant to the use of the plaintiff. The verdict established that the defendant had not made the bets. Mr. Baron Huddleston therefore held that the decisions in cases where the agents had made the bets were not in point. He said : " The contract of agency for the breach of which the plaintiff sues the defendant is one by which the plaintiff

(s) Story on Agency, 7th edit. sects. 466—488.

(t) *Cohen* v. *Kittell*, 22 Q. B. D. 680; 58 L. J. Q. B. 241; 60 L. T. N. S. 932; 37 W. R. 400; 53 J. P. 469.

employed the defendant to enter into contracts which, if made, would have been null and void, and the performance of which could not have been enforced by any legal proceeding taken by the defendant for the benefit of the plaintiff. The breach of such contract can give no right of action to the principal. I see no difference between the case and the employment of an agent to do an illegal act (*u*). The section of Story on Agency (*x*) which has been cited shows that the right of the plaintiff to have recovered in respect of the contract to have been made by the agent on his behalf is an 'essential ingredient' in the case against the agent for negligence in not contracting. In this case this 'essential ingredient' is wanting, and *Webster* v. *De Tastet* (*y*) shows that, this being so, the consideration urged on behalf of the plaintiff, that the losers of the bets to the defendant would probably have paid them as debts of honour, is wholly immaterial." Manisty, J., after referring to *Read* v. *Anderson*, said: "We are now invited to go a step further and to hold that a principal, who employs an agent to make bets on his account, can maintain an action for negligence against the agent should the latter refuse to bet for him. The custom of Tattersall's is again invoked, this time to make the agent responsible. It is clear, however, that the action cannot be maintained. . . . A principal can suffer no real loss through the refusal of his agent to make bets on his account." The probability that the defendant was a member of some club, which constituted itself a conventional forum for the enforcement of such payments, was as immaterial as the probability that the defendant would have

(*u*) *Ante*, pp. 123 *et seq.*
(*x*) Sect. 222.
(*y*) *Webster* v. *De Tastet*, 7 T. R. 157.

G.   N

paid without such pressure. It is impossible to separate the question whether an action would lie from the damage sustained; it is a case in which the law cannot imply nominal damages. Every *injuria* implies damages; here damages cannot be implied; so the neglect of the act of making the wager cannot be an *injuria*. The defendant's contract was to do that which in law is equivalent to nothing; he did nothing.

Agent's rights as against principal in respect of disbursements and commissions.

It will be remembered that the agent cannot recover any disbursements made for the purpose of effecting an illegal transaction (*z*). The question now is, whether an agent for making a void, as contradistinguished from an illegal, contract, can recover his disbursements. In 1854 this question was raised in the case of *Jessop* v. *Lutwyche* (*a*). The declaration was for money paid and on accounts stated; the plea was that the causes of action accrued after 8 & 9 Vict. c. 109, under and by virtue of certain contracts made between the plaintiff and defendant by way of gaming upon the market price of shares. Baron Parke held that the plea was consistent with a state of facts which would enable the plaintiff to recover, viz., that a third person had won the money, and that the plaintiff had requested the defendant to pay the money over to him. Similarly, in 1855, in *Knight* v. *Cambers* (*b*), the plea to the same effect was, for the same reason, successfully demurred to. In the case of *Rosewarne* v. *Billing* (*c*), the two earlier cases

(*z*) *Clayton* v. *Dilley*, 4 Taunt. 165; *ante*, Chap. VI. p. 124.

(*a*) *Jessop* v. *Lutwyche*, 10 Exch. 614; 3 C. L. R. 359; 24 L. J. Ex. 65.

(*b*) *Knight* v. *Cambers*, 15 C. B. 562; 3 C. L. R. 565; 24 L. J. C. P. 121; 1 Jur. N. S. 525.

(*c*) *Rosewarne* v. *Billing*, 15 C. B. N. S. 316; 33 L. J. C. P. 55; 10 Jur. N. S. 496; 9 L. T. 441; 12 W. R. 104.

were followed, and Erle, C. J., in the course of his judgment, said: "I am clearly of opinion that if a man loses a wager and gets another to pay the money for him, an action lies for the recovery of the money so paid (d). . . . I should incline to think that if one requests another to make a wagering contract on his account, and pay the loss if loss happens, that would be a continuing request to pay until revoked. If the party were a broker, who, by usage of the share market, was bound in all events to pay, it might be a question whether the principal could be allowed to rescind." Williams, J.: "It is quite consistent with the plea that the plaintiff, having made the contract in his own name, and being by force of the statute able to resist payment of the money, might have been minded to resist but for the defendant's request to him to pay."

So far these cases are authorities to show that the agent having made the wager, and the wager having been lost, an express direction from the principal to the agent to pay the amount lost founds an obligation between the principal and agent. But the case of *Ex parte Godefroi, In re Hart* (e), goes further. In that case a stockbroker sought to have the defendant made a bankrupt. The debt arose from transactions which the respondent had authorized him to effect on the Stock Exchange, and the money due on such transactions from the respondent had been paid by the peti-tioner. The defence of gaming transactions was set up. The Chief Judge held that the petitioner was merely agent, and "since the respondent must be taken to have known that by the rules of the Stock Exchange

(d) See *Alcinbrook* v. *Hall*, 2 Wils. 309; *ante*, p. 55.
(e) *Ex parte Godefroi, In re Hart*, W. N. (1870) 95.

N 2

the petitioner was bound to pay members of the Stock Exchange any sums of money which might be due from the respondent to them in regard to the transactions, a request to pay such sums must be implied." In the next case of *Ex parte Pyke, In re Lister* (*f*), there was an express request, after the loss of the wager, to the agent to pay on behalf of the principal. The case of *Lynch* v. *Godwin* (*g*), which is briefly reported, was an action to recover 40*l.* paid by the plaintiff for the defendant on a betting transaction. In 1878 the plaintiff was instructed by the defendant to bet 40*l.* on a horse called Vril for the Ascot Stakes. The plaintiff did so. In the result the horse lost, and the plaintiff paid the money. The defendant declined to repay. Lord Coleridge, C. J., held that the plaintiff could recover, for whilst the wager was void, transactions arising out of it were not. In the Court of Appeal this judgment was affirmed. Jessel, M. R., said : " The employment of an agent to bet was not in itself illegal ; and a bet was void, but not illegal. If you employ an agent to make a bet for you, you know you must pay, or be subject to very unpleasant consequences. If you do not withdraw your request, it must continue, and if he bet at your request, he paid at your request ; you were liable for the money so paid." Lindley, L. J., is reported to have enunciated the principle : " A request to pay the bet if lost was implied in the request to bet." Bowen, L. J., concurred.

(*f*) *Ex parte Pyke, In re Lister*, 8 Ch. Div. 754 ; 47 L. J. Bk. 100 ; 38 L. T. 923 ; 26 W. R. 806 ; see *ante*, p. 55, where the case is cited on the question whether the security for the advance was within the statute of Anne.

(*g*) *Lynch* v. *Godwin*, 26 Sol. Jour. 509.

The case of *Read* v. *Anderson* (*h*) was tried before *Read* v.
Anderson.
Hawkins, J., without a jury. It arose on the following facts :—The plaintiff was a turf commission agent, and a member of Tattersall's. According to well-established usage, known to the defendant, a turf commission agent instructed by an employer to back a horse backs it in his own name, and becomes himself alone responsible to the person with whom the bet is made ; and, on the settling day, he receives or pays, as the case may be, rendering his own account to his employer, paying to or receiving from him the balance of moneys won or lost. During the Ascot meeting of 1881, the plaintiff at Ascot received a telegram from the defendant instructing him to back certain horses for him. As to the horses in the first race, the telegram came too late to be acted on. As to the second race, the plaintiff carried out the defendant's instructions by backing the horses for the amounts named in his (the plaintiff's) name. The result was that 175*l.* was lost. The plaintiff did not telegraph to the defendant that he was "on" before the race; but after the race was over he telegraphed the result. The same evening the defendant repudiated the bets, "as I cannot stand messages being sent away after the race is over to say I am 'on.'" The plaintiff, in reply, sent to the defendant particulars of the bets, and an account. On the settling day the plaintiff paid the bets in question to the winners of them. Had he not Penalty on a
defaulter at
Tattersall's.
done so he would have been a "defaulter" within the meaning of one of the rules of Tattersall's subscription room, and upon complaint made to the committee of

(*h*) *Read* v. *Anderson*, 10 Q. B. D. 100; 13 Q. B. D. 779; 25 L. J. Q. B. 214; 48 L. T. 74; 31 W. R. 453; 47 J. P. 311.

the room he would have been liable to exclusion from the room, and under the rules of the Jockey Club he would have been liable to disqualification as to entering and running horses. The report does not say that the defendant was aware of these specific consequences.

The plaintiff brought this action to recover 175*l.*, the amount of the three bets so made by the plaintiff in his own name at the request of and for the defendant, and paid by the plaintiff to the winners thereof.

On behalf of the defendant, the first and unimportant contention was advanced, that because a telegram was not handed in before the race to say the defendant was "on," he was entitled to repudiate the bets. Such contention was based on an express condition to that effect, or one implied by universal custom. Hawkins, J., decided that such a condition was neither expressed nor implied, and found, as a fact, that the bets were *bonâ fide* made on behalf of the defendant. This alleged condition was not raised in the Court of Appeal.

On behalf of the defendant, the second and important contention was, that he had never authorized the plaintiff to pay the bets, and, even if he had, that authority *Judgment of* was revoked before the money was actually paid. In *Hawkins, J.* the course of his judgment, the learned judge points out the wagers were void and not illegal, and that the defendant might lawfully authorize the plaintiff or anyone to pay the amount of the losses; and if by his request or authority another person paid his lost bets, the amount so paid could be recovered from him as so much money paid to his use. "The request or authority to make such payments may be either express, or it may be implied from usage or from the nature of the dealings between the parties themselves" (*i*). He found, as a fact, that at the time the defendant gave the authority to make the bets he gave also an implied authority to pay them if they should be lost. On the basis of that finding, the learned judge found, as a fact, that the authority had not been revoked, and further concluded that such *de facto* revocation (if there had been any) would have been inoperative at law. He calls attention to the *dicta* of Erle, C. J., in *Rosewarne* v. *Billing*, and proceeds to state his reasons for so holding, which briefly were, that the plaintiff's authority was coupled with an interest, and, therefore, was irrevocable : " It was the plaintiff's security against any loss by reason of the obligation he had personally incurred on the faith of the authority to pay the bets if lost; the consideration for that authority was the taking upon himself that responsibility at the defendant's request." The point at which the authority becomes irrevocable is the act on the agent's part of making the bet. The learned judge states the principle in other words, as follows: " If a principal employs an agent to do a legal act, the doing of which may in the ordinary course of things put the agent under an absolute or contingent obligation to pay money to another, and at the same time gives him an authority if the obligation is incurred to discharge it at the principal's request, the moment the agent, on the faith of that authority, does the act and so incurs the liability, the authority ceases to be revocable." Another ground is suggested, namely, an implied contract to indemnify ; and Hawkins, J., says:

(*i*) The authorities cited are *Bubb* v. *Yelverton*, L. R. 9 Eq. 471 ; 39 L. J. Ch. 428; 22 L. T. 258; 18 W. R. 512 ; *Oldham* v. *Ramsden*, 44 L. J. C. P. 309 ; 32 L. T. 825 ; *Rosewarne* v. *Billing*, 15 C. B. N. S. 316 ; 33 L. J. C. P. 55 ; 10 Jur. N. S. 496 ; 9 L. T. 441 ; 12 W. R. 104 ; *Lynch* v. *Godwin*, 26 Sol. Jour. 509.

"I think it signifies nothing that such obligation (against
which the indemnity is to operate) is not enforceable
in a court of justice if the non-fulfilment of it would
entail serious inconvenience or loss upon the agent."

It will be seen that the bases of this decision are in-
applicable where the agent makes the contract in the
name of the principal. The irrevocability of the agent's
implied authority to pay is thus based on the fact that
he is taken to have incurred an absolute or contingent
obligation to pay. But in strictness an obligation
means a duty, a *vinculum juris :* that, however, is exactly
what the agent had not incurred; the only *quasi* duty
he had incurred is one known not to the law, but
only to a conventional form itself unknown to the law.
From the standpoint of indemnity, he is allowed protection against damages which could not be recovered
at law.

Lord Esher's dissentient judgment. In the Court of Appeal (*k*), Lord Esher, M. R., said:
"The real question is whether the defendant, as princi-
pal, could revoke the authority given to the plaintiff as
agent. The evidence proves that when a member of
Tattersall's makes bets and does not pay them if lost,
he is liable to be turned out of the room; and if he is
turned out, he cannot carry on his business as a turf
commission agent. The question is whether the law
implies an undertaking by the defendant that he will
not revoke the plaintiff's authority to pay bets which
have been lost. If a principal employs an agent to
perform an act, and if, upon revocation of the authority,
the agent will be by law exposed to loss or suffering,
the authority cannot be revoked. But in the present
case no claim could be lawfully enforced against the
agent. It is true that the betting contract was made

(*k*) *Read* v. *Anderson,* 10 Q. B. D. 100; 13 Q. B. D. 779; 52
L. J. Q. B. 214; 48 L. T. 74; 31 W. R. 453; 47 J. P. 311.

by the plaintiff in his own name on behalf of his principal; nevertheless it could not be enforced against him.
If the other party to the bet had lost it, and had declined
to pay it, he could not have been compelled to do so.
But it has been contended that, although this view is
true, the law puts it into the plaintiff's power to enforce
payment by the defendant of the amount of the bet,
because, unless it is paid, the plaintiff will suffer a loss
in his business; but the plaintiff's business, although it
may not be illegal, is directly objected to by the law,
and the contracts made by him in his business cannot
be enforced; it is a business of which the law ought not
to take notice, and, therefore, the inconvenience and the
loss which the plaintiff may suffer in his objectionable
business form no ground for an action for revoking an
authority which the principal ought not to have given.
The cases in which an authority cannot be revoked ought
to be confined to those cases in which the agent will upon
revocation suffer what the law deems to be an injury."

Bowen, L. J., whilst he felt the force of the point Bowen and
Fry, L.JJ.
that the obligation to pay a lost bet, relied upon by the
plaintiff, is not recognised by law, held, as an inference
of fact, that the contract of employment was such that
thereunder, and as a part thereof, there was an obligation on the principal to recoup his agent, and not to
revoke his authority to pay, but to indemnify the agent
against all payments made in the regular course of
business. Fry, L. J., agreed with Bowen, L. J.

It follows from this decision that as such contract of
employment is valid, the agent can recover his agreed
commission.   In *Bridger* v. *Savage* (*l*), such amounts
were allowed.

(*l*) *Bridger* v. *Savage*, 15 Q. B. D. 363; 54 L. J. Q. B. 464;
53 L. T. 129; 33 W. R. 891; 49 J. P. 725.

When and from whom winnings may be recovered.　The winner of a wager may recover his winnings when the loser has paid them to the winner's agent. It will be remembered that such a right exists even when the transaction, as between the winner and the loser, out of which the winnings have arisen, is illegal (*m*). In the case of *Beyer* v. *Adams* (*n*), it was held that the winner could not recover from his agent. The cases of *Tenant* v. *Elliott* and *Farmer* v. *Russell*, were cited in argument: but Stuart, V.-C., considered that section 18 destroyed the right of action. Such an action, he held, was clearly within the prohibition of the statute, and such prohibition could not be confined to actions against the loser of the wager. The question came before the Court of Appeal in the case of *Bridger* v. *Savage* (*o*), with the result that *Beyer* v. *Adams* was overruled. It was an action by the plaintiff to recover the sum of 131*l*. 17*s*. 6*d*. due to him on the balance of accounts for money had and received to the use of the plaintiff. The case for the plaintiff was that it was arranged between him and the defendant that the latter, for a commission of 5*l*. per cent. on winnings, was to make bets for the plaintiff by laying money for him on various horses at starting prices, and that he, the defendant, had accordingly done so, and had received 212*l*. 10*s*. from the losers; and that on the balance of account there was due the sum claimed in the action, after deducting the agent's commission. The case for the defendant was that there was no such arrangement as the plaintiff alleged, but that the bets on the horses were made

(*m*) See Chap. VI., pp. 125, 126.

(*n*) *Beyer* v. *Adams*, 26 L. J. Ch. 841; 3 Jur. N. S. 709; 5 W. R. 795.

(*o*) *Bridger* v. *Savage*, 15 Q. B. D. 363; 54 L. J. Q. B. 464; 53 L. T. 129; 33 W. R. 891; 49 J. P. 725.

by the plaintiff with the defendant personally, and that as such they were not recoverable at law. The action was tried before Lord Coleridge, C. J., without a jury, when his lordship disbelieved the defendant, and gave judgment for the plaintiff for the amount claimed. The defendant appealed : first, as against the finding of the facts ; secondly, against the legal conclusion to be drawn from the facts as found. Brett, M. R., said it was impossible to dissent from the Lord Chief Justice on the question of fact (p), and in the course of his judgment puts the question thus: " the defendant has received money which he contracted with the plaintiff to hand over to him when he had received it. That is a perfectly legal contract; but for the defendant it has been contended that the statute 8 & 9 Vict. c. 109, s. 18, makes that contract illegal. The answer is, that it has been held by the Courts on several occasions that the statute applies only to the original contract made between the persons betting, and not such a contract as was made here between the plaintiff and defendant." The learned judge then cites a passage from the judgment of Eyre, C. J., in *Tenant* v. *Elliott*, which points out that the defendant is not in the position of a stakeholder. The decision of the case in favour of the plaintiff would follow from the *ratio decidendi* of *Read* v. *Anderson*, that such contract of employment was valid. Bowen, L. J., said : " If the person who has betted pays his bet, he does nothing wrong ; he only waives a benefit which the statute has given to him, and

---

(p) In *Read* v. *Anderson*, the Master of the Rolls said the Court of Appeal were not bound by the findings of facts of Hawkins, J., trying the case without a jury : *Read* v. *Anderson*, 10 Q. B. D. 100; 13 Q. B. D. 779; 52 L. J. Q. B. 214; 48 L. T. 74; 31 W. R. 453; 47 J. P. 311.

confers a good title to the money on the person to whom
he pays it. Therefore, when the bet is paid, the transaction is completed, and when it is paid to an agent, it
cannot be contended that that is not a good payment
for his principal. If not, how monstrous it would be
that the agent who has received money which belongs
to his principal, and which he has received for his principal, and only on that account, should be allowed to
say that the payment was bad and void." The cases of
Johnson v. *Lansley* and *Beeston* v. *Beeston*, which will be
considered hereafter (*q*) as illustrating the rights of partners in void contracts, are to the same effect. The
decision was influenced by the case of *Sharp* v. *Taylor*,
which was criticised by Jessel, M. R., as shown in
Chapter VI.

The facts of the case of *Bridger* v. *Savage*, stated
above, exemplify the nature of the burden of proof
which lies on the plaintiff: first, the contract of
agency; secondly, the receipt of the money in respect
of bets entered into pursuant to such contract. The
second onus will commonly be discharged by proving
the agent's accounts as rendered by him to the principal (*r*). The agent is in general estopped from denying the accuracy of accounts rendered by him to his
principal, except in the case of an error arising by mis-
take (*s*).

(*q*) Page 195.

(*r*) *Bittleston* v. *Cooper*, 14 M. & W. 399; *Standish* v. *Ross*,
3 Ex. 527; 19 L. J. Ex. 185; *Lucas* v. *Jones*, 5 Q. B. 949; D. &
M. 774; 13 L. J. Q. B. 208; 8 Jur. 422; *Gingell* v. *Purkins*, 4
Ex. 720; 19 L. J. Ex. 129.

(*s*) *Skyring* v. *Greenwood*, 4 B. & C. 281; 6 D. & R. 401; 1 C. &
P. 517; *Shaw* v. *Picton*, 4 B. & C. 715; 7 D. & R. 201; *Cave* v.
Mills, 31 L. J. Ex. 265; 6 L. T. N. S. 650; 8 Jur. N. S. 363;
10 W. R. 471.

In the case of *Moore* v. *Peachey* (*t*), the same defence was raised as in the above case of *Bridger* v. *Savage*, namely, that the bets had been made between the plaintiff and defendant as principals. The plaintiff proved the employment, and put in accounts received by him from the defendant, wherein he was given credit for amounts purporting to have been received by the defendant, who charged him commission. He also produced letters, in some of which the defendant spoke of not being able " to get on " certain horses, and of persons with whom he had made bets refusing to pay him. The defendant struggled to rebut this evidence by swearing that he had " never placed," and had never received the money, and that the expressions in his letters had reference to his inability to make " hedging " bets, or of his loss in respect of hedging bets, and that the charges for commission were really charges for expenses. The evidence of the clerk and other bookmakers disclosed facts which showed that " bookmakers" and " commission agents " were practically and in many cases identical. Charles, J., however, could not accept the defendant's statement that he never made bets with other people, and was of opinion that the defendant was estopped by his conduct from saying that he betted as principal.

At one time it was thought that a stakeholder, who receives deposits from the parties to a contract by way of gaming and wagering was the agent of all the parties, or rather their trustee, instead of being the agent severally of each of the depositors with regard to the respective deposits. The effect of the former view

Stakeholders. Position of.

(*t*) *Moore* v. *Peachey*, 7 T. L. R. 748.

was that the several contracts of gratuitous bailment did not exist; the depositary was the trustee of all the parties, and as such, where the trust was a legal one, the request of any individual depositor for a return of his deposit did not ground an obligation on the trustee (*u*). But there was a decision to the contrary in the case of *Eltham* v. *Kingsman* (*x*), and also in *Hastelow* v. *Jackson* (*y*). In the case of *Hampden* v. *Walsh* (*z*), in the unanimous judgment of the Court (Cockburn, C. J., and Mellor and Quain, JJ.), it was decided and stated : " It may be true that he (the stakeholder) is the agent of both parties in a certain sense, so that, if the event comes off, and the authority to pay over the money by the depositor be not revoked, he may be bound to pay it over. But primarily he is the agent of the depositor, and can deal with the money deposited so long only as his authority subsists." Hence, then, in considering the obligations of the stakeholders, the several contracts of gratuitous bailment have to be looked at, and the purpose or final object of the bailment, whether valid, illegal, or void, will be immaterial so far as the right of the depositors to rescind the bailee's authority is concerned.

Rescission of stakeholder's authority.

The authorities on the revocation of a stakeholder's authority will now be reviewed. It will be seen that the power of rescission exists even after the decision of the event, until there has been an actual payment over to the

(*u*) *Brandon* v. *Hibbert*, 4 Camp. 37 ; *Bland* v. *Collett*, 4 Camp. 157 ; *Emery* v. *Richards*, 14 M. & W. 728 ; 15 L. J. Ex. 49; *Marryat* v. *Broderick*, 2 M. & W. 369 ; 1 Jur. 242.

(*x*) *Eltham* v. *Kingsman*, 1 B. & Ald. 683.

(*y*) *Hastelow* v. *Jackson*, 8 B. & C. 221.

(*z*) *Hampden* v. *Walsh*, 1 Q. B. D. 189 ; 45 L. J. 238 ; 33 L. T. 852 ; 24 W. R. 607.

winner.   In the case of *Varney* v. *Hickman* (a), which
is a leading authority on the construction of section 18
of 8 & 9 Vict. c. 109, the facts were as follows:—The
plaintiff and one Isaacs had deposited 20*l.* each with
the defendant on the event of a match between two
horses.   Before the race was run the plaintiff gave
notice to the defendant that he declined the bet, and
demanded back his deposit.   The plaintiff not attend-
ing to contest the race, Isaacs was declared the winner,
and the amount of the two deposits was handed over to
him by the defendant.   The plaintiff brought his action
to recover his deposit as money had and received.   The
defendant relied on section 18 of the statute to show
that the action could not be maintained.   Maule, J.,
said : " This cannot be considered to be an action
brought for recovering a sum of money alleged to be
won on a wager ; nor do I think it is an action to
recover a sum deposited in the hands of the defendant
to *abide* the event of the wager.   That must necessarily
mean an action to be sustained on the ground of the
existence and the determination of the wager. . . . .
As soon as the defendant received notice from the
plaintiff that he declined to abide by the wager, the
money ceased to be money deposited in the hands of
the former to abide the event, and became money of
the plaintiff's in his hands without any good reason
for detaining it."   Similarly, in *Martin* v. *Hewson* (b),
Parke, B., held that the statute did not apply where
a party seeks to recover his stake upon a repudiation of
the wagering contract.   In that case the repudiation

(a) *Varney* v. *Hickman,* 5 C. B. 271 ; 5 D. & L. 364 ; 17 L. J.
C. P. 102 ; *ante,* p. 140.

(b) *Martin* v. *Hewson,* 10 Exch. 737 ; 24 L. J. Ex. 174 ; 1
Jur. N. S. 214.

was prior to the ascertainment of the event of the wager. In the Irish case of *Graham* v. *Thompson* (c) a plea in a similar action was advanced, namely, " that the money was money deposited in the hands of the defendant to abide an event on which a wager had thereupon been made, to wit, &c., and that that wager had not been repudiated, or any demand of the said money, or any part thereof, made upon him by the plaintiff before the event on which the said wager had been made had taken place, and the said wager had been decided." But the demurrer to the plea succeeded on the ground that it was consistent with it that the plaintiff had repudiated the wager before the defendant had paid over the money to the winner. This case carries the power to rescind one step further forward, viz., to a period after the event, which shows that the bailment is revocable until finally executed by payment over pursuant to its terms. The decision of *Hampden* v. *Walsh* (d) is to the same effect. The wager in that case was about the possibility of proving the rotundity of the world. The wager was decided according to the agreement. The plaintiff lost the wager, and gave the stakeholder notice, prior to his having done so, not to pay over the plaintiff's deposit to the winner. It was held, on the principles of bailment above explained, and on the authorities hereinbefore reviewed, that the plaintiff, under the circumstances, was entitled to recover his deposit. The case of *Diggle* v. *Higgs* (e), which is stated at some length in Chapter VII. on the construction

(c) *Graham* v. *Thompson*, Ir. Rep. 2 C. L. 64.

(d) *Hampden* v. *Walsh*, 1 Q. B. D. 189; 45 L. J. Q. B. 238; 33 L. T. 852 ; 24 W. R. 607.

(e) *Diggle* v. *Higgs*, L. R. 2 Ex. Div. 422; 46 L. J. Ex. 721; 37 L. T. 27 ; 25 W. R. 607, 777.

of the proviso clause of section 18 of the statute, is a further authority to same effect. Similarly, in the Privy Council, in the case of *Trimble* v. *Hill* (*f*).

The case of *Savage* v. *Madder* (*g*), at least so far as obiter dicta contained in it, has been finally overruled. Martin, B., in that case said, the effect of the statute was to prevent any action being brought by the winner himself in respect of moneys deposited in the hands of a stakeholder to abide the event. But the plea in that case, in answer to the plaintiff's declaration for money had and received to the use of the plaintiff, and for interest, and on accounts stated, was " That the said money is money deposited in the hands of the defendant to abide the event on which a wager was made, and is claimed by the plaintiff as the winner of the said wager, together with other money won thereon, and the plaintiff did not repudiate the said wager, or demand back his said money before the event of the said wager, and has never repudiated the said wager or claimed the said money on any other ground than as winner of the said wager, and no part of the said money was or is a subscription or prize contribution, nor was or is due on any agreement to subscribe or contribute for or towards any plate, prize, or sum of money to be awarded to the winner or winners of lawful game, sport, pastime, or exercise." Hence it appears that the plaintiff was claiming not only his own deposit, but also winnings.

It is clear that a depositor, whether winner or loser, can recover his deposit prior to payment over pursuant

Savage v. *Madder.*

(*f*) *Trimble* v. *Hill*, 5 App. Cas. 342; 49 L. J. P. C. 49; 42 L. T. 103; 28 W. R. 479.

(*g*) *Savage* v. *Madder*, 36 L. J. Ex. 178; 16 L. T. 600; 15 W. R. 910.

to the agreement. If A. had been declared the winner, but the stakeholder refused to hand over the stakes, A. could sue him for his deposit. In the case of *Batty* v. *Marriott* (*h*), on the basis of an erroneous construction of the proviso clause of sect. 18 of the statute 8 & 9 Vict. c. 109, it was held that the winner might recover the whole of the stakes, but *Diggle* v. *Higgs* (*i*) is a binding decision to the contrary.

As the stakeholder's authority can thus be revoked, it follows that he could not maintain an action to obtain a deposit from an intended depositor : *Clayton* v. *Dilley* (*j*).

The Gaming Act, 1892, has not altered the depositor's rights, as will be seen in the next chapter.

Partnership.　　There appear to be two commonly occurring instances of partnership, namely, where two or more persons contribute to a fund to be applied by them in particular wagering transactions, or where they conduct the business of commission agents generally. It is a common rule that, between partners, whether they are so in general or for a particular transaction only, and whatever be the nature of the partnership venture, no account will be taken at law. The rule applies where all the moneys have been received and paid by one partner (*k*). If the partners cannot agree on their accounts, the same must be taken in a properly constituted partnership action in the Chancery Division. Where, however, no general account is involved, or where one partner has given the other a security, an action at law can be maintained.

(*h*) *Batty* v. *Marriott*, 5 C. B. 818; 17 L. J. C. P. 215; 12 Jur. 462. See Chap. VII. p. 156.

(*i*) *Diggle* v. *Higgs*, 2 Ex. Div. 422; 46 L. J. Ex. 721; 37 L. T. 27; 25 W. R. 777 (C. A.), reversing 25 W. R. 607.

(*j*) *Clayton* v. *Dilley*, 4 Taunt. 165.

(*k*) *Bovill* v. *Hammond*, 6 B. & C. 149; 9 D. & R. 186.

An instance of an action at law, upon an account stated between partners and a security given for payment of the balance, is found in the case of *Johnson* v. *Lansley* (*m*). The plaintiff and one Hunt jointly made bets with third persons on horse races. Hunt received the winnings, and accepted a bill drawn on him by the defendant, who subsequently indorsed it to the plaintiff. The defendant contended at the trial that the original wagering contracts between Hunt and the third person were void or illegal, and that in effect the Court was asked collaterally to enforce the invalid contracts. But this contention failed. The losers had paid; Hunt had received the winnings on behalf of himself and the plaintiff; the losers could not recover back from Hunt the money which they had paid to him. Hence, as Maule, J., said in the course of the argument, "Surely a duty arises on the part of Hunt to pay over his share to his co-partner." Jervis, C. J., in his judgment, after referring to the statute 8 & 9 Vict. c. 109, stated that the transaction was not illegal, and that Hunt was bound on every principle of justice to pay this money to Johnson. The circumstance of Lansley being substituted for Hunt could not make that illegal which as between Johnson and Hunt would not have been so. Maule, J., said: "The money which was the consideration for this bill was money which Hunt was bound to account for to Johnson. The losers could not get it back from Hunt, and it would be a very unjust thing that he should keep the whole."

In the case of *Beeston* v. *Beeston* (*n*), the plaintiff declared on a cheque drawn by the defendant in his

(*m*) *Johnson* v. *Lansley*, 12 C. B. 468.

(*n*) *Beeston* v. *Beeston*, 1 Ex. D. 13; 45 L. J. Ex. 230; 33 L. T. 700; 24 W. R. 96.

favour on a certain bank and dishonoured. The plaintiff proved that the defendant had received money on his behalf, and that the cheque in question was given in payment thereof. The defendant contended that the plaintiff could not recover from him such money, as it was a share of winnings received in respect of joint wagering transactions, and that consequently the cheque was given without consideration. Amphlett, B., stated: "There is no illegality in A. saying to B., 'Go and make bets on our joint account, and whatever the winnings on such bets may be shall be shared between us.'" It is true that Baron Amphlett cites the case of *Sharp* v. *Taylor* (o) with approval; but that was unnecessary for the decision.

The cases of *Johnson* v. *Lansley* and *Beeston* v. *Beeston* were cited in argument in the case of *Higginson* v. *Simpson* (p). In the last-mentioned case the plaintiff brought his action to recover 50*l.* by way of compensation for giving the defendant the name of a horse likely to win the Grand National Steeplechase. The facts, as found by the jury, were as follows :—The plaintiff and defendant agreed together that the plaintiff (a professional betting man) was to lay out 2*l.* in betting on a horse Regal for a particular steeplechase at the odds of 25 to 1, *i. e.*, taking the odds or betting 1*l.* to 25*l.* on the horse. If Regal won, it was agreed that the plaintiff was to have 50*l.* from the defendant, to be paid out of the defendant's winnings if he (the defendant) backed Regal; if Regal lost, the plaintiff was to pay the defendant 2*l.* The defendant did back Regal, and the horse won, and the defendant thereby won 250*l.*

On these findings it was held in the Divisional Court

(o) *Sharp* v. *Taylor*, 2 Ph. 801.
(p) *Higginson* v. *Simpson*, 2 C. P. D. 76 ; 46 L. J. C. P. 192; 36 L. T. 17; 25 W. R. 303.

that, in substance and in fact, the plaintiff and defendant had *inter se* entered into a wagering contract, and
that whether or not the object of the transaction was to
remunerate the plaintiff for his " tip," the contract itself
was none the less void. It will be seen, however, that
the facts are distinguishable from the cases in which A.
employs B. as his agent to make a bet with C., and then
sues B. for money paid to B. by C. to the use of A.;
and, further, are distinguishable from, though somewhat
akin to, cases in which A. and B. enter into a particular
transaction on their joint behalf—for instance, by jointly
wagering with C., and B. subsequently receives winnings from C. on behalf of himself and A. The facts,
therefore, distinguish the case from that of *Tenant* v.
Elliott on the one hand, and *Beeston* v. *Beeston* on the
other.

No case is reported in which the Court of Chancery
or the Chancery Division has taken the accounts. But
if there be a legal obligation between the partners, it is
impossible to see on what ground the Chancery Division
could refuse to take such accounts. In *Read* v. *Anderson* the employment of commission agents was held to
be a valid occupation; if that be so, then any partnership for the same purpose must be lawful : a partnership
action would lie (*q*). The submission here made must,
however, be sharply and decisively contrasted with those
cases where the partnership is illegal. It is apprehended
that if, in the course of taking the accounts in an action
for the dissolution of a partnership in a commission
agent's business, it was found that the partners had
been offending against the Betting House Acts, the
chief clerk would certify accordingly, and the Court
would then refuse to proceed.

(*q*) *Post*, pp. 204 *et seq*.

CHAPTER IX.

THE GAMING ACT, 1892.

THE chief practical differences in a civil Court between holding a transaction to be illegal and holding the same to be void appear to arise in connection with the rights of agents, and of third persons, who make payments in respect of the invalid transaction, and in respect of partnerships, for the purposes of effecting the invalid transactions. The difference is also strongly marked in respect of securities; but with regard to gaming and wagering, the effect of the statutory enactments has, in respect of such securities as are comprised within the statute 5 & 6 Will. IV. c. 41, been to remove such distinction.

The Gaming Act, 1892.

On the 20th May, 1892, a statute was passed, intituled "An Act to amend the Law concerning Games and Wagers," whereby it was enacted that any promise, express or implied, to pay any person any sum of money paid by him under or in respect of any contract or agreement rendered null and void by the Act of the 8 & 9 Vict. c. 109, or to pay any sum of money by way of commission, fee, reward, or otherwise in respect of any such contract, or of any services in relation thereto or in connection therewith, shall be null and void, and no action shall be brought to recover any such sum of money."

Effect.

The effect, then, of this amendment of the law is to remove some of the more substantial differences which

existed in the consequences of the statute of 8 & 9 Vict.
c. 109, having enacted that contracts therein comprised
should be null and void, as contradistinguished from
being illegal. It prevents the agent who has negotiated
a bet, or the third party who has discharged another's
debt of honour, from maintaining an action in respect
of his services or disbursements. It thus abrogates the
principles which underlaid the cases of *Jessop* v. *Lutwyche*, *Knight* v. *Cambers*, *Rosewarne* v. *Billing* and others,
and *Read* v. *Anderson* (a).

The Act is not retrospective. In the case of *Knight* v.
Lee (b), the plaintiff, a betting agent, sued the defendant in respect of a cause of action analogous to that in
the case of *Read* v. *Anderson*. The transactions in question had been effected prior to the passing of the Act;
but the action was not commenced until after that date.
It was held that the Act only applied to transactions
posterior to the date of its passing, and that in respect
of disbursements by an agent prior to such date, an action
could be maintained to recover such money (c).

In the case of *Tatam* v. *Reeve* (d), it was unsuccess- *Tatam* v.
fully contended that the Act did not apply to the fol- *Reeve.*
lowing facts :—The defendant requested the plaintiff to
settle an account which he forwarded to him. The
account purported to show that the defendant was indebted to four persons named in certain sums set opposite their names. The plaintiff paid the sums to the
persons named on the same day. The sums were due

(a) *Ante*, pp. 166, 178.

(b) *Knight* v. *Lee*, (1892) 1 Q. B. 41; 62 L. J. Q. B. 28; 67
L. T. 688; 41 W. R. 125.

(c) A similar decision on 8 & 9 Vict. c. 109, is *Moon* v.
Durden, 2 Ex. 22; 12 Jur. 138.

(d) *Tatam* v. *Reeve*, (1893) 1 Q. B. 44; 62 L. J. C. L. 30; 5 R.
83; 67 L. T. 683; 41 W. R. 174; 57 J. P. 118.

from the defendant to the persons named for bets on
horse races which the defendant had made and lost, and
the payments were made after the 20th May, 1892.
The plaintiff stated that the amounts paid by him were
not in respect of any bets made by him on behalf of the
defendant; that he had simply paid them on the defendant's request, and was not in any way liable to pay
them. It was not stated that the defendant knew that
the payments were for bets. On behalf of the plaintiff
it was contended that he did not pay the money " under
or in respect of " any contract rendered void by 8 & 9
Vict. c. 109, and that he merely paid upon the request
of the defendant, and under a .promise to repay him
implied from that request. Lord Coleridge, C. J., said,
with regard to *Read* v. *Anderson*, that it really cut at
the root of the value and principle of the statute, because
it was a decision that if you employed somebody else to
do that which you could not, so as to make it effectual
at law, do yourself, you could, in effect, make a good
contract in respect of a gaming debt. After citing the
Act of 1892, the Lord Chief Justice added : I cannot
feel any doubt or hesitation in coming to the conclusion
that " the payments were in respect of a contract or
agreement rendered null and void by 8 & 9 Vict. c. 109.
I agree that they were not paid ' under ' such a contract or agreement, because there was no contract of
betting or gaming between the plaintiff and the defendant; but the money was paid in respect of gaming
debts which the defendant owed to persons to whom the
plaintiff paid it, and it was paid in order to discharge
those debts. . . . If it was the case of a man deceived
into making payments in respect of a matter he knew
nothing whatever about, there would, at any rate, be
something to make us sorry to come to the conclusion

that he could not recover." Wills, J., was of the same opinion. He disclaimed the suggestion that the object of the Act was solely to get rid of the decision of *Read* v. *Anderson*. He held that the words "in respect of" were inserted purposely, and with the intention of striking at transactions such as the one before the Court. He further pointed out that this construction would not work any great injustice, because if a person pays money for another upon what amounts to a representation that it is not payable in respect of any contract or agreement which comes within the Act, the person on whose behalf the money is paid would be estopped from setting up the Act as an answer to the claim of the person who paid it. With regard to this principle of estoppel, the cases of its operation in reference to securities given for an illegal consideration were considered in Chapter VI., and may be consulted on its probable application to this question (c). "Estoppel," said Bowen, L. J., in the case of *Low* v. *Bouverie* (d), "is only a rule of evidence; you cannot found an action upon estoppel. Estoppel is only important as being one step in the progress towards relief on the hypothesis that the defendant is estopped from denying the truth of something which he has said. An illustration of a case of that kind of estoppel filling up the gap in the evidence which, when so filled up, would produce this right to relief, is found in the case of *In re Bahia and San Francisco Railway Company* (e). *Burrowes* v. *Lock* (f)

Estoppel.

(c) *Ante*, pp. 88 *et seq.*
(d) *Low* v. *Bouverie*, (1891) 3 Ch. 82; 60 L. J. Ch. 594; 65 L. T. 533; 40 W. R. 50.
(e) *In re Bahia and San Francisco Railway Company*, L. R. 3 Q. B. 584; 37 L. J. Q. B. 176; 18 L. T. 467; 16 W. R. 862.
(f) *Burrowes* v. *Lock*, 10 Ves. 470.

was a case of estoppel. It was a case where there was a right to relief on the hypothesis that the defendant was precluded from denying the truth of a particular fact:" The facts in *Low* v. *Bouverie* were as follows :—An intending lender applied to the trustee for information as to previous charges on certain trust property ; the trustee returned an equivocal answer, and not such a clear and unambiguous one as would raise an estoppel. The intended incumbrancer advanced the money, and took a charge on the trust funds; he subsequently discovered that there were prior incumbrances to a large amount. He sought to fix the trustee with liability. There was no actual fraud, and there was no warranty given by the trustee, and the facts did not support an estoppel. Hence there was no relief.

Result.
The result is, that where a debtor requests a third person to pay and discharge a debt for him, such third person is put on inquiry, aye or nay, is the debt in respect of a contract of gaming and wagering? A false and definite answer would ground an action for deceit or raise an estoppel in such an action as *Tatam* v. *Reeve*.

Loan by third person.
The effect of the Gaming Act, 1892, has not been decided with reference to a loan by a third person to a debtor who owes money under a gaming or wagering contract. As in *Tatam* v. *Reeve* (g), the advance by the third person would not be under the wager, and the question is, whether the fact that the payment was not made to the creditor on the wager would suffice to render the payment one not in respect of the wager. Two positions seem to be clear : first, if the lender had

(g) *Tatam* v. *Reeve*, (1893) 1 Q. B. 44 ; 62 L. J. C. L. 30; 5 R. 83; 67 L. T. 683; 41 W. R. 174; 57 J. P. 118.

no knowledge of any wagering transactions of the
borrower, and was ignorant of his probable application
of the money, the lender would be entitled to recover;
secondly, if the lender agreed with the borrower that
the borrower should apply the money so lent to the discharge of the latter's gaming or wagering debts, the
lender would not be entitled to recover. In the first
case the lender would have made no payment either
under or in respect of a wagering debt; in the second
case, he would have done so in respect of a wagering
debt, seeing that he has expressly stipulated that the
loan shall be applied for the purpose of paying the
debt. The difficulties will arise when the facts bring
cases between the two positions. Further, if a loan
were made to the debtor, with a knowledge that he
might use it for the discharge of his gaming or wagering debts, the lender, it is submitted, would still be
entitled to recover (*h*); but if the loan were made for
the purpose of the debtor's discharging therewith his
gaming and wagering debts, though without express
stipulation in that behalf, then the loan, though not
directly in respect of, is yet indirectly in respect of,
such void transaction (*i*), and it is suggested that the
lender would be disentitled to recover.

The right which was recognised in the case of
Bridger v. *Savage* (*j*), of the winner to recover money
actually paid by the loser of a wager to the winner's
agent, or to some third person on his behalf, has not

Right to recover win-nings from agent or third person who has received them.

(*h*) *Bagot* v. *Arnott*, Ir. Rep. 2 C. L. 1.
(*i*) *Pearce* v. *Brooks*, L. R. 1 Ex. 213; 35 L. J. Ex. 134; 12
Jur. N. S. 342; 14 L. T. 288; 14 W. R. 614; *Cannan* v. *Bryce*,
3 B. & Ald. 179; *M'Kinnell* v. *Robinson*, 3 M. & W. 434; *Foot*
v. *Baker*, 5 M. & G. 335; see *ante*, pp. 112 *et seq.*
(*j*) *Bridger* v. *Savage*, 15 Q. B. D. 363; 54 L. J. Q. B. 464;
53 L. T. 129; 33 W. R. 891; 49 J. P. 725.

been affected by the Act. In the case of *Benjamen* v. *De Mattos* (*k*), the plaintiff's right was recognised, and the adverse contention was treated almost as incapable of serious argument. The judgment was:—" The Act is very plain in its terms. It did not enable a person who had received money on behalf of another to retain it to his own use."

Power, on rescission, to recover a deposit from a stakeholder.

The right of a depositor to recover his deposit is also unaffected by the Act. In the case of *O'Sullivan* v. *Thomas* (*l*), the plaintiff had agreed to run one Hughes for 5*l.* a side, and the 10*l.* had been deposited in the hands of the defendant as stakeholder. The race was run. The plaintiff lost the race, whereupon he directed the defendant not to pay over to the winner the sum of 5*l.* deposited by him (the plaintiff). The plaintiff subsequently sued to recover his 5*l.*, and in the County Court he obtained judgment. As a result of an appeal to the Divisional Court, Wills, J., in the course of his judgment, stated:—" The only question was whether the money deposited to abide the result of the bet to be paid over to the other party to the bet if he won came within the terms of the Act— ' any sum of money paid by the person making the bet under a wagering contract . . .' I am of opinion that the action will lie, and that paid means paid ' out and out.' It does not mean money merely deposited for the purpose of paying some other party." Wright, J., was also of opinion that the terms of the Act referred to an actual and absolute payment, and pointed out

(*k*) *Benjamen* v. *De Mattos*, 63 L. J. Q. B. 248; 70 L. T. 560; 42 W. R. 284; 38 S. J. 238; 10 T. L. R. 221.

(*l*) *O'Sullivan* v. *Thomas*, (1895) 1 Q. B. 698; 64 L. J. Q. B. 398.

that the opposite construction would tend to defeat the
Act by allowing retention of the deposit, and so giving
the other party the practical certainty of being paid the
bet.

On the footing of this decision, the law being un- Partnership.
altered by the Act, it follows that the decisions in
Johnson v. *Lansley, Beeston* v. *Beeston,* are still law,
and that one partner in a wagering transaction could
recover from the other his share of the balance of
winnings on account stated. The one partner who
sued on such an account would admit the validity as
against himself of the payments and disbursements
made by the other. But the Act appears to have
accentuated a difficulty. In the absence of authority,
a hypothetical case alone can be stated. A. and B.
contribute a fund of 1,000l. for embarking on a series
of difference transactions. The possession of the fund,
and actual management of the business, is left to B.
B. operates. He makes some losses, part of which he
pays, but he receives winnings in excess of the losses.
B. renders an account to A., who asserts it to be fraudulent. A. thereupon issues a writ claiming dissolution
of partnership and consequential relief. In taking the
accounts, the following difficulties may arise: First,
A. objects to the payment of the then unpaid losses,
which he contends are not debts within section 44
of the Partnership Act, 1890 ; secondly, A. objects to
the allowance of the disbursements made by B. in respect of the losses, setting up the Gaming Act, 1892.
If both these objections are allowed, the items would
be struck out. Can it be that A. would be entitled to
a certificate bringing out the winnings without any
deductions in respect of the paid losses ? In the particular instance of an actual contribution by A. to the

partnership fund, B. would have paid the losses out of property belonging jointly to himself and A., and such payments would be voluntary payments made by B. with the joint property; B.'s position would not be. the same as if he had made these disbursements with his own separate property, and then claimed indemnity against the firm. Similarly, so far as he made payments of the losses out of the winnings, such payments would have been made out of joint property. A.'s position with regard to the losses paid would be the same as if he had handed over the amount of his share thereof to B., and directed B. to make the payment therewith. To that extent the payment would be a voluntary payment made by A. through the medium of his agent B., and with such payment he would be properly charged (*m*). The unpaid losses, however, are a difficulty, and the Court would not compel an unwilling partner to discharge them.

(*m*) *Bayntun* v. *Cattle*, 1 M. & R. 265.

CHAPTER X.

THE Stock Exchange and the operations conducted there to a considerable extent lie on the borderland of the subject of gambling. The chief legal problem which is presented is the distinction between speculative sales and purchases on the one hand, and difference transactions on the other. The rules of the Stock Exchange are so framed as to render mere wagering transactions at least a theoretical impossibility. It is deemed desirable to give a succinct account of the operations on the Stock Exchange and of its rules.

The chief legal questions: speculative sales and purchases not wagering.

There are two classes of members of the Exchange— the jobbers and the brokers. The jobbers are principals in all contracts, and deal solely with the brokers. The brokers are never principals, but agents only of their outside clients; of course, the rules do not prevent a broker from dealing on his own account, and not on behalf of a client, and, in fact, brokers do so deal. The clients instruct their brokers to buy from or to sell to the jobbers. The broker's remuneration is his commission. The jobber, when applied to by the broker, gives a quotation for the stocks or shares, at the lower figure he offers to buy, and at the higher figure to sell. The jobber, knowing nothing of the outside clients, deals with the broker on the footing that the latter is personally responsible to him on every contract entered

Machinery of the Exchange. Brokers and jobbers.

into. The majority of the transactions for sale and purchase are made for completion on periodical days, occurring either monthly or bi-monthly, according to the stock dealt in; such days are called settling days.

Settling day. On settling day, on the one hand, there must be a payment in cash; and, on the other, the short, though reasonable, time, which is usually some ten days within which actual delivery and transfer of the stock or shares must be made, begins to run. If the jobber does not deliver to the purchasing broker within the time allowed, the latter may instruct the official broker to the Stock Exchange to buy in the stock against the jobber, who will be liable for all charges incurred thereby. The penalty which a member of the house incurs on failure to meet his obligations is the liability of immediately being declared a defaulter, which determines his membership of the house, and prevents him from dealing on or entering the Stock Exchange.

It will thus be seen that this machinery is as applicable for the purchase of consols or other gilt-edged securities for the purposes of investment as for the purchase for a rise, or the sale for a fall, of shares of a speculative character. In the former case, the transaction is really closed on the settling day; but in the latter it may only be nominally closed then, and, in reality, by other transactions be continued until the next settling day.

Bulls and bears.
Continuations.
Contango and backwardation.
A bull—*i. e.*, one who buys for a rise—or a bear—*i. e.*, one who sells for a fall—may on settling day be unable or undesirous of taking or making delivery, or willing upon terms to forego his rights; but, at the same time, he may deem it advisable to continue his speculation. The operations which follow are known by the general term, "continuations." The speculator then instructs

his broker to carry over. Assuming the speculator to have been a bull, the broker then endeavours to resell the shares which the bull desires to carry over; on such resale, the purchaser may be the original vendor or another jobber; the price at which this repurchase would be effected would generally be the making-up price of the day, which would be fixed by the orders of the committee of the Stock Exchange. By a collateral agreement the broker then repurchases the stock or shares from the jobber at the same price, plus a premium for the accommodation; this premium is called a contango. Similarly, when the speculator is a bear, a similar set of transactions would result in a contango being paid by the bear for the accommodation of not making delivery on the settling day. Where the broker arranges the carrying over with the same jobber as was concerned in the original transaction, the contango is simply the consideration for the postponement of the completion of the contract. But where the broker does not or cannot arrange the continuation with the original jobber, he completes the original contract with him, and on the security of the stocks or shares, purchased by the bull, borrows the required money from another jobber; such other jobber " takes in " the stocks or shares, and the property in the particular parcel of stocks or shares vests in him, though with an obligation to deliver on the next settling day a like parcel of the same stocks or shares. The transaction is more than a mere pledge. On the other hand, the market may have run in favour of the bull, and then, instead of needing accommodation at the expense of a contango, he may be in a position to offer accommodation on terms advantageous to himself. For instance, a large amount of stock may have been withdrawn from the market, and the jobber may be

G. P

unable to deliver to the broker the stock which he has purchased on behalf of the bull. The jobber must obtain accommodation, and if necessary pay for it; a premium so paid by him is called a backwardation.

When the continuations are ended, the final settlement is brought about, either by an actual delivery of the stocks or shares purchased, or by a reverse contract of sale, whereunder the original purchaser becomes a vendor of an equivalent number of stocks or shares. The final result to the outside speculator is a gain or a loss. The result to the speculator may be the same as if he had entered into a mere difference transaction. But he has employed a different machinery, and has utilized separate legal obligations, which could have been specifically enforced, or for a breach of which damages of an ascertainable amount could have been recovered.

From an affidavit, sworn by some of the leading members of the Stock Exchange, and used in the case of *Ex parte Grant, In re Plumbly* (a), it appears that in order to avoid delivery a similar amount of (but not the identical) stocks or shares may be sold or purchased, as the case may be. As, then, one member of the house cannot sell to another certain shares, numbered say, 1 to 20, at the then market price, and at the same time agree to repurchase from him the same shares at the market price at some future date, an obstacle, at least formal, is placed in the way of transacting a mere difference bargain. But, as a fact, stock is not numbered, and contracts for sale or purchase of a parcel of shares do not earmark the particular shares by reference to their numbers.

(a) *Ex parte Grant, In re Plumbly*, 13 Ch. Div. 667; 42 L. T. 387; 28 W. R. 775.

In *Grizewood* v. *Blane* (b), the jury found as a fact that certain transactions between a jobber, a member of the Exchange, and a non-member, who had operated through a broker, were mere wagering contracts. But this finding of fact was stated by Brett, L. J., in *Thacker* v. *Hardy* (c), to have been probably due to the misunderstanding by the jury of the nature of the evidence before them, and Cotton, L. J., said the finding could not easily be justified, having regard to the mode of doing business on the Stock Exchange (d). In each of the judgments in *Thacker* v. *Hardy* the transactions on the Exchange are recognized as real sales and purchases.

But from time to time the allegation will be advanced that the rules have been departed from. For instance, in the case of *Ex parte Rogers, In re Rogers* (e), it was sought to distinguish the transactions from those in *Thacker* v. *Hardy* by the contention that the broker had not, in fact, acted as agent for his client, but had constituted himself a principal. If that contention had been established, the sole parties to the contracts would have been Rogers (the speculating non-member of the house) and Evans (the broker); and as to such contracts there was evidence that Rogers and Evans understood that Rogers was only speculating for the rise of the stocks which he bought, and never intended to accept delivery, but meant to sell them

Alleged departure from the rules.

(b) *Grizewood* v. *Blane*, 11 C. B. 526; 12 L. J. C. P. 46.

(c) *Thacker* v. *Hardy*, 4 Q. B. D. at pp. 695, 696; *Ex parte Marnham*, 2 De G. F. & J. 634; 30 L. J. Bk. 1; 6 Jur. N. S. 1273; 3 L. T. 516; 9 W. R. 131.

(d) See Evidence before Stock Exchange Commissioners, 1878.

(e) *Ex parte Rogers*, 15 Ch. Div. 207; 43 L. T. 163; 29 W. R. 29.

again before the account day, and to receive or to pay the difference between the prices at which he bought or sold. If there had been evidence of a correlative intention on the part of Evans, then the contracts would have been wagering contracts. But the contention failed that Evans had acted otherwise than as the broker of Rogers; hence, the contracts were between Rogers of the one part, and the jobber of the other part, and whatever may have been Rogers' intention, communicated or not to his broker, Evans, there was no evidence that the jobber intended to do otherwise than to make real sales and purchases: therefore the contracts in question were not wagering contracts.

Options, calls, and puts. The form of speculation known as dealing in "options" requires notice. A man holds a number of particular shares which at the present time are quoted at a certain figure. The holder thinks the shares will increase in value; he is in a position to offer to sell those shares at a future date at an enhanced price, or which is equivalent, at the present price plus a premium. If the holder can find a purchaser for the future date, he resolves the uncertainty of the accretion in value to him of the shares into the certain gain represented by the increase of price at which he has sold. But the holder, instead of selling for a future day, may sell the right of being called on to sell at a future date, if so requested. The holder then sells an "option," viz., the right to buy from him the particular shares on a particular day at a fixed price. Either the purchaser of the option exercises the right or he does not: if he does, then he pays the price, and accepts delivery; if he does not, then he pays the difference between the price which he would have paid if he had exercised the option, and the present price, *i. e.*, the premium agreed on. Such an option to buy is known as a call. The other species of options are options of selling, and are called "puts." The grantor of a "put" incurs the obligation to the grantee of buying from him particular stock on a particular day at a fixed price. By the exercise of this right the grantee can limit his risk of a fall in value of the shares. In addition to the foregoing, there is a third kind of option, which is merely a combination of a put and call, and confers the rights which either the put or the call severally would have given.

Perhaps the grantor of the option to call may not be possessed of the shares in respect of which he has given the call at the time of granting it, and when the option is exercised he may be compelled himself to buy. In the event of his buying from the grantee of the option, the result of the transactions would be the payment of a difference. But this ultimate result would not make the original transaction a wagering one. But if the parties never intended a real purchase, or to give the right, and desired merely to give form to a transaction whereunder the one must either lose the difference between the then market value and the agreed price or gain the premiums, and the other must make the correlative gain or loss, then the whole transaction, *ab initio*, was a mere wagering one. Similarly, the option of a "put" might formally be made an element in a wagering transaction. However, according to the rules of the house, the transactions of sale and purchase, or the options of sale and purchase, must be real.

Options: when not entitled to the shares, &c.

The rules of the Exchange forbid members to enter into bargains in prospective dividends in shares or stock of railway or other companies. This rule is not in-

Prospective dividends; rules of the Exchange.

volved in one forbidding wagering transactions. A man who holds shares on which a dividend is about to be declared, though of uncertain amount, is at liberty to sell his right to the receipt of this uncertain sum in consideration of a fixed sum. In *Martin* v. *Gibbon* (e), the defendant instructed the plaintiff, who was his broker, to sell for him the next dividend on 50,000*l.* of South Eastern Railway "A" Deferred Stock. The plaintiff sold to a dealer, and, after the dividend had been declared, paid to the dealer the difference between the actual dividend declared and the amount of the purchase-money. The contract was held not to be a wagering one (e). The plaintiff recovered his disbursement from the defendant. This right to indemnity would remain under the general principles of agency, and would not be affected by the Gaming Law Amendment Act, 1892, which only has reference to transactions rendered void by 8 & 9 Vict. c. 109.

If, however, the vendor of the prospective dividend was not entitled to, and had no intention of becoming entitled to, the stocks or shares in respect of which the dividends sold were to accrue due, and the purchaser was aware that the vendor was not entitled, and did not intend to become entitled, the jury on such facts might reasonably conclude that the transaction was a wagering contract.

A species of dishonest user of the Stock Exchange is involved in the operations known as "making a market" or "rigging the market." A market is made for shares by buying or pretending to buy the same at a premium, with the intent thereby to induce the public to come in and subscribe for the shares in the company,

Martin v.
Gibbon.

"Rigging the market."

(e) *Martin* v. *Gibbon*, 33 L. T. N. S. 561; 24 W. R. 87.

under the false notion that there is a *bonâ fide* premium to be obtained by subscribing. An agreement by two or more persons thus to cheat and defraud others is a criminal conspiracy (*f*).

But, apart from such criminal acts, the speculative transactions are subject to legislative interference only to a slight degree. The Bankruptcy Act imposes some sanction. In the Bankruptcy Act, 1883, s. 28, one of the grounds on which the Court could either refuse or suspend the order for discharge, or grant it subject to conditions, was the following:—"That the bankrupt has brought on his bankruptcy by rash and hazardous speculations or unjustifiable extravagance in living." That section of the Act of 1883 has now been repealed and replaced by section 8 of the Bankruptcy Act, 1890, whereunder the Court may either (i) refuse the discharge, or (ii) suspend the discharge for a period of not less than two years, or (iii) suspend the discharge until a dividend of not less than ten shillings in the pound has been paid to the creditors, or (iv) grant it on conditions as to judgment being entered, on proof (*inter alia*) "That the bankrupt has brought on, or contributed to, his bankruptcy by rash and hazardous speculations, or by unjustifiable extravagance in living, or by gambling,

Sanction on speculation.

B. A. 1890, s. 8.

(*f*) *Scott* v. *Brown, Dœring, McNab & Co.*, (1892) 2 Q. B. 724; 4 Rep. 42; 61 L. J. Q. B. 738; 67 L. T. 782; 41 W. R. 110; 57 J. P. 213; *R.* v. *De Berenger*, 3 M. & S. 67; *Reg.* v. *Aspinall*, 2 Q. B. D. 48; 46 L. J. M. C. 145; 36 L. T. 297; 25 W. R. 283; 13 Cox, C. C. 563, C. A.: affirming, 1 Q. B. D. 730; 13 Cox, C. C. 230; 35 L. T. 738; 24 W. R. 921; *Bigbie* v. *Phosphate Sewage Company*, 1 Q. B. D. 679; 35 L. T. 350; 25 W. R. 85, C. A.: affirming, L. R. 10 Q. B. 491; 44 L. J. Q. B. 233; 33 L. T. 470; 24 W. R. 115; *Marzetti's Case*, 42 L. T. 206; 28 W. R. 541; *Twycross* v. *Grant*, 2 C. P. Div. 469; 46 L. J. C. P. 636; 36 L. T. 812; 25 W. R. 701; *Gray* v. *Lewis*, L. R. 8 Ch. 1035; 43 L. J. Ch. 281; 29 L. T. 12; 21 W. R. 923.

or by culpable neglect of his business." If a man speculates beyond his means of meeting possible losses, his speculations are rash and hazardous (*g*).

These sections last cited will be seen to be an extension of the principle of section 201 of the Bankruptcy Law Consolidation Act, 1849 (*h*), whereunder it was provided that "no bankrupt shall be entitled to a certificate of conformity under this Act, and any such certificate, if allowed, shall be void if he shall within one year next preceding the issue of the fiat or the filing of such petition have lost 200*l*. by any contract for the purchase or sale of any government or other stock, where such contract was not to be performed within one week after the contract, or where the stock bought or sold was not actually transferred or delivered" (*i*).

Right of official assignee. When a member of the house becomes a defaulter, then under the rules the official assignee winds up his business; he collects the differences due from other members of the house, and holds the fund upon a mandate to apply it amongst those members who would have had claims against the defaulter in respect of current transactions. It has been held that the assignee holds this artificial fund by a title adverse to the trustee in bankruptcy of the defaulter (*k*).

(*g*) *Ex parte Rogers*, 13 Q. B. D. 438; 33 W. R. 354; 1 M. B. R. 159; *Ex parte Salaman*, 14 Q. B. D. 936; 54 L. J. Q. B. 238; 52 L. T. 378; *Ex parte Young*, 2 M. B. R. 37; *Re Burlow, Ex parte Thornber*, 3 Mor. 304; 56 L. T. 168; *Re Rankin*, 5 Mor. 23; *Re Nicholas*, 7 Mor. 54; *Re Jenkins*, 8 Mor. 36; 39 W. R. 430; *Re Keays*, 9 Mor. 18.

(*h*) 12 & 13 Vict. c. 106.

(*i*) *Ex parte Matheson*, 1 De G. M. & G. 448; 21 L. J. Bk. 18; 16 Jur. 769; *Ex parte Ryder*, 1 De G. & J. 317; 26 L. J. Bk. 69; 3 Jur. N. S. 1159; *Ex parte Copeland*, 2 De G. M. & G. 914; 22 L. J. Bk. 17; 17 Jur. 121; *Ex parte Buckland*, 1 Font. Cas. in Bk. 250; *Ex parte Wade*, 8 De G. M. & G. 241.

(*k*) *Nicholson* v. *Gooch*, 5 E. & B. 999; 25 L. J. Q. B. 137; 2

But speculation on the Stock Exchange was not Barnard's Act. always thus free from legislative interference. From the year 1734 until 1860, the statute known as Barnard's Act was in force (*l*). It was aimed at "the wicked, pernicious, and destructive habit of stockjobbing," in so far as that habit tended to disturb the stability of the public stocks, which, as Sir John Romilly explained, in *Williams* v. *Trye* (*m*), were stocks ordinarily considered as public funds or securities, guaranteed as to dividends and capital. Options, whether as puts or calls, and all wagering contracts, were declared null and void; difference transactions subjected the parties thereto to penalties, as did contracts for the sale of stock of which the vendor was not possessed.

Speculative dealings in bank shares are, owing to the Leeman's Act. dangerous influence on commerce, subject to statutory restrictions. In the years 1864 to 1866, bank shares were made the subject of bull operations, and the shares were carried up to fictitious values. When the fall came, panic ensued. Hence the statute known as Leeman's Act (*n*) was passed. Section 1 thereof enacts that "All contracts or agreements and tokens of sale and purchase which shall, from and after the 1st day of July, 1867, be made or entered into for the sale or transfer, or purporting to be for the sale or transfer of any share or shares, or of any stock or other interest in any joint stock banking company in the United King-

Jur. N. S. 303; *Ex parte Grant, In re Plumbly*, 13 Ch. Div. 667; 42 L. T. 387; 28 W. R. 775.

(*l*) Barnard's Act, 7 Geo. 2, c. 8, repealed by 23 & 24 Vict. c. 28.

(*m*) *Williams* v. *Trye*, 23 L. J. Ch. 860; 18 Beav. 366; 18 Jur. 442. See also *Lyne* v. *Siesfeld*, 1 H. & N. 278; *Wells* v. *Porter*, 3 Scott, 141; 2 Bing. N. C. 722.

(*n*) 30 & 31 Vict. c. 29.

dom of Great Britain and Ireland, constituted under or
"regulated by the provisions of any Act of Parliament,
royal charter, or letters patent, issuing shares or stock
transferable by any deed or written instrument shall be
null and void to all intents and purposes whatsoever,
unless such contract, agreement, or other token shall
set forth and designate in writing such shares, stock, or
interest by the respective numbers by which the same
are distinguished at the making of such contract, agreement, or token in the register or books of such banking
company as aforesaid, or where there is no such register
of shares or. stock, by distinguishing numbers, then,
unless such contract, agreement, or other token shall set
forth the person or persons in whose name or names
such shares, stock, or interest shall at the time of making
such contract stand as the registered proprietor thereof
in the books of such banking company, and every
person, whether principal, broker, or agent, who shall
wilfully insert in any such contract, agreement, or other
token any false entry of such numbers, or any name
or names other than that of the person or persons in
whose name such shares, stock, or interest shall stand
as aforesaid, shall be guilty of a misdemeanour and be
punished accordingly."

Custom of
the Stock
Exchange.
The usage of the Stock Exchange has been to dis-
regard this statute. In the case of *Perry* v. *Barnett* (*o*),
Bowen, L. J., said: "It has been denied that it is
practicable to make valid contracts on the Stock
Exchange for bank shares in compliance with Leeman's
Act. I do not believe this. No doubt speculative
contracts cannot be made, and because the great object
of the Stock Exchange is to deal in speculative con-

(*o*) *Perry* v. *Barnett*, 15 Q. B. D. at p. 397.

tracts, Leeman's Act is not complied with, and contracts are made which are void by that Act, and there is a custom of the Stock Exchange that when such contracts are made the brokers are to be bound as if the contracts were valid." With regard to this custom, it has been sought unsuccessfully to bring it within the principle that if a person employs a broker to buy or sell on a market of the usage of which such person is ignorant, he authorizes him to make contracts upon the footing of such usages as are reasonable, and as do not alter the character of such contracts (*p*) ; both in *Neilson* v. *James* (*q*), and in *Perry* v. *Barnett*, it was held to be an unreasonable custom, which altered the character of the contract : in the former case, Cotton, L. J., intimated that the sooner the custom was altered the better.

The consequence of the illegality of this custom has been to render, in some instances, the brokers liable in damages for negligence, and to deprive them of any right of indemnity. In *Neilson* v. *James*, the plaintiff, who was the registered holder of certain shares in a joint stock bank, instructed the defendant, his stock-broker, to sell the shares. The defendant entered into a contract with a stock jobber whereunder, as usual (*r*), the jobber agreed at the settling day either to take the shares himself or give the names of responsible trans-

(*p*) *Robinson* v. *Mollett*, L. R. 7 H. L. 802 ; 44 L. J. C. P. 362 ; 33 L. T. 544.

(*q*) *Neilson* v. *James*, 9 Q. B. D. 546 ; 57 L. J. Q. B. 369 ; 46 L. T. 791.

(*r*) *Paine* v. *Hutchinson*, L. R. 3 Ch. 388 ; 37 L. J. Ch. 485 ; *Coles* v. *Bristowe*, L. R. 4 Ch. 3 ; 38 L. J. Ch. 81 ; 19 L. T. 403 ; 17 W. R. 105 ; *Cruse* v. *Paine*, L. R. 6 Eq. 641 ; 37 L. J. Ch. 711 ; 19 L. T. 127 ; 17 W. R. 44 : affirmed L. R. 4 Ch. 441 ; 38 L. J. Ch. 225 ; 17 W. R. 1033.

ferees. But this contract was invalid by reason of non-
compliance with the Act. The bank failed before the
date at which the jobber in the ordinary course would
have named the transferees, and he repudiated the contract. By reason of the default of the broker, the
plaintiff lost at any rate the purchase money; the broker
had entered into an invalid contract instead of such a
valid one as would have complied with the duty undertaken by him. The defendant was, on appeal, mulcted
in damages to the extent of the purchase money. The
Court refused to afflict the plaintiff with presumptive
knowledge of the illegal custom of the Stock Exchange.

In the case of *Perry and Another* v. *Barnett* (s), the
plaintiffs were stockbrokers, and having received instructions from the defendant to purchase shares in a
certain bank, they entered into a contract with a jobber.
According to the usage of the Exchange, the contract
did not comply with the Act, though under the custom,
when the defendant repudiated such void contract, the
plaintiffs were compelled to pay the jobber. They
thereupon brought an action against the defendant for
an indemnity; but Grove, J., found as a fact that the
defendant had no actual knowledge of the custom;
hence having regard to the character of the custom the
plaintiffs failed.

If the client of the broker can be proved to have had
knowledge of the custom, and to have acquiesced in it,
then he cannot maintain an action for damages as in
Neilson v. *James*, and under such circumstances, on the

(s) *Perry* v. *Barnett*, 14 Q. B. D. 467: affirmed on appeal, 15
Q. B. D. 388; 54 L. J. Q. B. 466; 53 L. T. 585.

principle of *Read* v. *Anderson* (*t*), it has been held that
the broker is entitled to an indemnity (*u*).

Pursuant to such void contracts, there may subsequently be made actual transfers of the stock or shares,
and such transfers when made will create perfectly valid
obligations (*x*).

(*t*) *Read* v. *Anderson*, 13 Q. B. D. 779 ; 52 L. J. Q. B. 214 ;
48 L. T. 74 ; 31 W. R. 453 ; 47 J. P. 311.

(*u*) *Seymour* v. *Bridge*, 14 Q. B. D. 460 ; 54 L. J. Q. B. 347 ;
29 S. J. 480 ; *Barclay* v. *Pearce*, n. to *Seymour* v. *Bridge*, 14
Q. B. D. at p. 462.

(*x*) *Mortimer* v. *M'Calln*, 9 M. & W. 636 ; 4 Jur. 172 ;
Loring v. *Davis*, 32 Ch. Div. 625 ; 55 L. J. Ch. 725 ; 54 L. T.
899 ; 34 W. R. 701.

Part II.—CRIMINAL.

—◆—

CHAPTER XI.

INTRODUCTORY.

At the risk, on the one hand, of treating of topics which are expounded in the standard text books relating to summary jurisdiction (a); and, on the other hand, of stating elementary matters of criminal procedure, it is, nevertheless, deemed desirable to give the following account of the criminal procedure as an introduction to the consideration of the substantive offences.

Summary Jurisdiction.

Statutes.
The procedure in accordance with which the powers of summary jurisdiction have to be exercised is contained in the Acts known as the Summary Jurisdiction Acts: Jervis's Act, 11 & 12 Vict. c. 43, the Summary Jurisdiction Act, 1879 (42 & 43 Vict. c. 49), the Summary Jurisdiction Act, 1884 (47 & 48 Vict. c. 43); and in the several Acts giving cognizance of the offences.

Information.
The function of the Court, exercising its powers, is the investigation of a definite charge, to which all the evidence must be material. Under the 14th section of the Summary Jurisdiction Act, 1848, the making of the charge is described as the statement to the defend-

(a) Paley's Summary Convictions; Oke's Synopsis and Formulist; Stone's Manual.

ant of the substance of the information. The information is the "statement by which the magistrate is informed of *the offence* for which a summons or warrant is required" (*b*). The laying of the information is the initial step in the proceedings: at the outset the offence must be specified. Whilst the statement of the offence need not be in writing, yet the Summary Jurisdiction Act, 1848, contemplated that it would be: in the absence of writing, there is extreme danger that an offence may not be specifically stated. Where there is laxity in the description of the offence in the information, it is probable that the summons or warrant issued to obtain the appearance of the defendant will not be duly accurate, and that the looseness of the information will be reproduced in the actual charge made, and subsequently in the evidence adduced; the final result, as in the case of *R.* v. *McKenzie* (*c*), may be the quashing of the conviction. Formerly, it was a matter of difficulty to describe the offence, because in all cases it did not suffice to use the description contained in the statute creating the offence; but by the Summary Jurisdiction Act, 1879, s. 39, sub-s. 1, it has been enacted that " the description of any offence in the words of the Act. . . . or in similar words, shall be sufficient in law " (*c*). It is unnecessary in the information to specify or negative an exception, exemption, proviso, excuse, or qualification (*d*). The facts which constitute the offence should be set out; the defendant must be enabled to judge whether the statement discloses an offence, and, if so, whether it is one to which he can plead *autrefois* acquit,

Description of the offence in the information.

(*b*) Per Huddleston, B., *R.* v. *Hughes*, 4 Q. B. D. at p. 633.

(*c*) *R.* v. *McKenzie*, (1892) 2 Q. B. 519; 61 L. J. M. C. 181; 67 L. T. 201 ; 41 W. R. 144; 56 J. P. 712.

(*d*) S. J. Act, 1848, s. 14; S. J. Act, 1879, s. 39, sub-s. (2).

or convict; the statement must not be alternative, for the defendant can only be called upon to show cause against one charge at a time (e). By sect. 10, Summary Jurisdiction Act, 1848, it has been enacted that the information must relate to one offence only. But the difficulty arises in deciding what is one offence. In the case of *Milnes* v. *Bale* (f), Brett, J., called attention to the manner in which the offence could be proved: if a succession of acts can be adduced in proof of the offence, then those acts taken together constitute but one offence. Thus, where the offence was keeping an unlicensed dancing-house, proof might be obtained from acts done on many days; the offence is single (g). In each case the nature of the offence and the actual wording of the statute must be considered; particular care is needed in such Acts as the Gaming and Betting House Acts, where the several sections contain in each several offences which must be dissected. Where an information contains more than one offence, it is defective in substance within sect. 1, Summary Jurisdiction Act, 1848; the magistrates may and should put the prosecutor to his election as to which single offence he should proceed with (h). The magistrates must dispose of one charge before they proceed to hear the evidence of another; for otherwise the evidence material to the second charge might influence their determination of

One offence only.

(e) *R.* v. *Marsh*, 4 D. & R. 260; *R.* v. *Daman*, 1 Chitty, 147; 2 B. & Ald. 378; *R.* v. *Trelawney*, 1 T. R. 222; *R.* v. *Hoard*, 6 J. P. 445; *Cotterill* v. *Lempriere*, 24 Q. B. D. 634; 59 L. J. M. C. 133; 62 L. T. 695.

(f) *Milnes* v. *Bale*, L. R. 10 C. P. 591; 44 L. J. C. P. 336.

(g) *Garrett* v. *Messenger*, L. R. 2 C. P. 583; 16 L. T. N. S. 414; 15 W. R. 864; 36 L. J. C. P. 337; 10 Cox, C. C. 498.

(h) *Rodgers* v. *Richards*, (1892) 1 Q. B. 555; 66 L. T. 261; 40 W. R. 331; 56 J. P. 281; 17 Cox, C. C. 475.

the first charge (i). An information differs, then, essentially from an indictment, in so far as it can only contain one count; where several counts are required several informations must be laid.

Knowledge of the fact that an information has been laid is communicated to the defendant by means of a summons, which states the offence contained in the information, and which requires his appearance as therein specified. If the defendant fails to appear in answer thereto, or if it be thought probable that the defendant, on being served with the summons, will abscond, then a warrant may be issued for his apprehension, after the information has been reduced to writing, and been substantiated on oath or affirmation (k). The summons or warrant.

In the case of *R.* v. *Hughes* (l), it was argued that the defendant, though he had sworn falsely, had not done so in the course of a judicial inquiry. This contention raised the important question whether the magistrates who heard the inquiry had, under the circumstances, any jurisdiction to entertain the charge. The circumstances were such that the process used for obtaining the appearance of the defendant to the original charge were hopelessly irregular. The defendant had been arrested on a warrant without any previous information having been laid; but he appeared and answered to the charge. Voluntarily or involuntarily, the defendant was before the magistrates, and in his presence a charge was made. It was held by the Court for Crown Cases Reserved (Kelly, C. B., diss.), that the irregularity or regularity of the processes *R.* v. *Hughes.* Effect of appearance on prior irregularity,

(i) *Hamilton* v. *Walker*, (1892) 2 Q. B. 25; 61 L. J. M. C. 134; 67 L. T. 200; 40 W. R. 476; 56 J. P. 583.

(k) S. J. Act, 1848, s. 1.

(l) *R.* v. *Hughes*, 4 Q. B. D. 614; 48 L. J. M. C. 151.

G.   Q

THE LAW OF GAMBLING.

whereby the defendant had been caused to appear were
not essential to the jurisdiction of the justices; the
making of a charge in the presence of a defendant who
answers thereto is all that is necessary. In that case
the regular order was inverted, the information did not
precede the charge ; but a certain oral statement was at
once the charge and the information. In that case, the
defendant to the original charge did not protest on the
ground of the irregularity of the warrant. Hawkins, J.,
said, "Had he known of the illegality of his arrest, he
might have demanded his release from it, and prayed
for an adjournment to a future day, to enable him to
prepare his defence. This, I think, would have been
the duty of the magistrates to grant (*m*). A refusal to
do this, however, would not have destroyed their jurisdiction, though it might possibly have afforded good
ground for setting aside the conviction, on the ground
that they had not allowed the accused sufficient opportunity to answer the charge." In the later case
of *Dixon* v. *Wells* (*n*), the effect of a protest by a defendant was considered. In the course of the case it
was stated that it had become a general practice for the
magistrate's clerk to hear complaints without any
written or other information, fill up a form of summons,
obtain the signature of any magistrate, and so cause
the man to be summoned, and perhaps exposed to a
heavy penalty, although the magistrate signing the
summons may not have ascertained whether there was
a *primâ facie* case against the person summoned.

together with
a protest then
made.

(*m*) *Turner* v. *Postmaster-General*, 5 B. & S. 756; 10 Cox, C.
C. 15; 11 Jur. N. S. 137; 11 L. T. 369; 13 W. R. 89; 34 L. J.
M. C. 10; *R.* v. *Shaw*, 34 L. J. M. C. 169; 10 Cox, C. C. 66;
L. & C. 579; 11 Jur. N. S. 415; 12 L. T. 470; 13 W. R. 692.

(*n*) *Dixon* v. *Wells*, 25 Q. B. D. 249; 59 L. J. M. C. 116 ; 62
L. T. 812; 38 W. R. 606.

Animadverting on this practice, Lord Coleridge, C. J., said, " If it be, indeed, the practice to sign a summons without hearing an information, and for one person to hear the information and another to sign the summons, a practice more loose or likely to lead to injustice . . . I can hardly conceive. . . . The practice seems to me to be in direct contravention of the provisions of Jervis's Act, sect. 1." After stating the rule of *R.* v. *Shaw*, *R.* v. *Hughes*, the Chief Justice held that the case then before the Court was distinguishable on two grounds : " First, in all the cases to which our attention has been called there was no protest made by the persons who appeared, and the Courts said, applying a well-known rule of law expounded centuries ago, that faults of procedure may generally be waived by the person affected by them. They are mere irregularities, and if one who may insist on them waives them, submits to the judge, and takes his trial, it is afterwards too late for him to question the jurisdiction which he might have questioned at the time. In this case there was a protest . . . . The appellant objected that there was no summons and no information, and that the whole proceeding was irregular, and that the Court had no jurisdiction to try him, because he was not properly brought there . . . . I do not, however, feel able to decide in his favour on that point alone, for, although the fact of his protest ought to be a complete answer to the assumed jurisdiction, I cannot disguise from myself the fact that from the language of many of the judges in *R.* v. *Hughes*,—although, perhaps, not necessary for the decision of that case—and the judgments of Erle, C. J., and Blackburn, J., in *R.* v. *Shaw*, they seem to assume that if the two conditions precedent of the presence of the accused and jurisdiction over the offence were ful-

filled, his protest would be of no avail. It would have
been easy to say that a protest would have made a
difference . . . It is an important question well worth
consideration in the Court of Appeal."

The evidence given in support of the summons may
disclose, not the offence charged, but another; this
variance can be met by an adjournment (o). In the
case of *R.* v. *Hughes* (*p*), the defendant to the original
charge had been charged with an indictable misdemeanour created by 24 & 25 Vict. c. 100, and evidence
had been taken in support of that charge; but the
magistrates finally convicted summarily under a different statute, 34 & 35 Vict. c. 112, without any new
information or charge for the latter offence. "In
short," said Hawkins, J., "they convicted him of an
offence with which he had never been legally charged.
In this, I am of opinion, they were wrong; and upon
this ground I am strongly inclined to think the conviction may be quashed." In support of that view, the
learned judge refers to *Martin* v. *Pridgeon* (*q*), and *Reg.*
v. *Brickhall* (*r*). Under the circumstances of *Reg.* v.
Hughes, it was, however, unnecessary to decide the
point. In the earlier case of *Blake* v. *Beech* (*s*), the

only information was that on which the warrant was
issued under 8 & 9 Vict. c. 109, s. 3, namely, for keeping a common gaming house. But the charge made
when the defendant was brought up was a charge which

(o) S. J. Act, 1848, ss. 1, 3, 9.

(p) See *ante*, p. 225.

(q) *Martin* v. *Pridgeon*, 1 E. & E. 778; 28 L. J. M. C. 179;
5 Burr. N. S. 894; 7 W. R. 412; 8 Cox, C. C. 170; 33 L. T. 119.

(r) *R.* v. *Brickhall*, 33 L. J. M. C. 156; 10 Jur. N. S. 677;
10 L. T. 385.

(s) *Blake* v. *Beech*, 1 Ex. Div. 320; 45 L. J. M. C. 111; 34
L. T. N. S. 764; 4 J. P. 678.

could not be made under 8 & 9 Vict. c. 109, and it was made under the Betting House Act (16 & 17 Vict. c. 119). It appeared, to Cleasby, B., and Grove, J., that this made the proceedings irregular. " It would be extremely inconvenient to enter in each case into the consideration of the similarity or dissimilarity of different charges. It is better, especially in cases involving an imprisonment for six months, to abide by the rule established by the authorities, that the charge must be comprised within the information, and not different from it." Where, then, such a variance develops, the magistrates should exercise their powers of adjournment, and a fresh information should be laid and processes issued.

When the defendant has been held to be guilty of *The conviction.* the offence, there remains, after the adjudication, the drawing up of the conviction or order. The original design of this document was such as thereby to demonstrate that all the proceedings required by justice had been regularly observed, and that the sentence could be legally supported by the evidence. The conviction is now a mere memorandum of the judgment. But, as such, it does not enjoy the protection given by sections 1, 3, and 9, of the Summary Jurisdiction Act, 1848, in respect of objections to form and variances, to complaints, summonses and warrants. Statutory forms are provided (*t*), and must be followed with accuracy. The form of the *Parts of.* conviction or order consists of three parts : first, the recitals, which no longer contain the information, summons or warrant, and the evidence ; secondly, the statement that the prisoner is guilty of the offence therein set out, which part is called the conviction, and is thus

(*t*) Rules of 1886, Summary Jurisdiction Acts. See Appendix of Forms.

designated by the same name as the whole document; thirdly, the adjudication, setting out the penalty, and providing for the payment of costs by the defendant. With regard to the second part—the conviction in the narrow sense, the offence must be stated with precise accuracy, and the remarks that were made on the description of the offence in the information apply here. The offence may be described in the words of the statute whereby it is created (*u*) ; but it should be noticed that section 14 of the Summary Jurisdiction Act, 1848, and section 39 (2), Summary Jurisdiction Act, 1879, do not remove the need which theretofore existed of negativing an exception, exemption, proviso, excuse, or qualification, &c., in the conviction. As the information must only contain the allegation of one offence, so, as a matter of practice, it would seem preferable to draw separate convictions in respect of the several informations. There is, however, no statutory prohibition against including in one conviction two or more convictions and their attendant adjudications. If the description of the offence in the adjudication be insufficient, or otherwise wrong in point of form, advantage may be taken of the power to amend given by Baines' Act (12 & 13 Vict. c. 45, s. 7).

Autrefois convict or acquit.

The defendant, when called on to answer to the charge, may plead guilty or not guilty, or that he has been previously convicted or acquitted of the offence charged against him. He would prove the previous conviction by production of the copy of the conviction, or, in the instance of an acquittal, by the production of the magistrates' certificate, granted under section 14, Summary Jurisdiction Act, 1848, or by other evidence.

(*u*) S. J. Act, 1879, s. 39 (1).

The acquittal, to avail, must have been on the merits. It seems that a conviction, though followed by no punishment other than the giving of a security to be of good behaviour, as may be inflicted by the magistrates under their important discretionary powers (x), would support the plea; otherwise it would follow that a person whose offence, at the most, deserved nothing beyond a nominal punishment, would be in a worse position than one whose offence had been visited by a substantial punishment, which he had suffered (y). Strictly, a plea of autrefois convict or acquit can only be supported where the form as well as the substance of the second charge is identical with that of the first. But the maxim, *Nemo debet bis puniri pro uno delicto*, cannot be avoided by merely changing the form on the second charge. The common law rule, as stated by Cockburn, C. J., in *Reg.* v. *Elrington* (z), is, "A series of charges shall not be preferred, and, whether a party accused of a minor offence is acquitted or convicted, he shall not be charged again on the same facts in a more aggravated form;" or, as Blackburn, J., enunciated it, in the case of *Wemyss* v. *Hopkins* (a), "whenever a person has been convicted and punished for an offence by a court of competent jurisdiction, *transit in rem judicatum* —that is, the conviction shall be a bar to all further proceedings for the same offence, and he shall not be punished again for the same matter; otherwise there

(x) S. J. Act, 1879, s. 16, sub-ss. 1, 2.

(y) Per Hawkins, J., *Reg.* v. *Miles*, 24 Q. B. D. 423; 59 L. J. M. C. 56; 62 L. T. 572; 38 W. R. 334; 54 J. P. 594; 17 Cox, C. C. 9.

(z) *R.* v. *Elrington*, 1 B. & S. 688; 31 L. J. M. C. 14; 8 Jur. N. S. 97; 5 L. T. 284; 10 W. R. 13; 9 Cox, C. C. 86.

(a) *Wemyss* v. *Hopkins*, L. R. 10 Q. B. 378; 44 L. J. M. C. 101; 33 L. T. 9; 23 W. R. 691.

might be two different punishments for the same offence." The difficulty lies in the application of the rule to the particular facts of the cases which arise. It is well established that a former acquittal or conviction may be pleaded in bar to a subsequent prosecution for the same offence, whether with or without circumstances of aggravation, and whether such circumstances of aggravation consist of the offence having been committed with malicious or wicked intent, or by reason that the offence was followed by serious consequences. It will be found, on examination of the Betting House Acts (16 & 17 Vict. c. 119), that the different offences thereby created have not been created with a due regard to this common law principle.

Appeals.

A right of appeal to a Court of Quarter Sessions from the Court of Summary Jurisdiction is given either by the Act which creates the offence, or in other cases, where the right is not so conferred, it will be found to arise under section 19 of the Summary Jurisdiction Act, 1879. This section in terms only applies where the defendant has not pleaded guilty, and is not otherwise authorized to appeal. Whencesoever the right may come, the procedure regulating its exercise is contained in the sub-sections of section 31 of the Summary Jurisdiction Act, 1879 (b). It will be noticed that by sub-section 5 of that section, the Court of Appeal may confirm, reverse, or modify the decision. Hence, the Court of Appeal, exercising its jurisdiction,

---

(b) The words "by this Act or by any future Act" in sect. 31, S. J. Act, 1879, are repealed by the S. J. Act, 1884, whereunder, by sect. 6, the provisions of sect. 31, S. J. Act, 1879, are made applicable to appeals authorized by any Act prior to the S. J. Act, 1879. See *Reg.* v. *Glamorgan JJ.*, (1892) 1 Q. B. 620; 61 L. J. M. C. 169; 66 L. T. 444; 40 W. R. 436; 56 J. P. 437.

may now be asked to modify the adjudication part of the conviction without altering the conviction, using the word in its narrower sense. An appeal against a sentence will lie where the right to appeal arises otherwise than under section 19, whether the defendant does or does not plead guilty; but where the only right of appeal is that which arises under that section, the defendant would not thereunder be able to appeal if he had pleaded guilty. In the case of *Reg.* v. *The Justices of Surrey, and Bell* (c), the right of appeal arose under the statute 12 & 13 Vict. c. 92; the defendant either pleaded guilty or was found guilty, but on the appeal he did not dispute his guilt, and asked the Court of Quarter Sessions merely to modify the sentence. When the appeal was called on the respondents did not appear, hence the conviction was quashed. A writ of certiorari was refused, on the ground that the appeal was in order, and that under the circumstances the Court of Quarter Sessions took the proper course in quashing the conviction.

An appeal upon a point of law can be obtained from Special cases. the Court of Summary Jurisdiction, either by means of a case stated under 20 & 21 Vict. c. 43, or by means of a special case under the Summary Jurisdiction Act, 1879, s. 3 (d).

An illustration of the application of the special case is afforded by the case of *Downes* v. *Johnson* (e), commonly known as the *Albert Club* case. The magistrate found certain facts, namely, that a house was in the

- (c) *R.* v. *Justices of Surrey, and Bell*, (1892) 2 Q. B. 719; 61 L. J. M. C. 200; 66 L. T. 578.

(d) This subject is fully treated in Oke's Magisterial Synopsis, 14th ed. p. 129 *et seq.*, also in Trotter's Appeals from Courts of Summary Jurisdiction.

(e) *Downes* v. *Johnson*, (1895) 2 Q. B. 203; 64 L. J. M. C. 238.

occupation of the Albert Club, Limited, of which there were some 700 and more shareholders, who used it for the purpose (*inter alia*) of betting *inter se* on horse races—some of the members usually laid odds against, and others usually backed, the horses; but frequently the positions were reversed. But it was not proved that members made bets with non-members on the club premises. On such facts the learned magistrate decided that the defendant had not been brought within the words of the Act, "using a place for the purpose of betting with persons resorting thereto." Hence the question was asked in special case, Whether on such facts the magistrate came to a correct determination and decision in point of law.

It need hardly be said that a special case is not the means to review a decision of a question of fact. In the recent *Newmarket case* (*f*), in which the stewards of the Jockey Club were summoned for that they, being the occupiers of a certain place, knowingly and wilfully permitted the same to be used for an illegal purpose, the magistrates decided that the evidence did not satisfy them that the defendants knowingly and wilfully permitted the enclosures to be kept or used for the purposes of betting within the meaning of the Act of 1853. The magistrates were asked to state a case, but refused. After some delay a rule was obtained for an order *nisi* calling upon the justices of Cambridgeshire and the stewards of the Jockey Club to show cause why the justices should not state a case for the opinion of the Court upon the summons. The magistrates, in showing cause against the order *nisi* in their affidavits, stated that they had decided a question of fact, and of

(*f*) *R.* v. *Godfrey and others*, reported in the newspapers, August 1st, 1895.

fact only, namely, that there was no sufficient evidence to prove what was charged against the defendants. The Court held that they could not go behind that statement and compel the magistrates to state a case. Wright, J., pointed out that the proper course for the applicant to have followed, would have been to have applied for an order requiring the bench to hear and determine the matter, and if on such an application it had been shown that their decision on the facts was contrary to their oath to decide without favour or affection, or in any way corrupt or perverse, or made on personal grounds, they might have been compelled to hear the case and decide it as if it had not been heard before. Or, again, in such circumstances as indicated, leave might have been given to file a criminal information against them. The learned judge was pointing out the way in which, if there was misconduct, it could be dealt with; he, of course, expressed no opinion on the success or failure of any such application in that case. .

The reader is referred to Short and Mellor's Practice of the Crown Office for the practice relating to writs of mandamus or certiorari.

Under section 17, sub-sections (1) and (2) of the Summary Jurisdiction Act, 1879, the defendant, when charged before a court of summary jurisdiction with an offence which may render him liable to be imprisoned for a term exceeding three months, may, on appearing before the Court, and before the charge is gone into, but not afterwards, claim to be tried by a jury. Thereupon he will be dealt with as if charged with an indictable offence. The accused must be informed of this right in time to exercise it. *Right to be tried by a jury.*

If the accused elects to exercise this right, the posi- *Procedure when the*

right is
exercised.
tion of matters thereafter becomes the same as if the
defendant had been charged with an indictable offence,
and not with an offence punishable on summary conviction. The procedure is different. The justices have
to satisfy themselves that the evidence discloses a *primâ
facie* case of the commission by the accused of an indict-
11 & 12 Vict.
c. 42, s. 25.
able offence. Under section 25 of the statute 11 & 12
Vict. c. 42, it is enacted, " that when all the evidence
offered upon the part of the prosecution against the
accused party shall have been heard, if the justice or
justices of the peace then present shall be of opinion
that it is not sufficient to put such accused party upon
his trial for *any* indictable offence, such justice or justices
shall forthwith order such accused party, if in custody,
to be discharged as to the information then under
inquiry ; but if, in the opinion of such justice or justices,
such evidence is sufficient to put the accused party upon
his trial for *an* indictable offence, or if the evidence
given raise a strong or probable presumption of guilt of
such accused party," then the accused should be committed for trial with or without the benefit of the exercise of the powers of admitting to bail contained in
section 23. Therefore, in cases in which the magistrates
send a case for trial before a jury, the question is,
whether the evidence given on the hearing of the summons covers the charges in the indictment. Hence,
also, applications are commonly made to add fresh
counts to indictments founded on the evidence in the
depositions. In fact, where the provisions of the Vexatious Indictments Act (22 & 23 Vict. c. 17) do not
apply, a bill may be presented to a grand jury without
any preliminary inquiry. But the last-mentioned
statute applies (*inter alia*) to the misdemeanour of
keeping a gambling house; and so in respect of that

offence no bill of indictment can be presented to or
found by any grand jury, unless the prosecutor or other
person presenting such indictment has been bound by
recognizances to prosecute or give evidence against the
person accused of such offence, or unless the person
accused has been committed to, or detained in, custody,
or has been bound by recognizance to appear to answer
to an indictment to be preferred against him for such
offence. By the second section of the same Act, if the
justices at the hearing of the information shall refuse
to commit or to bail the person charged with such offence
to be tried for the same, then the prosecutor may require the justices to take the prosecutor's recognizances
to prosecute such charge. By a later Act, being an 30 & 31 Vict.
"Act to remove some Defects in the Administration of c. 35, s. 1.
the Criminal Law," it was provided that the Vexatious
Indictments Act should not preclude the presentation or
finding of any bill or indictment containing counts for
any of the offences mentioned in 22 & 23 Vict. c. 17,
"if such counts be such as may now be lawfully joined
with the rest of such bill of indictment, and if the same
count or counts be founded (in the opinion of the Court
in or before which the same bill of indictment be preferred) upon the facts or evidence disclosed in any
examination or deposition taken before a justice of the
peace, in the presence of the person accused or proposed
to be accused by such bill of indictment and transmitted
or delivered to such Court in due course of law." . . . .
In the case of *Reg.* v. *Brown* (*g*), an information was *Reg.* v.
laid, and a summons obtained against the defendant for *Brown.*
using a house for betting; subsequently he was charged
. . . . "that he, being the occupier of a certain house,

(*g*) *R.* v. *Brown*, (1895) 1 Q. B. 119; 64 L. J. M. C. 1.

unlawfully did use the house for the purpose of betting with persons resorting thereto upon certain events and contingencies of and relating to certain horse races, contrary to the statute (*h*)." The defendant claimed to be tried by a jury. The indictment contained four counts.

Counts in indictment.
The first count charged him, as the occupier of a certain house and rooms therein, with unlawfully opening, keeping, and using the said rooms in the said house for the purpose of betting with persons resorting thereto. The second count charged him, as such occupier, with opening, keeping, and using the rooms for the purpose of money being received by him and on his behalf, as and for the consideration of an undertaking, promise, and agreement to pay thereafter money on the contingency of and relating to horse races. The third and fourth counts merely varied the first and second by charging the defendant, not as the occupier of the house and rooms, but as being a person using the same for the purposes aforesaid respectively. The evidence given before the magistrates, and contained in the depositions, amply covered the whole of the counts. The Court of Crown Cases Reserved unanimously held that the indictment was perfectly legal.

(*h*) The summons should have stopped in the description of the offence at the word "thereto."

CHAPTER XII.

OFFENCES RELATING TO GAMING HOUSES.

Gaming Houses.

In Chapter II., it was shown that a common gaming house is a common nuisance, and that the keeper thereof is indictable for such keeping. Common gaming houses were and are obnoxious to the law, as affording temptations to idleness, and as encouraging excessive play and its attendant evils; not unfrequently such houses draw together numbers of disorderly persons (a). It will be remembered that this indictable offence existed side by side with the legality of any game at common law; the playing of any game was not unlawful, but it was criminal to keep a house whereto many persons might resort, with or without disorder, for the purpose of gaming.

Common gaming house.

The indictment may still be preferred, though, as a matter of practice, the summary offences next hereafter to be mentioned have largely superseded its use. The indictment need not contain a statement of the particular facts which support the allegation of keeping the common gaming house; on the authorities, it is sufficient that the description be general. In *R*. v. *Dixon* (b), a husband and wife were indicted that they

Indictment for keeping.

(a) See *ante*, p. 41, and the authorities there cited.
(b) 2 Geo. I.; *R*. v. *Dixon*, 10 Mod. 336 (case 176).

and each of them on a certain day and on other days
did unlawfully keep a common gaming house, and in
R. v. *Mason* (c), Grose, J., was of opinion that a general
description would suffice. In the case of *R.* v. *Rogier* (d),
the indictment particularized; for, after charging that
the defendants unlawfully did keep and maintain a
certain common gaming house, it continued: and in the
said common gaming house, for lucre and gain, unlawfully and wilfully did cause and procure divers idle and
evil-disposed persons to frequent and come to play
together at a certain unlawful game at cards, called
rouge et noir; and in the said common gaming house
unlawfully and wilfully did permit and suffer the said
idle and evil-disposed persons to be and remain playing
and gaming in the said unlawful game called rouge et
noir for divers large and excessive sums of money, to
the common nuisance of, &c. Holroyd, J., was of
opinion that it was sufficient merely to have alleged
that the defendants kept a common gaming house. On
a motion in arrest of judgment, it was argued on behalf
of the defendants that it was not a nuisance, because
the indictment did not show that any inconvenience
had accrued to the neighbourhood; and, further, that
gaming was not illegal at common law, and that no
statute had made rouge et noir an illegal game. It was
held, that the indictment disclosed an offence at common
law. Abbott, C. J., pointed out that, if any confirma-
tion of the authority of *Hawkins* were wanted, it was
supplied by the enactments of the legislature. The 25
Geo. II. c. 36, s. 5 (e), after reciting that, in order to

R. v. *Rogier.*

(c) *R.* v. *Mason*, 1 Leach's C. C. 487.
(d) *R.* v. *Rogier*, 1 B. & C. 272; 2 D. & R. 431.
(e) Sects. 5 and 8 of this statute are unrepealed and unaltered.

encourage prosecutions against persons keeping bawdy houses, gaming houses, or other disorderly houses, enacts, that if any two inhabitants of any parish give notice in writing to a constable of any person keeping a bawdy house, gaming house, or any other disorderly house, the constable shall go with such inhabitants to a justice of the peace, and shall, upon such inhabitants making oath that they believe the contents of the notice to be true, enter into a recognizance to prosecute such offence, and the constable is to be allowed the expenses of the prosecution, and each of the inhabitants is to receive 10*l.* By section 8, the difficulty of proving who is the real owner or keeper is overcome by the provision " that any person who shall appear, act, or behave himself as master, or as the person having the care and management of any such house, shall be deemed to be the keeper thereof, and shall be liable to prosecution as such, although he be not the real owner." The Chief Justice then refers to the provisions of the 9 Anne, c. 14, s. 2, whereunder the playing at any game is unlawful, if more than 10*l.* be lost. He subsequently adds : " The playing for large and excessive sums of money would of itself make any game unlawful ; and, if so, there can be no doubt that this is an offence at common law."

The absence of an allegation in the indictment that the neighbours had suffered inconvenience is immaterial. Gaming houses are a species of disorderly houses, and, to support a conviction for keeping a disorderly house, it is unnecessary to prove that there was any external manifestation of the internal pursuits (*f*). In Chapter II.

The Stat. Law Rev. Act, 1867, and 38 & 39 Vict. c. 21, s. 1, do not touch these sections.

(*f*) *Reg.* v. *Rice and Wilton*, L. R. 1 C. C. R. 21 ; 35 L. J. M.

G.   R

it has been submitted that gaming—playing at a game for money (g)—does not at common law become unlawful because the stakes are excessive. But, whilst at common law all gaming was lawful, provided there was no foul play, yet a common gaming house, of which the *indicia* have been stated above, was a well-recognized nuisance.

The Statute 33 Hen. VIII. c. 9.

This Act has the merit that, by section 17, all previous statutes made against unlawful games were repealed. The statute has been followed by that of 8 & 9 Vict. c. 109, and 17 & 18 Vict. c. 38 ; these three statutes create specific offences, and confer executive powers, and make procedural provisions.

In Chapter III., a general account has been given of the Act 33 Hen. VIII. c. 9, but here only such portions as are unrepealed will be considered.

The offences. The offences created under this Act are—

Keeping a house of, &c. (A.) By section 11—That no person by himself, factor, deputy, servant, or other person shall for his or their gain, lucre, or living, keep, have, hold, occupy, exercise, or maintain any common house, alley, or place, of dicing-table, carding, or any other manner of game prohibited by any statute heretofore mentioned, or any unlawful new game now invented or made, or any other new unlawful game hereafter to be invented, found, had, or made, upon pain to forfeit and pay for every day keeping, having, or maintaining, or suffering any such game to be had, kept, or maintained, executed, or played within any such house, garden, alley, or other place contrary to the form and effect of this statute, forty shillings.

C. 93 ; 12 Jur. N. S. 126 ; 13 L. T. 382 ; 14 W. R. 56 ; 10 Cox, C. C. 155.

(g) *R*. v. *Ashton*, 1 E. & B. 286 ; 22 L. J. M. C. 1 ; 17 Jur. 501.

(B.) By section 12—And also every person using Using such
and haunting any of the said houses and plays and house.
there playing, to forfeit every time so doing six shillings
and eightpence.

(C.) By section 16—That no manner of artificer or Certain
craftsman of any handicraft or occupation, husbandman, classes of people play-
apprentice, labourer, servant at husbandry, journeyman ing at unlaw-
or servant of artificer, mariners, fishermen, watermen, ful games.
or any serving man shall play at dice, cards, or any
other unlawful game under the pain of twenty shillings
to be forfeited for every time.

In order to render the Act effectual for the suppression of the offences a power of search was given by section 14; and the justices were subsequently authorized
to bind with recognizances those found on the premises
(2 Geo. II. c. 28, s. 9). This power, having become obsolete by reason of the larger powers of the later statutes,
was repealed by the Statute Law Revision Act, 1863 (h).

This statute, by creating the offence of keeping for
gain a house of playing unlawful games, did not destroy
the common law offence of keeping a common gaming
house. That such had been its result was unsuccessfully contended in *R.* v. *Dixon* (i).

The Statute 8 & 9 *Vict. c.* 109.

In Chapter VII., it was necessary to cite the preamble
and the earlier sections of the statute 8 & 9 Vict. c. 109,
in order to exhibit the policy of the Act as leading up
to the detailed consideration of the 18th section. A
reference back will show that this statute was of the

(h) Hawkins, J., in *Jenks* v. *Turpin*, 13 Q. B. D. 505; 53 L,
J. M. C. 161; 50 L. T. 808; 49 J. P. 20; 15 Cox, C. C. 486;
says that sect. 14 does not seem to have been repealed.
(i) *R.* v. *Dixon*, 10 Mod. 336 (case 176).

highest importance with regard to the policy of the law in respect of games of skill, removing the impediments imposed on the exercise thereof by the statute 33 Hen. VIII. c. 109.

Offences.

The offences described in this statute are—

(D.) By section 4—That the owner or keeper of any common gaming house, *and* every person having the care or management thereof, *and* also every banker, croupier, *and* other person who shall act in any manner in conducting the business of any common gaming house,—shall, on summary conviction, in addition to any penalty or punishment to which he may be subject under 33 Hen. VIII. c. 9, be liable to forfeit and pay a penalty not exceeding 100*l.*, or may be imprisoned with or without hard labour for any period of time not exceeding six calendar months.

This is the only offence relating to gaming houses described in the Act. Substantially this offence is identical with that of section 11 of 33 Hen. VIII. c. 9. In terminology, the slight difference is, that the earlier statute speaks of the keeping of a house of playing unlawful games, and the later one substitutes the term, the keeping of a common gaming house. It is worthy of notice that the 4th section contemplates dual punishment for the same acts, namely, the penalties and punishments of the earlier statute *plus* the penalties and punishments of the later. But the same section, possibly with reference to the contention which was raised in *R.* v. *Dixon* (*k*), enacts, that nothing therein contained should prevent any proceeding by indictment against the owner or keeper or other person having the care or management of a common gaming house;

(*k*) *R.* v. *Dixon*, 10 Mod. 336 (case 176).

though it provides that no person who shall have been summarily convicted should be liable to be indicted for the same offence.

This Act does not directly impose any penalty on persons haunting and playing in common gaming houses; if it does so at all, it must be indirectly, by incorporating the offence contained in section 12 of the earlier statute and the powers of section 14, as extended by 2 Geo. II. c. 28, s. 9.

The practical weakness of this Act lay in its defective executive powers. It will be remembered that it had repealed the duty imposed, by the earlier statute, on justices to make search. But it is provided by section 3 that, outside the metropolitan police district, in every case in which the justices of peace in every shire, and mayors, sheriffs, bailiffs, and other head officers within every city, town, and borough within the realm now had power to enter into any house, room, or place where unlawful games should be suspected to be holden, it should be lawful for any justice of the peace, upon complaint made before him on oath that there was reason to suspect any house, room, or place to be kept or used as a common gaming house, to give authority, by special warrant under his hand, when in his discretion he should think fit, to any constable to enter, with such assistance as might be found necessary, into such house, room, or place, in like manner as might have been done by such justices, &c., and, if necessary, to use force for making such entry, whether by breaking open doors or otherwise, and to arrest, search, and bring before a justice of the peace, all such persons found therein as might have been arrested therein by such justice of the peace had he been personally present; and *all such persons should be dealt with according to law as if they had been arrested in such house, room, or place by the*

The weakness of the Act.

Outside the metropolitan police district: search warrant, sect. 3.

justice before whom they should be so brought. The form of the search warrant is given in the Appendix to the Act (*k*).

Within the metropolitan police district. Prior to the passing of the 8 & 9 Vict. c. 109, there was power within the metropolitan police district for any superintendent of the metropolitan police to make a written report to the commissioners of police that there were good grounds for believing that a house or room within the district was kept or used as a gaming house, and on two or more householders dwelling within the district, and not belonging to the police, making oath in writing, to be taken and subscribed before a magistrate, and annexed to the report, then the commissioners might make an order in writing, whereby the superintendent was authorized to enter such house, with force if necessary, and to take into custody all persons found therein, and to seize and destroy all instruments of gaming, and to seize all moneys and securities. This Offence under 2 & 3 Vict. c. 47, s. 48. power was given by the 2 & 3 Vict. c. 47, s. 48. The section also provided (offence E.) that the owner or keeper, or other person having the care or management of the gaming house, and also every banker, croupier, and other person acting in any manner in conducting the said gaming house, should be liable to a penalty of 100*l.*, or to not more than six calendar months' imprisonment, with or without hard labour; and, further, that every person found in the premises without lawful excuse should be liable to a penalty of not more than 5*l.*

Search warrant under sects. 6 and 7 of 8 & 9 Vict. c. 109. However, the process of obtaining a search warrant within the metropolitan police district was simplified by the 6th section of the statute 8 & 9 Vict. c. 109, whereunder it was provided that if any superintendent belonging to the metropolitan police force should report

---

(*k*) See Appendix, Form No. II.

in writing to the commissioners of the police that there are good grounds for believing, and that he does believe, that a house, &c., within the district is kept as a common gaming house, then either of the commissioners may, in writing, authorize the superintendent to enter, with force if necessary, to take into custody all persons found therein, and to seize all instruments of gaming and all moneys and securities for money found therein. Thus the procedure is more simple than that under the Metropolitan Police Act (2 & 3 Vict. c. 47, s. 48). Further, by section 7, on making such entry, a search of the whole house is authorized, and of all persons found therein.

The statute 8 & 9 Vict. c. 109, does not define a common gaming house. But section 2, after reciting that doubts had arisen whether certain houses, reputed to be opened for the use of subscribers only, or not open to all persons desirous of using the same, are to be deemed common gaming houses (*l*), states that it shall suffice for a conviction in default of other evidence; namely, that it shall be sufficient to prove that such house or place is used for playing at any unlawful game, and that a bank is kept there by one or more of the players exclusively of the others, or that the chances of any game played therein are not alike favourable to all the players, including amongst the players the banker or other person by whom the game is managed, or against whom the other players stake, play, or bet, and provides that every such house shall be deemed a common gaming house such as is contrary to law, and forbidden by the statute of 33 Hen. VIII. and by all other Acts containing provisions against unlawful games or

Evidence required for a conviction.

(*l*) *Crockford* v. *Lord Maidstone*, 8 L. T. 217; Oliphant's Law of Horses, p. 281.

What is not required. gaming houses. And section 5 provides that it shall not be necessary, in support of any information for gaming in, or suffering any games or gaming in, or for keeping or using, or being concerned in the management or conduct of a common gaming house, to prove that any person found playing at any game was playing for money, wager, or stake. To the same effect is section 49 of the Metropolitan Police Act (2 & 3 Vict. c. 47). By section 8 of the statute it is enacted that **Effect of finding instruments of gaming.** where any cards, dice, balls, counters, tables, or other instruments of gaming used in playing any unlawful game, shall be found in any house, &c., suspected and entered, or about the person of any of those found therein, it shall be evidence, until the contrary be made to appear, that such house, &c., is used as a common gaming house, and that the persons found in the room where such instruments of gaming shall have been found were playing therein, although no play was actually going on in the presence of the officer entering or of those with him. The destruction of all such instruments of gaming may be ordered forthwith.

Obtaining witnesses. Persons concerned in the unlawful gaming may, with a view to the conviction of keepers of gaming houses, be examined as witnesses, and, under section 9, may obtain a certificate, which indemnifies them against their acts in respect of such unlawful gaming.

Appeal. A person summarily convicted under this Act is empowered to appeal against such conviction, and the right must be exercised in accordance with the general procedure directed by the Summary Jurisdiction Acts, as explained in Chapter XI.

Distress. Tender of amends. By the 21st and 22nd sections provisions are made with a view to relieving against the liabilities that might be incurred through making a distress upon a process not in proper form ; the 23rd section provides for the limitation of actions.

By virtue of the 25th section no information, con- *Conviction,* viction, or other proceeding, before or by any justice *&c. not to be quashed for* under this Act can be quashed or set aside, or adjudged *informality, &c.* void or insufficient for want of form, or be removed by *certiorari* into her Majesty's Court of Queen's Bench.

The Statute 17 & 18 Vict. c. 38.

An Act for the Suppression of Gaming Houses.

Experience proved that the last-mentioned and the *Occasion fo* other Acts were inadequate for the suppression of *statute.* gaming houses, because the keepers thereof obstructed the entrance of the police, and whilst the police were using force the instruments of gaming were removed or destroyed, with the result that sufficient evidence could not be obtained. Hence the offences (F.) and (G.) were created :—

Offence (F.), *by section* 1.—Any person who shall wil- *Offences* fully prevent any constable duly authorized to enter *thereunder.* any suspected house from entering, and any person who by any bolt, bar, chain, or other contrivance, shall secure any external or internal door of or means of access to any house, &c., or shall use any means or contrivance whatsoever for the purpose of preventing or obstructing such entry, may for every such offence, on summary conviction, be fined 100*l.*, or be imprisoned with or without hard labour for not more than six calendar months.

Offence (G.), *by section* 3.—If any person found in any house, &c., entered as aforesaid, upon being arrested or upon being brought before any justices, on being required to give his name and address, shall refuse or neglect to give the same, or shall give any false name and address, he may, on summary conviction be fined not more than 50l. or be imprisoned for not more than one month. And further, to increase the stringency of the law by inflicting penalties on some people who had previously escaped, higher penalties and pains were attached than had theretofore been applied to the summary offences. The offence (H.) in section 4 is *not* defined in terms of a common gaming house as was offence (D.), but substitutes therefor the term "*for the purpose of unlawful gaming.*" The offence is—

Liability of: i. owner, &c.; ii. owner, &c. wilfully permitting; iii. any manager or assistant; iv. person lending money.

Any person, being the owner or occupier, or having the use of any house, room, or place, who shall open the same for the purpose of unlawful gaming being carried on therein, and any person who being the owner or occupier of any house or room, shall knowingly and wilfully permit the same to be opened, kept, or used by any other person for the purpose aforesaid, and any person having the care or management of or in any manner assisting in conducting the business of any house, room, or place, opened, kept, or used for the purposes aforesaid, and any person who shall advance or furnish money for the purpose of gaming with persons frequenting such house, room, or place, may, on summary conviction, be fined not more than 500l. or be imprisoned with or without hard labour for not longer than twelve calendar months.

Evidence. Effect of obstructions, alarms, &c.

The provisions of the statute 8 & 9 Vict. c. 109, were supplemented as to the evidence required to support a conviction, for, by section 2, the wilful obstruction of an officer in entering, the barring of the means of access, or facilities for giving alarm in case of such entry, or any means or contrivance for concealing, removing, or destroying any instruments of gaming, are deemed to

OFFENCES RELATING TO GAMING HOUSES.

be evidence until the contrary be shown that the house, &c., is used as a common gaming house within the meaning of this Act, and of former Acts relating to gaming, and that the persons found therein were unlawfully playing.

It will be remembered that under the statute 8 & 9 Vict. c. 109, s. 9, the persons concerned in the unlawful gaming might, with the benefit of an indemnity, give evidence. But under the present Act (section 5) any persons arrested on entry may be compelled to take oath and give evidence as if subpœnaed for that purpose ; and having thus on compulsion given evidence, they could under section 6 claim a certificate which would operate as a stay to any proceedings against themselves relating to any such matter.

Penalties and costs may be levied by distress (section 7), and, by section 8, it is provided that one-half of any penalty which should be adjudged to be paid, should be paid to the person laying the information, and the remainder to the relief of the poor-rate, as therein specified. A question arose as to the effect (if any) of this 8th section on the 47th section of the Metropolitan Police Act (2 & 3 Vict. c. 71). Within the police district a penalty of 50l. was recovered in respect of an offence under the statute 17 & 18 Vict. c. 38, one-half, about which no question arose, was paid to the informer, and the other half was paid to the overseers of the poor. The receiver of the metropolitan police district claimed the moiety which had been paid to the overseers of the poor. The receiver's claim was based upon the 47th section of the Metropolitan Police Act. It was held, that the 17 & 18 Vict. c. 38, s. 8, had not repealed the 2 & 3 Vict. c. 71, s. 47, so far as concerned the application of penalties recovered under the former Act before

Power to compel persons to give evidence.

Levy and application of penalties, &c.,

within the metropolitan police district.

a police magistrate of the metropolis, and that section 8 impliedly contained the reservation "unless recovered or adjudged before the police courts in the metropolis" (*m*).

Appeal from summary conviction. Under this Act, as under the 8 & 9 Vict. c. 109, a right of appeal from a summary conviction is conferred. With reference to such appeals, it is expressly provided by section 11 that no objection shall be allowed to the information whereon the conviction had taken place, or to such conviction on any matter of form or on any insufficiency of statement, provided that it shall appear that the defendant had been sufficiently informed of the charge intended to be made against him and that the conviction was proper on the merits of the case. Further, no information, conviction, or judgment can be removed by certiorari into the Court of Queen's Bench.

The sections relating to an informal distress, to tender of amends and limitation of actions (sections 12, 13, 14), are literal reproductions of the corresponding sections of the 8 & 9 Vict. c. 109.

Questions of law arising on the offences (A.) to (H.). It now remains to consider the questions of law which have arisen out of the foregoing enactments. The offence (A.) is that of keeping for lucre a house, &c. for playing unlawful games; the offences (D.) and (E.) relate to keeping a common gaming house; the offence (H.) relates to keeping a house for the purpose of unlawful gaming. A subsidiary question as to the extension and meaning of the term "place," which occurs in offences (A.) and (H.), may conveniently be reserved until the authorities are considered which arise immediately out of its use in the Betting House Act (16 & 17 Vict. c. 119).

(*m*) *Wray* v. *Ellis*, 28 L. J. M. C. 45; 1 El. & El. 276; 23 Jur. 624; 32 L. T. 157.

The first general question is, What constitutes a "keeping, having, holding, occupying, exercising, or maintaining," or an opening, within the meaning of these offences? By section 11 of the statute of 33 Hen. VIII., c. 9, the keeping contemplated is *by way of business*, for lucre, gain, or living; by section 2 of the 8 & 9 Vict. c. 109, it suffices to show that the house *is used* for playing, and the increased executive powers under the 17 & 18 Vict. c. 38, clearly contemplate an organized and systematic user of the premises. It is not contemplated that the owner of a house should offend if he once and again *by way of recreation* there play baccarat or other game with his friends. There are two cases in point arising under the Act which restricted cock-fighting (12 & 13 Vict. c. 92, s. 3). In *Clarke* v. *Hague* (*n*), cocks were fought on one occasion in a bowling-alley, and on no other occasion had cocks been fought there. It was held that such user did not constitute a user within the meaning of the Act. In *Morley* v. *Greenhalgh* (*o*), there was a cock-fight in a quarry, on one occasion and no more; it was held that the once using did not make it a place used for cock-fighting. On the other hand, the gaming need not be the sole purpose for which the house is used. In the leading case of *Jenks* v. *Turpin* (*p*), Mr. Justice Hawkins said, "If the house had been kept open for a double purpose, viz., as a honest, social club for those who did not desire to play, as well as for the purpose of gaming for those who did, it would none the less be a

"Keeping" within the meaning of the statutes.

Unlawful gaming one purpose amongst others.

(*n*) *Clarke* v. *Hague*, 2 E. & E. 281; 8 Cox, C. C. 324; 29 L. J. M. C. 105; 6 Jur. N. S. 273; 8 W. R. 363.

(*o*) *Morley* v. *Greenhalgh*, 3 B. & S. 374; 32 L. J. M. C. 93; 9 Jur. N. S. 745; 7 L. T. 624; 11 W. R. 263.

(*p*) *Jenks* v. *Turpin*, 13 Q. B. D. 505; 53 L. J. M. C. 161; 50 L. T. 808; 49 J. P. 20; 15 Cox, C. C. 486.

house opened and kept *for the purpose of gaming*." In
that case, the main and principal object of the club was
gaming at baccarat. From half-past four in the afternoon till eight on the following morning those who
liked could play. A night steward, whose duties were
in the card-room, was kept. Baccarat was the game
throughout the night, and at it thousands were nightly
won and lost. At baccarat as there played no bank
could be less than 50*l.*; and the ordinary regulation
banks ranged from 50*l.* to 300*l.*; and the open banks
sometimes reached 1,000*l.* Ordinarily, there would be a
fresh bank every twenty minutes: a special table and
arrangements were provided for the banker and the
punters: for each bank three packs of cards were used.
For such accommodation the proprietor received from
each banker 1 per cent., and each punter 5*s.* as card
money, up to 2 A.M., after which 5*s.* an hour till 5 A.M.,
and after that time, to make playing prohibitory, 1*l.* an
hour. Members' cheques were cashed by the proprietor
at a charge of 1 per cent. This case affords an illustration of a strong instance of a house kept for the
purpose of gaming.

The house need not be kept for the purpose of gaming
by all or any person who comes thereto. The doubt as
to whether a house kept for the purpose of subscribers,
and no others, resorting thereto could be a common
gaming house, was alluded to in section 2 of the 8 & 9
Vict. c. 109, and it was enacted that it could be.
Hawkins, J., in *Jenks* v. *Turpin*, points out that to no
gaming house is the public at large invited to go without restriction of some sort or other. The keeper of
such a house has always the right to admit or refuse
admission to anyone he pleases, or to make such rules
as he may think fit for the regulation of such admission.

Common, not public gaming house.

In that case the keeper had placed himself in the hands
of a committee to elect whom they would, provided only
the number of members did not exceed five hundred.
If the admission of five hundred persons to a gaming
house does not make it a common gaming house, it
might equally be said that the admission of five thousand
would not. "The law does not require that it shall be
a public gaming house : a *common* gaming house is that
which is forbidden, that is, a house in which a large
number of persons are invited habitually to congregate
for the purpose of gaming."

In the case of *Jenks* v. *Turpin* (*q*), the proprietor of
the club had been convicted, under section 4 of the
17 & 18 Vict. c. 38, of keeping and using the house
for the purpose of unlawful gaming, the committee of
management had been convicted under the same section
as persons assisting in conducting the business of the
house so kept for the purpose of unlawful gaming. On
the case stated, the question was raised as to what constituted unlawful gaming within the section. The contention was advanced that the unlawful gaming struck
at was gaming at ace of hearts, pharaoh, basset, and
hazard (12 Geo. II. c. 28, s. 1), at passage or any game
with dice (13 Geo. II. c. 19), or roulet (18 Geo. II.
c. 34), and at none other. Smith, J., decided against
that contention on the ground that, "in 1854, it is
common knowledge that the games of ace of hearts,
pharaoh, and basset had fallen into disuse. I cannot
suppose that the statute was passed simply to meet the
game of hazard and games played with dice, and the
keeping of a house in which to play roulet. These were
by no means the only games by which gambling was

Definition of a common gaming house.

Jenks v. Turpin.

Unlawful gaming.

(*q*) *Jenks* v. *Turpin*, 13 Q. B. D. 505; 53 L. J. M. C. 161; 50
L. T. 808; 49 J. P. 20; 15 Cox, C. C. 486.

carried on at that period. If this had been the intention of the legislature, in my judgment it would have
particularized these three games, and not have used the
most general words possible, viz., unlawful gaming.
The real answer appears to me to be this : to play at a
game of chance with cards for money in a common
gaming house is unlawful gaming." Hawkins, J., discussed in detail the question whether the house was
kept for the purpose of *unlawful* gaming in the sense of
gaming at *unlawful* games. He commences with the
freedom allowed at common law, whereunder the playing
at any game was legal; he then passes to the statute
of 33 Hen. VIII. c. 9, whereunder no game is made
absolutely unlawful, though the offences (A.), (B.), and
(C.) are created; he points out that the 16 Car. II. c. 7,
and 9 Anne, c. 14, declared no game unlawful, though
excessive or fraudulent gaming at any game was made
a penal offence ; he then reviews the 12 Geo. II. c. 28,
relating to ace of hearts, pharaoh, basset, and hazard,
and the 13 Geo. II. c. 19, touching passage and every
other game invented or to be invented with a die or
dice ; and then the 18 Geo. II. c. 34, s. 1, regarding
roulet or any other game with cards or dice already
prohibited by law. By such an examination, the learned
judge exhibits the reference in the first section of the
8 & 9 Vict. c. 109, to the laws theretofore made in
restraint of *unlawful* gaming, and, commenting on that
section, he says : " Nothing could more clearly indicate
the intention of the legislature to legalise to all persons
and at all times mere games of skill, but to preserve in
their integrity all the penalties which then attached to
the playing of unlawful games anywhere, *or gaming at
all* (even at lawful games) *in common gaming houses.*
The 17 & 18 Vict. c. 38, is an extension of the 8 & 9

Legality of
games of
skill.

Vict. c. 109, and in the former *unlawful gaming* has as wide a meaning as in the latter Act. "Since that statute (8 & 9 Vict. c. 109) the only games made unlawful by 33 Hen. VIII. c. 9, are games of dice and cards, whether such games were known at the time of the passing of that statute, or have been since invented. All such games, if they are games of chance, or games of chance and skill combined (which cannot be called games of mere skill) are, in my opinion, clearly within the meaning of the words unlawful games in 17 & 18 Vict. c. 38. The language of the first section of 8 & 9 Vict. c. 109, referring to 33 Hen. VIII. c. 9, and repealing only so much of it as applies to games of skill, is a strong indication of the intention of the legislature that all the other games mentioned in the statute of Hen. VIII. were to continue to be treated as unlawful in the sense in, and to the extent to which, they were made unlawful by that statute, viz., unlawful if played in a house kept for playing them." Baccarat being a game of cards which is not a game of mere skill, it is "a new unlawful game hereafter to be invented" (*r*) (sect. 11, 33 Hen. VIII. c. 9), and the evidence established the offence (A.) described in that section, or the offence (D.) of sect. 4 of the 8 & 9 Vict. c. 109 ; and, further, as baccarat is an unlawful game within the statute, the occupier was properly convicted of offence (H.), described in sect. 4 of the statute 17 & 18 Vict. c. 38, viz., of opening and keeping a house for the purpose of unlawful gaming. Hawkins, J., further stated, "Having regard to the house being a common gaming

(*r*) In *Fairtlough* v. *Whitmore*, 64 L. J. Ch. 386; W. N. (1895) 52, Stirling, J., held that "*chemin de fer*," though differing somewhat from "*baccarat banque*," *i.e.*, the game played in *Jenks* v. *Turpin*, was equally an unlawful game.

house, I am of opinion that the conviction may also be
supported upon the ground that *all* gaming therein,
even at lawful games, was *unlawful gaming*."

Liability of
managers.

The committee of management of the club having in
some manner assisted in conducting the business thereof
were respectively properly convicted. The remaining
question in the case arose out of the conviction of certain
players who were merely players. It was held that they
had not assisted in conducting the business of the club,
and had therefore been improperly convicted. But it was
not decided whether the players could have been punished
otherwise than under section 4 of the 17 & 18 Vict. c. 38.

Players.

There was no specific imposition of penalties as on
players of ace of hearts, pharaoh, basset, hazard, passage,
roulet. But as the keeper might have been convicted,
(offence (A.)), under section 11 of the 33 Hen. VIII. c. 9,
the players might have been convicted under section 12
of the same Act (offence (B.)). Under section 14 of the
same Act, the justices had power to bind the players
by recognizances, by themselves or else with sureties,
"no more to play, haunt, or exercise from thenceforth,
in, at, or to any of the said places, or at any of the said
games." This power was extended by the statute
2 Geo. II. c. 28, s. 9, which recited that under the
statute of Hen. VIII. the justices had not power to
take any security other than the recognizances of the
persons so found playing, and enacted that any justice
who should find that any person had been exercising any
unlawful games should have full power to commit such
offenders to prison, without bail or mainprize, until
they should enter into one or more recognizances, with
or without sureties, at the discretion of the said justice,
not to play or use such unlawful game. The section 14
of the statute of Hen. VIII. has been repealed, but the

extending Act, 2 Geo. II. c. 28, s. 9, does not appear
to have been repealed. The powers seem to be incorporated by section 3 of the 8 & 9 Vict. c. 109.
Within the metropolitan district, by the Metropolitan
Police Act (2 & 3 Vict. c. 47, s. 48), persons found on
the premises without lawful excuse are liable to a
penalty (s). In inflicting penalties upon the players it
would appear that the common law has been supplemented; the only offence known to the common law
was the keeping of a common gaming house (t).

(s) See *ante*, p. 246.
(t) See Hawkins, J., *Jenks* v. *Turpin*, 13 Q. B. D. at p. 517;
cf. Smith, J., at p. 535.

CHAPTER XIII.

OFFENCES RELATING TO BETTING HOUSES.

Section (A.)—*The Statute* 16 & 17 *Vict. c.* 119.

The business of betting offices.
IN 1853, there existed, in the large, and even in small towns, offices and houses where a regular business of betting was carried on. The offices and houses were sometimes conducted by the owner or occupier whose business it might be said to be, or by a manager or sometimes the offices or houses were entrusted to a servant. The business was of this kind—A list of races about to take place and the current odds against each horse were placarded, and the proprietor, who, either himself or by another conducted the business, received deposits from all sorts of persons, to abide the event of races on which they were willing and anxious to bet, and they in return for their deposits usually received a ticket which enabled them when the race was over to obtain the money from the office if they won, and if they lost the deposit was gone and they had no further interest in the bet (a). The keeper, or his servants on his behalf, held the bag against all comers (b). The preamble of the Act recites that a kind of gaming has sprung up tending to the

(a) *Reg.* v. *Cook*, 13 Q. B. D. 377; 51 L. T. 21; 32 W. R. 796; 48 J. P. 694.

(b) Hansard's Parliamentary Reports.

injury and demoralization of improvident persons by
the opening of places called betting houses or offices,
and the receiving of money in advance by the owners
or occupiers of such houses or offices, or by other persons acting on their behalf, on their promises to pay
money on the events of horse races and the like contingencies. The enacting parts of the Act, with the object
of rendering evasions difficult, have gone beyond the
preamble; and in attaining that object, have involved
the limits of the offences in considerable uncertainty.
Thus, in each offence the following sequences of terms
are used:—"House, office, room, *or other place*" (hereinafter for brevity spoken of under the single term
"place"); "opened, kept, or used" (hereinafter denoted
by the term "used").

The following are the offences created by this Act:—

Offence (A.) *under section* 1.—Any place used by any
person [*that is to say*, (α) by the owner, occupier, or
keeper thereof, or any person using the same; or (β) any
person procured or employed by or acting for or on
behalf of such owner, occupier or keeper, or person
using the same; or (γ) by any person having the care
or management or in any manner conducting the business thereof] for either or both of two specified purposes
(namely), first, for the purpose of betting with persons
resorting thereto; secondly, for the purpose of receiving
money on deposit [*that is to say*, by or on behalf of such
person as and for the consideration for any assurance,
undertaking, promise or agreement, express or implied,
to pay or to give thereafter any money or valuable
thing on any event or contingency of or relating to any
horse race or other race, fight, game, sport or exercise,
or as and for the consideration for securing the paying
or giving by some other person of any money or valu-

Analytical
statement of
the offences.

able thing on any such event or contingency as aforesaid], shall be a common nuisance.

One place cannot be two common nuisances at the same time. A place used for the first purpose only, where no money was received in advance, would be a common nuisance. Blackburn, J., in the case of *Haigh* v. *The Town Council of Sheffield* (c), expressed a doubt whether an offence could be established without showing that money had been deposited. But in *R.* v. *Preedie* (d), it is pointed out that the first section extends the preamble, in so far as it says for the one purpose *or* for the other; similarly in section 3. In the recent case of *Bond* v. *Plumb* (e), the disjunctive character is clearly recognized. Whilst, then, a common nuisance can be so constituted either in the one way or in the other, it is submitted that one place could not at one time be two common nuisances ; if evidence of both purposes were forthcoming, the offence might possibly be aggravated, but it is difficult to think that two indictments could lie, under the circumstances.

Offence (B.) *under section 2.*—Any place, a common nuisance within section 1, shall be a common gaming house within the 8 & 9 Vict. c. 109. Again, it is submitted that one place could at one time only be one common gaming house.

Offence (C.) *under section 3.*—Any owner or occupier of a place, or person using the same, who shall use the same for the purposes mentioned in section 1, or either of them, shall be liable. . . . .

Offence (D.) *under section 3.*—Any owner or occupier of a place, who shall knowingly and wilfully permit the

(c) *Haigh* v. *The Town Council of Sheffield*, L. R. 10 Q. B. 102 ; 44 L. J. M. C. 17 ; 31 L. T. 536 ; 23 W. R. 547.

(d) *R.* v. *Preedie*, 17 Cox, C. C. 433.

(e) *Bond* v. *Plumb*, (1894) 1 Q. B. 169 ; 70 L. T. 405 ; 42 W. R. 222 ; 58 S. J. 99.

same to be used by any other person for the purposes aforesaid, or either of them, shall be liable. . . . .

Offence (E.) *under section* 3.—Any person having the care or management of or in any manner assisting in conducting the business of any place used for the purposes aforesaid, or either of them, shall be liable . . . . (C.) (D.) or (E.), on summary conviction before two justices of the peace, to be fined a sum of 100*l*., or to be imprisoned with or without hard labour for not longer than six calendar months.

A question, which is not free from doubt on the present state of the authorities, is whether or not each of the offences (C.) (D.) and (E.) contain two severable offences. After a raid on a betting house, it is not unusual for a considerable number of summonses to be issued. Thus, the occupier may be summoned separately for using, on a given date, the place for the first purpose and for the second purpose. If he elects to be tried by a jury, the indictment will contain two counts, one charging the user for the one purpose, the other charging the user for the other purpose. If the offences are distinct, the defendant will be liable on conviction to separate penalties. But if the submission above made is correct, namely, that the place at one time would only be one common nuisance and one common gaming house, it would seem that definite indication would be required in section 3 that the same acts should, on summary conviction, constitute two offences; so far from that definite indication being found, the section says, "for the purposes hereinbefore mentioned, or either of them," whereas it would have been quite easy to have provided that a person who used a place for both purposes should be liable to double penalties. In the recent

Whether by using a place for the two purposes, two offences are committed.

case of *R.* v. *Brown* (*e*), Hawkins, J., expressed the opinion that the double purpose carried but the single penalty; Lord Russell, C. J., pointed out that the evidence which would establish the user for the second purpose would go far to establish the user for the first purpose, so much is the second involved in the first; but Wright, J., differed from the opinion of Hawkins, J. Undoubtedly it is a complete offence under this section to use a place for the purpose of betting with persons resorting thereto, even though no money be deposited in advance: *R.* v. *Preedie* (*f*), *Bond* v. *Plumb* (*g*); but it is submitted that, at the same time to use a place for the two purposes, involved as the first is in the second, does not constitute two offences.

Offences continued.

Under section 4, offence (F.)—Any person being the owner or occupier of any place used for the purposes aforesaid, or either of them . . .

Offence (G.)—or any person acting for or on behalf of such owner or occupier, or any person having the care or management, or in any manner assisting in conducting the business thereof . . .

(F.) *and* (G.)—who shall receive, directly or indirectly, any money or valuable thing as a deposit on any bet on condition of paying any sum of money or other valuable thing on the happening of any event or contingency of or relating to a horse race, or any other race, or any fight, game, sport, or exercise, or as or for the consideration for any assurance, undertaking, promise, or agreement, express or implied, to pay or give thereafter any

(*e*) *R.* v. *Brown*, (1895) 1 Q. B. 119; 64 L. J. M. C. 1.

(*f*) *R.* v. *Preedie*, 17 Cox, C. C. 433.

(*g*) *Bond* v. *Plumb*, (1894) 1 Q. B. 169; 70 L. T. 405; 42 W. R. 222; 38 S. J. 99.

money or valuable thing on any such event or contingency, shall be liable . . .

Offence (H.)—And any person giving any acknowledgment, note, security, or draft on the receipt of any money or valuable thing so paid or given as aforesaid, purporting or intended to entitle the bearer or any other person to receive any money or valuable thing on the happening of any such event or contingency as aforesaid, shall be liable to . . .

(F.), (G.), *or* (H.)—upon summary conviction before two justices of the peace, to be fined a sum of 50*l.*, or to be imprisoned, with or without hard labour, for three calendar months.

There appears to be no authority on this section and the relation of the offences (F.), (G.), or (H.) to the major offences of sect. 3. A typical charge is, that A. B., being owner of a certain house used by him for the purposes of receiving money on deposit, &c., did on a certain date receive a certain sum of money, to wit, &c., from one C. D., on a bet, &c. It is obvious that a large number of such summonses could be commonly issued. Before obtaining a conviction it would be necessary to prove the major charge—probably the defendant's books would be put in evidence—then the receipt of the specific deposit would be proved. But if the defendant be first punished for the major offence, it seems in the last degree unjust to make that the foundation of further convictions on a series of minor charges. The defendant received deposits at a place: *ergo*, he kept a place for the purpose, and accordingly was punished; but keeping a place for the purpose, he received — deposits: *ergo*, he committed — offences, and accordingly must be punished — times more. It is to be hoped that a defendant who has been tried on the major offence will meet the minor

Relation of the offences under sect. 4 to those under sect. 3.

summons with a plea in bar in the nature of autrefois convict or acquit. If he should plead guilty, understanding that the justices will bind him over to come up for judgment when called on, he may, if called up for judgment, find himself in an evil position (*f*). The difficulty arises on whatever construction is placed on the section. If the occupier were convicted on the major offence, his servant or agent might be convicted under sect. 4; but even then the agent himself might have been convicted on the same evidence under the 3rd section. As a matter of practice, the summonses issued under the 4th section are not commonly proceeded with after a conviction for the major offence.

Saving clause as to certain deposits.　There is an important qualification with regard to the receiving by way of deposit. By sect. 6 it is provided that nothing in the Act shall extend to any person receiving or holding any money or valuable thing by way of stakes or deposit to be paid to the winner of any race or lawful sport, game, or exercise, or to the owner of any horse engaged in any race. On this proviso, the cases and questions raised under the similar proviso in sect. 18 of the 8 & 9 Vict. c. 109, are in point, and will be found in Chapter VII., pp. 145 *et seq*. In the previous section (sect. 5), provision is made whereunder a depositor may recover his deposit, in spite of the illegality which attaches to the act of making the deposit. The *delictum* is not treated as *par* between the depositor and the holder of the bag against all comers.

Power to recover deposits in spite of illegality.

Offences of advertising.　　*Offence* (I.)—Under sect. 7, offences connected with the

(*f*) A client, to whom these remarks applied, appealed against a sentence of three months' imprisonment with hard labour; his view of the matter was, "First I was punished for getting drunk, next I am punished for the separate whiskies which made me so."

advertising of betting places are created; but, as these have been extended by a subsequent statute, it will be more convenient to consider the whole of such offences together.

As in the Gaming House Acts, so in this Act, the Executive justices of the peace have power to issue a special search powers. warrant; in fact, in identical form with that under the 8 & 9 Vict. c. 109. The complaint is made, before any justice of the peace, that there is reason to suspect a place to be used as a betting house or office contrary to the Act, thereupon the search warrant is issued, where-under the officers may, with or without force, enter and diligently search the suspected place, and search and arrest the keepers and all persons there haunting and resorting; within the metropolitan police district, the commissioners of police may authorize the superinten-dent of the police to search. The statute 16 & 17 Vict. c. 119, does not create any offence whereunder the mere resorters can be punished; in fact, by first speaking of them in the preamble as improvident persons, it shows, by sect. 6, that the policy of the Act is to protect such persons, and not to treat them as *participes criminis*. The Act, however, by sect. 2, has declared such a house to be a common gaming house within the statute 8 & 9 Vict. c. 109, and such persons might be dealt with as resorters to a common gaming house. There are no pro-visions in this Act against obstructing the officers in executing the search warrant; but if the place be deemed a common gaming house within the earlier statute, it is submitted that, as such, the provisions of the statute, 17 & 18 Vict. c. 38, would apply to that par-ticular species of gaming house as well as to any other.

The statute 16 & 17 Vict. c. 119, does not directly Witnesses. provide for the giving of evidence by persons found on

the premises, as was done in sect. 9 of the statute 8 & 9
Vict. c. 109, the provisions whereof were supplemented
by those of sect. 5 of the statute 17 & 18 Vict. c. 38.
As the statute created no specific offence, and did not
render such persons liable even to be bound by recognizances, it may have been thought unnecessary to provide an indemnity. As a matter of practice, people,
whose names are found in the books of the betting
house, are commonly served with subpœnas to give evidence. Men sending deposits to a bookmaker are aware
of the unpleasant chance of future publicity, and, in
order to evade it, not unfrequently use another person's
name. It ought to be an offence thus to involve an
innocent person in annoyance and loss of time.

Appeal, cer-
tiorari.

The Act contains a section which gives a right of
appeal from a summary conviction. That section (13)
and the sections relating to objections on matters of
form, and to the removal of process by certiorari, and
to distress on an informal process, and to tender of
amends and limitations of actions, are analogous to the
corresponding sections in the Gaming House Acts.

Order for
destruction of
books.

In an unreported case (g), the justices, after convicting a defendant of one of the major offences, made
an order for the destruction of his books, which had
been seized on executing the search warrant. The
defendant obtained a rule for an order nisi calling
on the justices to show cause why a writ of certiorari
should not issue directing them to bring up their
order for the purpose of being quashed. The justices relied on the 25th section of the statute, but it
was determined that that section, of course, did not

(g) *Moore and others* v. *Wilcox and others*, 1889, a decision of
Coleridge, L. C. J., and Bowen, L. J.

apply for the protection of order made without jurisdiction, and that the order in question was made without
jurisdiction; for, whilst under the 11th section of the
Betting House Act the books and documents were
properly before the magistrates, yet assuming that that
section could be combined with the 8th section of the
8 & 9 Vict. c. 109, the latter section only extended to
" cards, dice, &c., or other instruments of gaming," and
did not include such books and documents.

This statute extended to Ireland, but did not extend Statute
applied to
to Scotland, and hence, subsequently arose the occasion England and
Ireland only.
for the passing of Anderson's Act (37 Vict. c. 15).

The principal procedural matters are discussed in Procedure.
Chapter XI. But attention may again be called to the
case of *Blake* v. *Beech* (*h*). In that case, pursuant to the
powers of section 11 of the Act 16 & 17 Vict. c. 119, a
search warrant had been issued and executed; the house
searched was therein stated to be suspected of being
used as a common gaming house within the meaning of
the statute 8 & 9 Vict. c. 109; the information was to
the same effect. The appellant, however, was subsequently charged under the 3rd section of the statute
16 & 17 Vict. c. 119, for that he " on the 17th day of
October, 1875, at the borough aforesaid, being the person having the management of a room in a certain house
called the 'Angel,' situate, &c., did use such room for
the purpose of betting with persons resorting thereto
upon certain events and contingencies relating to certain
horse races, contrary," &c. (*i*). Before the magistrates

(*h*) *Blake* v. *Beech*, 1 Ex. Div. 320; 45 L. J. M. C. 111; 34
L. T. N. S. 764; 4 J. P. 678.

(*i*) The charge should have stopped at the words " resorting
thereto," that is, the complete offence; the additional words are

it was contended that, after the issue of the search
warrant, an information ought to have been laid, and
that a summons embodying the substance of such information ought to have been delivered to the appellant.
But the justices, whilst they were of opinion that it
was due to the defendant to have the information, did
not think it was sufficient ground for a discharge. The
judgment of Cleasby, B., with whom Grove, J., agreed,
turned on the point that the only information was that on
which the warrant was issued under 8 & 9 Vict. c. 109,
s. 3, namely, for keeping a common gaming house; but
the charge made when the defendant was brought up
was a charge which could not be made under 8 & 9 Vict.
c. 109, and it was made under 16 & 17 Vict. c. 119;
this made the proceedings irregular. It was also held,
that the sections of the Act, other than section 11,
showed that it was not intended by that section to
introduce an exceptional procedure of having a man put
on his trial without any previous notice: "it is an
important section, because, as the purposes for which the
house, &c., was used would be difficult of proof, and the
person managing the house not known, it enables the
magistrate to have the person found there brought up so
as to know who ought to be charged" (*l*).

Questions
arising out of
the foregoing
offences.

    The Act, unlike the Gaming House Act, does not
state what evidence shall suffice to support the offences.
The elements are, first, a place within the meaning of
the Act, and, secondly, a user for one or other of the

"Place"
cannot be
separated
from "user."

forbidden purposes. It is difficult to say to what extent
these two elements are severable. If the term "place"
means any *locus*, which could be used for either of the

---

frequently added, but they should be omitted when charging a
using for the first purpose.

(*l*) *Anderson* v. *Hume*, 46 J. P. 825.

mentioned purposes, then the two elements are not distinct. The question whether or not a given *locus* is a place within the meaning of the Act, is a question of fact which must depend on all the circumstances; similarly, the question whether there has been a user within the Act, is a question of fact which must also depend on all the circumstances of the case. The following cases will illustrate the inferences which have been drawn in particular instances, and will therefore serve as suggesting the probable inferences to be drawn from other sets of circumstances which may arise for adjudication.

In *Doggett* v. *Catterns* (m), the plaintiff sued the defendant in an action for money had and received by the defendant to the use of the plaintiff; the defendant pleaded that the money alleged to have been had and received by the defendant for the use of the plaintiff, was money deposited by the plaintiff with the defendant under a contract by way of wagering and gaming and illegal betting on horse races. The plaintiff argued that his right to recover was none the less owing to the operation of the 5th section of the statute. The circumstances under which the deposits had been made were as follows:—The defendant was in the habit of standing at a table placed under a tree in Hyde Park for the purpose of making bets with persons who resorted thereto, and of receiving deposits from the resorters. The Court of Common Pleas decided that, as the defendant was carrying on the trade of betting, he was using a "place" within the Act, and that the plaintiff was entitled to recover. The defendant appealed. It will be seen that, granting the illegality, the plaintiff was

Doggett v. *Catterns.*

Table in Hyde Park.

(m) *Doggett* v. *Catterns*, 19 C. B. N. S. 765; 34 L. J. C. P. 159; 11 Jur. N. S. 243; 12 L. T. 355; 13 W. R. 390.

alone entitled to recover (if at all) under the 5th section,
that is, by showing that the defendant was "such person"
as is therein mentioned.   On appeal, Crompton, J., held
that those words, " such person," in section 5, mean " any
person being the owner or occupier of any place," as
specified in section 4, and do not include a person using
a place of which he was neither the owner nor the occupier.   Pollock, C. B., with reference to the question at
issue, said that the *locus in quo* to be a place must be
capable of having an owner or occupier.   He added that
the fact of its being an open place without any house,
office, or room, would not alone prevent it from being a
place within the statute. - With this judgment Blackburn, J., and Channel, B., agreed.   Bramwell, J., based
his judgment on the ground that places to be within

*Decision con-
sidered.*

the statute must be ascertained places of resort.   This
case was considered by Hawkins, J., in *Reg.* v. *Preedie* (n) ;
the learned judge said the case had often been cited as
deciding that a man day after day, at a table placed
under a clump of trees in Hyde Park, carrying on his
business of betting, receiving money in advance on bets
on horse races, could not be convicted under section 3.
But the learned judge points out the consideration
advanced above, that the case turned on section 5,
involving section 4.   He adds : " For my own part, I
think it is not essential to a place within section 3 that
it should have an occupier, or that the person who uses
it for the illegal purpose should have permission to do
so from either the owner or occupier."

*Shaw v.
Morley.*

In the case of *Shaw* v. *Morley* (o), the appellant had
been convicted of " having the care and management of

(n) *R.* v. *Preedie*, 17 Cox, C. C. 433.

(o) *Shaw* v. *Morley*, L. R. 3 Ex. 137 ; 37 L. J. M. C. 105 ; 19
L. T. 15 ; 16 W. R. 763.

and assisting in conducting the business of an office and place at Doncaster, then and there opened, kept, and used for the purpose of betting with persons resorting thereto." The town council of Doncaster were owners of Doncaster Town Moor, where the Doncaster races were run; at various times race stands had been built on a portion of the ground fronting the racecourse, which was inclosed by iron railings, and was called the "inclosure," and to the grand stand and inclosure the public were admitted by guinea tickets during the four days of the September meeting. Along the east end of the inclosure, outside it, and at a distance of about six feet from the iron railing which inclosed it, ran a permanent wooden palisade, forming with the iron railing a space of about forty-four yards long and six feet wide. In 1867 this space was let to William Nicholl for the meeting. He divided it by partitions, and in each division a wooden structure of five feet high was erected, fronting both ways, the iron railing being on one side, the wooden palisade on the other. The structure, of which the appellant had the care and management, was covered with green baize, and had boards used as desks fronting each way; a man sat at each desk, who acted as clerk and recorded the proceedings in the book lying on the desk before him. Upon this structure was a board fronting both ways, bearing the words "William Nicholl, of Nottingham," and papers, partly printed and partly written, with the names of races, horses, and betting prices. The betting lists so exhibited had on them the odds for and against each horse in each race upon which William Nicholl, the proprietor of the structure, was prepared to bet. In respect of his care of the said structure, so used, the appellant was convicted, and appealed. For the appellant it was

Offices in an inclosure at a racecourse.

O.   T

contended that the Act did not apply to racecourses, and
that such a temporary roofless structure was not within

Absence of roof immaterial.
the Act.   But Kelly, C. B., said, "It is no matter
whether there is a roof or none, or whether the structure
is movable or fastened to the earth : it is clearly an
office within the Act. Then, was the business conducted
by the appellant the business prohibited by the Act ?
The preamble shows that it is within the intent of the
Act ; for the mischief recited is exactly gaming of the
description which was here conducted by the appellant,
carried on by means of an office."   Martin, B., in the
course of his judgment, said " the structure was both an
office and a place."   Pigott, B., whilst admitting that
the mischief chiefly aimed at was the establishment of
betting houses in towns, said, "fortunately, the language is large enough to hit those who are attempting
to evade its provisions by plying their trade upon a
racecourse."

Bows v. Fenwick.
In the case of *Bows* v. *Fenwick* (*p*), the appellant was
convicted that he, being the occupier of a certain place,
to wit, a standing on a certain racecourse, unlawfully
used the said standing for the purpose of betting with
persons resorting thereto. The facts were as follows :—

Umbrella fastened to ground.
The defendant was on the racecourse at Chester, standing on a stool about two feet six inches high, over which
was a large umbrella, similar to a carriage umbrella,
capable of covering several persons, the stock being
made in joints like that of a sweep's brush, so as to be
taken in pieces, and was fastened in the ground with a
spike. The umbrella, when opened, was seven or eight
feet high. It was a showery day, but the umbrella was
kept up, rain or dry. On the umbrella was painted, in

(*p*) *Bows* v. *Fenwick*, L. R. 9 C. P. 339 ; 43 L. J. M. C. 107 ;
30 L. T. 524 ; 22 W. R. 804.

large letters, " G. Bows, Victoria Club, Leeds." There
was also a card exhibited, on which were the words,
" We pay all bets first past the post." The defendant
was calling out, offering to make bets; and he was seen
to make several bets, and, at such time, to receive deposits of money, and for which he gave tickets. The
question raised by the case stated was whether the stool
and umbrella used as aforesaid by the defendant did
constitute a "place" within the terms of the Act. Lord
Coleridge, C. J., said : "It is plain that the appellant
was (provided the stool and umbrella constituted an
office, room, or place within the meaning of the Act)
publicly using them for a purpose prohibited by the
Act. The only question raised before us was, whether
or not they did constitute an office, room, or other place.
Now, the thing described clearly was not a house or a
room. Was it an office or other place ?. Possibly it
might be said to be in some sense an office ; but I am
of opinion that, at all events, it was a 'place.' It was
an ascertained spot, where the appellant, for the time at
least, carried on the business of betting with all persons
·who might resort thither for that purpose. The card,
connected with the umbrella and the inscription upon it,
clearly indicated a fixed and ascertained place used by
the appellant for a purpose prohibited by the Act."
Lord Coleridge, after stating that the Act, being an The Act to be construed strictly.
interference with the liberties of the subject, must be
construed strictly, held that the case was on all fours
with *Shaw* v. *Morley.* He added: "There is a sufficient
fixity of the structure, by means of the spiked umbrella,
to bring the case within the words of the Act, and it is
clearly within the mischief of the Act." Brett, J., said :
" It would seem that the kind of gaming prohibited is
the opening and keeping a place for the purpose of

gaming or betting with persons resorting thereto—a
fixed place to which all persons may resort. I agree
that it is necessary that it should be a fixed place,
Place must be   whether on a racecourse or elsewhere. . . . The place
fixed and
ascertained.   used need not be a house, office, or room, but that it
must be a fixed and ascertained place. Now, was this
a fixed place ? It was a place selected and fixed upon
by the appellant for persons who desired to deal with
him to resort to. . . . The appellant goes there with a
stool, and a thing which probably is not an umbrella,
but is more like an open tent. He takes it, not to
shelter him from the rain, but to be a fixed place. The
material part of the statement is that, having fixed this
umbrella or tent into the ground, with his name painted
on it, and a reference to a club at Leeds, he exhibits a
card with these words, ' We pay all bets first past the
post,' meaning obviously, we pay here ; or, in other
words, if the holders of tickets will resort to or come
under this umbrella, they will be paid, if winners. The
umbrella was intended as a fixed place for persons
desirous of making bets to resort to, and was clearly a
place within the contemplation of the Act, as inter-
preted by this Court, and by the Exchequer Chamber
in *Doggett* v. *Catterns*." Denman, J., concurred, and
added : " It was enough that there was a piece of
ground ascertained and appropriated by the appellant
for carrying on his proceedings."

These two cases of *Shaw* v. *Morley* (q), and *Bows* v. *Fenwick* (r), are of much importance with regard to betting
on racecourses. But whilst the facts therein respectively

  (q) *Shaw* v. *Morley*, L. R. 3 Ex. 137; 37 L. J. M. C. 105; 19
L. T. 15; 16 W. R. 763.
  (r) *Bows* v. *Fenwick*, L. R. 9 C. P. 339; 43 L. J. M. C. 107;
30 L. T. 524; 22 W. R. 804.

illustrate what will suffice to support a conviction, the false inference must not be drawn that no conviction could be obtained in the absence of the fixed umbrella and placard, as in the later case, or in the absence of a structure, as in the former case. The principle seems to be that the *locus* must be so fixed and ascertained, that persons may resort thereto for the purpose of betting with a person there carrying on the business of betting. In the two foregoing cases, the defendants adopted particular means for fixing and advertising the place.

In the case of *Eastwood* v. *Miller* (s), the appellant *Eastwood* v *Miller*. was charged that he did unlawfully use a certain place, A field. to wit, a field, for the purpose of betting on a certain pigeon-shooting match for money, contrary to 16 & 17 Vict. c. 119, s. 3. The facts were as follows:—The appellant was the occupier of the borough park ground; on payment, people were admitted to the grounds, which were inclosed, and were of over three acres in extent. A number of people were there, and amongst them two bookmakers, with books in their hands, shouting out, "Twenty to one on the match," being a certain pigeon-shooting match then and there to be held. Bets with the bookmakers prior to the match, and during the course of the match, were proved to have been made by the public. The appellant was convicted, and, on the appeal, raised two questions: first, whether the ground was used or permitted to be used by the appellant for the purposes of betting; secondly, whether the ground was a "place" within the meaning of the Act. Lush, J.: "It could hardly be contended that grounds uncovered cannot be a 'place' within the meaning of the

(s) *Eastwood* v. *Miller*, L. R. 9 Q. B. 440; 43 L. J. M. C. 139; 30 L. T. 716; 22 W. R. 799; 38 J. P. 647.

Act. I see no reason whatever, from the framing of
the Act, to hold that there cannot be a 'place' within
the meaning of the Act unless it is a structure of some
kind—a building or a tent. An inclosed area, though
uncovered, might as well be a 'place' within the Act as
a place either covered with canvas as a tent, or a light
structure as a building. It is an inclosed place, occupied exclusively by the appellant, and is therefore
within the language and intent of the Act. The fact
that it is a large inclosure cannot affect the question.
Whether it is a quarter, a half acre, or three acres,
cannot affect the question, if it is a 'place' occupied
and inclosed within the meaning of the Act, to which
persons were admitted by the sufferance of the occupier." Archibald, J.: "I think we should fall very far
short in carrying out the object of this Act if we were
to hold that it was necessary that there should be a
room, or house, or office, or erection of some kind, in
order to its being a 'place' within the meaning of the
Act. There may be a 'place,' although it is in the
open air; there may be a 'place' without any kind of
erection; and, of course, it must depend on the circumstances of each particular case whether it is brought
within the description of 'place.' Upon the facts, as
they appear here, the magistrates were justified in holding that this was a 'place.' The area is three or four
acres in extent. The 'place' is one inclosed, having a
gateway. Persons were admitted by ticket, and on
payment for a price of entrance. The appellant is the
occupier of this inclosed land, and received money from
the persons for admission into it. I think, under these
circumstances, it cannot be doubted that this was a
'place' within the meaning of the Act."

It is, perhaps, unfortunate that in this case of *East-*

wood v. *Miller*, neither *Shaw* v. *Morley*, nor *Bows* v. *Fenwick*, were cited to, or referred to by, the Court. The judgments were much influenced by *Doggett* v. *Catterns*, and the clear distinction between the facts in the two cases—in the former no occupier, in the latter an inclosed area with an occupier. It will be seen hereafter that it is not necessary that the "place" should have an occupier, as in *Eastwood* v. *Miller*. The decision, however, is that an inclosed area, to which admission is obtained by payment, may be a "place" within the statute. The conviction of the appellant that he did wilfully and knowingly permit the place to be used by persons for the purpose of betting, whilst it affords an illustration of what evidence did suffice, before that particular bench of magistrates, to support a conviction for wilfully and knowingly permitting, further involves the conclusion that the bookmakers were committing by their acts an offence against the Act, namely, an illegal user of the place.

In the case of *Haigh* v. *The Town Council of Sheffield* (t), the appellant was charged that he being the occupier of a certain place, to wit, Hyde Park Cricket Ground, situate, &c., unlawfully, knowingly, and wilfully, did permit the said place to be used by George Trickett and others for the purpose of betting with persons resorting thereto. The appellant occupied, as tenant, a house together with an inclosed piece of ground adjoining called Hyde Park Cricket Ground, used for cricket, foot racing, and other games and sports. On the day named in the summons foot racing took place in the grounds to which persons were admitted on payment of sixpence. Within the grounds, but outside the space

Haigh v. The Town Council of Sheffield.

A cricket ground.

(t) *Haigh* v. *The Town Council of Sheffield*, L. R. 10 Q. B. 102; 44 L. J. M. C. 17; 31 L. T. 536; 23 W. R. 547.

0
0

280   THE LAW OF GAMBLING.

reserved for the runners, and amongst the spectators, some fifteen or twenty persons, being clearly professional bettors (George Trickett being one of them), stood on chairs and stools in different spots, with books in their hands, calling out the odds on the various runners, and betting with different persons. A man behind each of the bettors recorded the bets in a book. The persons betting paid money (1s. each) and received a ticket. A large number of persons assembled in the grounds, to the number of upwards of 10,000. Although there was nothing to show the terms on which Trickett and the other professional bettors were admitted to the grounds, the evidence satisfied the magistrate that the appellant knew of what was going on, and took no steps to prevent it, and that he might have prevented it had he so minded. On such evidence the magistrate convicted the appellant. Blackburn, J., held, after all the previous cases had been cited, that the grounds were a "place" within the Act; for "it was completely under the control of the appellant just as much as an ordinary skittle ground is, and it is immaterial that it was not covered over." Mellor, J., said, "As to this not being a 'place,' I think that point quite unarguable," and he thus dealt with the argument that the word "place" in the Act must be construed *ejusdem generis* (*u*): "We must first look at the object of the Act, and we must also bear in mind that every word in succession in this enactment is larger in its meaning than the preceding word, until at last we come to 'other place,' so that assuming the rule of construction as to *ejusdem generis* to be applicable, we are not bound by the strict rule, or to give any narrow interpretation to the word 'place.'"

"Place" *ejusdem generis*, construction how far applicable.

(*u*) See also Grove, J., in *Gallaway* v. *Maries*, 8 Q. B. D. 275; 51 L. J. M. C. 53; 45 L. T. 763; 30 W. R. 151; 46 J. P. 326.

It was hardly argued that if the *locus in quo* was a place, and if user on one occasion constituted user within the Act, that what the bookmakers were doing was not illegal; but the point advanced for the appellant was that he had not knowingly and wilfully permitted the illegal user. But the Court held that the bookmakers were illegally using the place, and, on the evidence, might be held habitually to have used the place, if that were necessary, and that the occupier was within the principle that a man must be taken impliedly to be answerable for what he knows to be the ordinary consequence of what he expressly permits (*x*). It will have been noticed that in neither of the two last-mentioned cases were the bookmakers using any particular spot, fixed, as in *Bows* v. *Fenwick*, by the umbrella, or by the structure in *Shaw* v. *Morley*; they were simply using the inclosures.

In the case of *Gallaway* v. *Maries* (*y*), the respondent on the appeal had been charged with using a place for the purpose of betting with persons resorting thereto. The following facts were proved or admitted :—A race meeting was held in Four Oaks Park, a private park belonging to the Four Oaks Park Company, admission thereto being by payment. The respondent and John Schester paid for admission to the park and to the grand stand in the park, and during the races were in a railed inclosure attached to the stand, which inclosure was opened to persons admitted to the grand stand and was commonly called and known as the ring. Whilst in the inclosure Schester stood upon a small wooden box, which was not in any way attached to the ground,

Implication of owner, &c.

Gallaway v. Maries.

Wooden box in a railed inclosure on a racecourse.

(*x*) *R.* v. *Moore*, 3 B. & Ad. 184.

(*y*) *Gallaway* v. *Maries*, 8 Q. B. D. 275 ; 51 L. J. M. C. 53 ; 45 L. T. 763 ; 30 W. R. 151 ; 46 J. P. 326.

and he and the respondent, who were in company and
acting together, were calling out in the inclosure and
were offering to make, and they made, ready money
bets with other persons on some of the races. Schester
received the money for the bets made, and the respondent booked the same; they stood together in one place
within the inclosure during the races. The justices
were of the opinion that the inclosure was not a "place"
within the meaning of the Act, and that the box did
not constitute such a place. On a case stated, the
question was whether the respondent was, on the facts,
within the 3rd section of the Act. The respondent and
his companion had this small wooden box, not attached
to the ground, but defining a certain spot in a certain
limited railed inclosure, and there standing on and at
the box, they advertised by their shouts their willingness
to bet, and took and made bets, and remained in the
same spot during the races. Grove and Lopes, JJ.,
were of opinion that they were within the Act. Mr.
Justice Grove examined the case of *Bows* v. *Fenwick*,
and said that the judgment was based on two grounds:
first, that the appellant in that case was using an ascertained spot for his business of betting; and, secondly,
that the card and umbrella indicated a fixed and
ascertained place. He said, "I think the ground of
the judgment was that the place was fixed, and the
umbrella was only considered as indicating a place to
the public around. The question is, whether the Court
would have come to the same conclusion, if the umbrella
had been wanting and the man had used some other
means of attracting the public. I am inclined to think
that the more important consideration is the fixity of
the place, not, indeed, absolute fixity, as in the case of
fixtures, but in the sense of the "place" being and

Important consideration: the fixity.

remaining the same for a considerable time, long enough for the betting public to know where persons offering or willing to make bets might be found. . . . Coupling the judgment in *Shaw* v. *Morley* with the decision in *Bows* v. *Fenwick*, it would appear that the umbrella, being a mere advertisement, made no difference, but might be regarded only as indicating the fixed and ascertained place." The learned judge concludes, "Therefore I think all the cases show that a 'place,' to be within the statutes, must be a fixed ascertained place, occupied or used so far permanently that people may know that there is a person who stands in a particular spot indicated by a certain definite mark with whom they may bet. I do not decide whether a person standing on a carriage step or in a circle where the turf was cut away, or where a little heap of stones was put down during the races, would be within the Act if he offered to bet there. But I am far from saying that he would not be so. Here, however, there was in my opinion, a place within the meaning of the Act."

In the case of *Eastwood* v. *Miller*, it did not appear that the bookmakers stood still in the crowd on definite spots, and in *Haigh* v. *The Town Council of Sheffield*, the chairs used by the bookmakers were movable ; so that it must not on the authorities be concluded that, if a man continually moves about in a prescribed, though possibly large, area, amongst the persons resorting to that area, he cannot be convicted of using such *locus in quo* for the purposes and in the manner prevented by the Act. But *ex necessitate*, by moving about in the area and by not using any method of advertising his object, he would render the proof of illegal user of the place exceedingly difficult though not impossible, and similarly this difficulty would be experienced on attempting to convict the owner or occupier of knowingly and wilfully permitting such illegal user.

Snow v. *Hill.*   In the case of *Snow* v. *Hill*(z), the appellant had been convicted of illegally using a certain field. The following are the facts:—On a certain date, dog races for prizes open for public competition, after entries made by the owners of the dogs, were held in an inclosed

Alleged illegal user of a field. field, about four acres in extent. The ground had been let for hire for the purposes of the race meeting to a committee, who carried out the arrangements for the racing, and the admission of the persons who resorted to the ground. The public were admitted to one portion of the field (which was divided by a rope from that part of the field on which the races were run) on payment of an entrance fee. The public had access also to another portion of the field, also divided by a rope from that part of the field on which the races were run, and forming one side of such field, of the length of about a hundred yards, and about seven yards in depth, on payment of a higher entrance fee. A great number of persons were present at the race meeting within both the reserved portions of the field, the appellant being in the latter. The appellant was seen to receive from, and pay money to, persons with whom he had been heard to make bets. He had no particular location on the reserved space, but during the afternoon freely moved about in the reserved ground. He carried no umbrella, had no box, stool, or satchel, nor any distinctive mark, and did not exhibit his name. The magistrates thought the facts brought the case within *Eastwood* v. *Miller* (a), where the occupier was

(z) *Snow* v. *Hill*, 14 Q. B. D. 588; 54 L. J. M. C. 95; 52 L. T. 859; 33 W. R. 475; 49 J. P. 440; 15 Cox, C. C. 737.

(a) *Eastwood* v. *Miller, ante,* p. 277.

convicted of an offence in that he kept the whole of some inclosed grounds for the purpose of betting. But on appeal, it was held that Snow did not keep or use any place for the purpose of betting with persons resorting thereto. "He was simply walking about the field, making bets with the other persons who were present, and we do not think that what he did came within the purview of the Act."

In the case of *Reg.* v. *Preedie* (*b*), Mr. Justice Hawkins said :—" In all cases it will be found that one essential requisite to the constitution of such a place is that it must be fixed and ascertained. It must, too, be a place to which, at the time when the offence is charged to have been committed, persons were resorting, though with what primary object they were so resorting is, in my judgment, immaterial ; the Act is silent on that point. The temptation to gamble by betting was what the Act was intended to check, and the temptation to bet would be equally held out by a professional betting man plying his avocation in a crowd of persons assembled for the most innocent purpose unconnected with sport, as it would be in a crowd gathered together to witness the sport of racing. It need not be inclosed within walls or fences, or bounded by any defined line. Furthermore, it may extend over a considerable area—even acres of ground. Were it otherwise, many racecourses might be pointed out upon which a betting man might with impunity carry on such operations as the Act was intended to suppress. It must not, however, be supposed that I intended to say that a place to come within the statute may be unlimited in its area ; on the contrary, I am of opinion that, though it may be

Marginal notes:
Conviction wrong owing to absence of proof of illegal user.

R. v. *Preedie.* "Place," essential requisite of, fixed and ascertained.

Intention of statute.

(*b*) *R.* v. *Preedie*, 17 Cox, C. C. p. 433.

bounded by no defined line, it must, nevertheless, be limited in extent to the area occupied by the persons congregated together and resorting to it, and to such a space carrying on his business there as a betting man, might fairly and reasonably be said to be doing so in the immediate presence of those so congregated together.

The question of place is one of fact.

Whether that which is charged as a place within section 3 satisfied those requirements is a question of fact, to be determined by the tribunal before whom the matter comes for adjudication." The learned judge then examines the authorities for the view that the

The "spot," construction not adopted.

"place" must be a fixed particular spot. He admits that in the judgments of Lord Coleridge, C. J., in *Bows* v. *Fenwick*, and of Grove, J., in *Gallaway* v. *Maries*, expressions are to be found which might be thought to indicate their opinions to be that the word "place" in the statute means some particular ascertained spot just sufficient for a man to stand or sit upon. "I can hardly think," he says, "these learned judges intended by their expressions to lay it down as law that nothing would satisfy the term 'place' unless it was some particular spot on which a person stood, or which was appropriated by him exclusively for his own use, as a stall, or a standing in a fair or a market would be, or that they meant to convey more than this,—that the place must be fixed and ascertained." In support of this view, and against the "spot" construction, he cites the cases of *Eastwood* v. *Miller*; *Haigh* v. *The Town Council of Sheffield*.

Conclusion as to what may be a "place."

On the balance of the authorities, the law appears to be that it is not necessary that the *locus in quo* should be a particular fixed spot of small area, but, as an abstract proposition, any inclosed area might be a "place." In the passages cited above from *Reg.* v.

Preedie (c), Mr. Justice Hawkins expresses views which lead to the conclusion that any *locus in quo*, for the time being occupied by a crowd of changing and indefinite configuration, might be a "place," provided that a betting man there carrying on his business might be said to be doing so in the immediate presence of persons so congregated together. The difficulty of the last view arises from the ambiguity of the terms "betting man" and "his business." If these terms denote a person who by his user and practice offends against the Act, then the idea of "place" is not elucidated, for it becomes any *locus in quo* which may be used in contravention of the Act.

The foregoing cases illustrate the practical impossi- "User." bility of dissevering the question of "place" from the question of "user." In the last-mentioned case of *Reg.* v. *Preedie*, Mr. Justice Hawkins discusses at length what constitutes a "user" within section 3. The legislature did not intend to make all betting illegal. "It is just as lawful now as it ever was for persons to bet together casually at any place, and as often as, and to any extent, they please." But, on the other hand, the mischief to which the Act was directed was expressed by Erle, C. J., in *Doggett* v. *Catterns* (d), "The habit of using a particular place by persons skilled in gambling and betting, for the purpose of luring the ignorant and improvident to the ruinous courses to which the vice of gambling too frequently leads." Hence, Hawkins, J., said, "for the purpose of checking that habit, it was Description of illegal user forbidden to any person to use any place for the purpose by Hawkins, of *systematically carrying on a business* of betting with or J.

(c) *R.* v. *Preedie*, 17 Cox, C. C. 433.
(d) *Doggett* v. *Catterns*, 19 C. B. N. S. 765; 34 L. J. C. P. 159; 11 Jur. N. S. 243; 12 L. T. 355; 13 W. R. 390.

receiving deposits from persons resorting thereto.　It is not the mere act of betting frequently, or with many persons; it is *the carrying on the business of betting* and *announcing such business* to those assembled and *inviting the persons* resorting to the place to bet with such

Such description considered.

bettors which the law was intended to suppress."　The preamble to the Act in part supports this idea of business, and further, the persons who are liable under the Act include any person having the care or management or in any manner conducting the business.　But the Act does not indicate what evidence shall suffice to establish the carrying on of such a business.　A man in an inclosure to which a number of persons are resorting makes with such persons a large number of bets; either this man makes his living by his betting or amuses himself thereby, and in each case his object and desire is the acquisition of gain by speculation.　It is difficult to think that the same acts, namely, making the same bets with the same persons could constitute an offence in the case of "the well-known professional betting man," and not in the case of the amateur; the only possible distinction in the two cases appears to be that the former by his presence in the inclosure might, in the absence of any further overt act, be held impliedly to announce his business and to solicit customers.　In the case of *Snow* v. *Hill* (e), the appellant had merely conducted himself as one of the public, walking about making promiscuous bets with those whom he chanced to meet.　It was held that he himself was merely one of the persons resorting thereto; there was no proof that he was a professional bettor at all.　But even if he had been a professional bettor, the onus of proving that, on the

(e) *Snow* v. *Hill*, 14 Q. B. D. 588; 54 L. J. M. C. 95; 52 L. T. 859; 33 W. R. 475; 49 J. P. 440; 15 Cox, C. C. 737.

occasion in question he was infringing the Act would
lie on the prosecution, and that onus would not be discharged in the absence of proof that he was doing more
than appeared in the case of *Snow* v. *Hill* (f). To support
a conviction there should be in the case of any man,
professional or amateur, proof of some external manifestation of the carrying on of a business by announcing
it, and by explicit invitation.

The position, then, of bookmakers, in the view of the Bookmakers
law as determined by the Act and the authorities cited at race meetings.
supra, is one of much difficulty. The Act does not
recognize bookmakers, and there is no definition of the
term. The attempt to define would at once reveal the
difficulty of distinguishing such a one from the casual
bettor; some arbitrary line would have to be drawn.
It is certain that a man may make a book, *i.e.*, enter
into a considerable number of wagering contracts on a
given event, without committing an offence; for example, if, being a member of the Albert Club, Limited,
he made his book on the club premises with other members of the club. If, instead of making these same bets
on the club premises, he does so in some place such as
Tattersall's Ring at Newmarket, could it be said that
he would thereby be committing an offence? It is
submitted not. Yet the ring is a place, and there is a
user for the purpose of making a book with a class
of persons resorting thereto, namely, members of the
club. If the particular bond of common membership
of a club be dissolved, and if that of ordinary social in-
timacy be substituted, then, on such facts, A. would use
the ring (place) for the purpose of betting (making a
number of bets) with that class of persons resorting thereto

(*f*) *Snow* v. *Hill*, 14 Q. B. D. 588; 54 L. J. M. C. 95; 52 L.
T. 859; 33 W. R. 475; 49 J. P. 440; 15 Cox, C. C. 737.

G.   U

who are his friends. It would not seem that A. is committing an offence; nevertheless he would be using the place for the purpose of betting with some of the persons resorting thereto. The motive of the man who makes the book is, in every case, the desire of gain by speculation. No doubt, in neither of the non-criminal instances given above does the maker of the book consider whether those who wager with him are provident or not; he, chiefly, at any rate, concerns himself with the question whether they can pay, and is guided in the one instance by the fact of membership of the club and in the other by personal friendship. The practical conclusion from the above, then, is that a man, say a well-known bookmaker, a member of Tattersall's, can attend a race meeting and make his books amongst his co-members without doing any illegal act; though he would be well advised not to receive any deposits in advance for fear lest he should bring himself within the second illegal purpose. But, on the other hand, a man may make a book under circumstances which involve criminal liability. A bookmaker enters the 5s. ring at Newmarket, and more or less obtrusively announces his willingness to make a book on an event with any of the people resorting to such ring who can pay in advance. It would be idle for him to contend that the ring could not possibly be a "place;" and if the prosecution proved that the defendant made a large number of bets with a number of the resorters, who offered him deposits, and that he by the name on his satchel induced them so to bet, and offered facilities for so doing, and solicited them on that behalf, he could be properly convicted on the authorities of the offence of illegally using a place.

Resorters and resorting.   Apart from the inseparable questions of place and user, there have been decisions on that element of the

user denoted by the word *resorting*. In the case of
R. v. *Brown* (*f*), the defendant was indicted at quarter
sessions for using a house for the purpose of betting
with persons resorting thereto. The only evidence left
to the jury in support of this count was proof of the
receipt of a large number of telegrams and letters
giving directions as to bets. The Recorder ruled that
the persons, by so sending messages and telegrams, were
resorting to the house. But the Court of Crown Cases
Reserved was unanimously of opinion that there must
be actual physical resorting and haunting, and that a
man could not be said to resort to several places at one
and the same time.

The Act, whilst it thus aims at physical resorting, *The person
further contemplates that not only must there be such *using to be
*contrasted
resorters, but there must also be a person using the *with the
*resorters.
same for the illegal purpose. In the case of *Oldham* v.
Ramsden (*g*), the defendant had employed the plaintiff,
a member of a club called the Ellesmere Club, to make
bets on his behalf. The plaintiff did so by laying
wagers with another member of the club, and, after
such wagers had been lost, the plaintiff paid the amount.
The defendant refused to recoup him; hence the action.
The defendant, aware of his then liability, if the wager
was simply void, pleaded that the plaintiff had knowingly paid the money, and the same was received by or
on behalf of the owner, occupier, or keeper of a place
used for the purpose of betting with persons resorting
thereto. If the defendant had established this plea, the
payment by the plaintiff would have been tainted by
illegality. The sole evidence in support of the plea

(*f*) *R.* v. *Brown,* see *ante,* p. 237, where the indictment is
set out.
  (*g*) *Oldham* v. *Ramsden,* 44 L. J. C. P. 309; 32 L. T. 825.

The Ellesmere
Club.

was : That the Ellesmere Club was a limited company, with 1,400 to 1,500 members; the club premises were situate in a certain street; one room in the club was set aside for betting, where members made bets one with the other, though no non-members made bets on the premises. It was held that this evidence showed that the place was a club, an ordinary club at which bets were made. In the course of the argument, the fact was pressed on the Court that a number of bets were made on the premises. Grove, J., asked how the person using the same was distinguished from the persons resorting thereto?

Downes v.
Johnson.
The Albert
Club.

In the Albert Club case, which has already been referred to (*h*), it was proved : that on the premises there was a club room, which was used exclusively by the members of the club; that individual members had no prescribed places or pitches in the club room, and that no member could be accurately described as " holding a bag" against all comers; that certain members of the club usually laid odds against horses running in horse races ; that certain of the members backed horses so running, but frequently the respective positions were reversed, when the layers became backers, and *vice versâ;* that there was a tape machine in the club room, inclosed by a rail, within which a servant of the club stood during racing hours, and called out to the members the names of horses running, as they came up on the tape machine, together with the starting prices of the horses, as shown by the machine, and thereupon the members of the club made bets upon horses, either backing or laying odds against them respectively. The respondent to the appeal, on the days mentioned in the information, made numerous bets with members of the club, as shown

(*h*) *Downes* v. *Johnson*, (1895) 2 Q. B. 203; 64 L. J. M. C. 238.

by his betting book and eight settling books. On the
club premises were obtainable newspapers, time tables,
&c., and refreshments ; there was also a billiard table.
The attempt was unsuccessfully made to prove that non-
members of the club were admitted into the lobby of the
club, and that the respondent, on being called out, made
bets with them within the lobby.   Hence, in this case,
there was no distinction between the persons resorting
and the owners or occupiers.   On behalf of the appellant, it was contended that the user by Johnson was a
using of the premises for the purpose of carrying on his
business of betting systematically with persons resorting
thereto ; if such user was not an offence, then it would
follow, it was argued, that in a club of 1,000 members,
one member might lay odds with the other 999 every
day in the year.   Mr. Justice Wright, in the course of
the argument, put this case :—Twelve friends hire a
room one hour a day for the exclusive purpose of betting
inter se.   Mr. Poland, Q.C., admitted that such user was
probably not illegal, and contended that it was a question of degree, not being illegal unless, in fact, it
amounted to the carrying on of a business.   It was
held that the " resorters " must be strangers, as contradistinguished from members of the club.   Mr. Justice
Grantham, after referring to the preamble of the Act,
said : " If a person joined a club of this kind manifestly
for the purpose of meeting other members, it must be
assumed that he knew something about betting, and
that he was not one of those imprudent persons aimed
at by this statute.   It might be that he went to his
club to learn something. . . . The members were in the
same category, namely, people desirous of finding out
about betting and horses.   Mr. Poland said it was a
question of degree.   If not illegal for twelve, why for

*Bond fide
clubs for the
promotion of
betting.*

twenty or one hundred? Where is the line to be drawn? It is wholly legal or wholly illegal." Mr. Justice Wright concurred. But he pointed out that the club was a *bonâ fide* institution, established some thirty years; it was not a mere blind for carrying on the trade or business of betting by any proprietor or anyone else; it was not merely a club into which any solvent person could obtain admission for the purpose of betting.

On the one hand, then, the principle of the decision of *Downes* v. *Johnson* would apply to Tattersall's, *et hoc genus omne;* but on the other, if the club were a mere disguise to enable a man to carry on the business of betting with "resorters," then such a man and the owner or occupier would be within the reservation pointed out by Mr. Justice Wright.

Where club a mere disguise.

A good instance of a typical offence against the Act is afforded by the case of *Wright* v. *Clarke* (*i*). Ostensibly the business was that of a turf commission agent. Wright advertised freely in the newspapers that he, as agent, would execute commissions on all races at the best price. He desired that business should be conducted solely through the post. He stipulated for cash in advance in respect of all commissions. His remuneration purported to be five per cent. on winnings. His advertisements were answered by the police. Wright acknowledged their instructions, and sent a cheque for the winnings, less commission. A search warrant was obtained, and the documents and books showed that he was carrying on an enormous business. He was charged that he, being the occupier of a certain house and office, to wit, &c., and being a person using the same, did unlawfully keep and use the same for the purpose of

Wright v. Clarke.
Typical case of alleged business of agent.

(*i*) *Wright* v. *Clarke*, 34 J. P. 661.

receiving money on an undertaking to pay money on contingencies relating to horse racing. He was convicted, and thereupon appealed. It was argued that no one resorted to the house with whom he made bets, and, in fact, that he never acted as principal: this ground of contention appeared to be valid. But, Blackburn, J., said Wright was responsible for the payment of the bets, and that an implied undertaking would suffice to bring the case within the statute, and on the facts there could be no doubt that the depositors understood that the winnings would be paid by Wright. Hence Wright failed in his contention that the vouchers which he sent on receipt of the deposits did not amount to an undertaking to pay money on a bet, and were no more than advice as to the mode of obtaining payment.

This case shows that a commission agent who receives money in advance will be held criminally liable in respect of the implied promise. However, it would appear that if such a man did not receive deposits in advance, he would not be within the Act. It may seem paradoxical that if he affords temptation to the public to gamble, he may do so provided he encourages them or gives them facilities for cheating him as well. Practically, however, such a proviso stops the promiscuous business. No such practical justification can be alleged in connection with the distinction of resorting physically and of sending messages for the purposes of betting. Commission agents with responsible customers receive instructions by letter or telegram, and execute the same by wagering at their clubs: thus, in fact, under the present condition of the law, the betting of the country is in a large measure conducted.

In the above case of *Wright* v. *Clarke*, the deposits were received on the premises. Obviously, if one place

Immunity of agent who does not receive deposits in advance.

Where the receipt must be.

was used for receiving deposits, proof of that fact would not support a conviction for using another place for that purpose. A bookmaker might be convicted of using a box at a post office for that purpose; but it would be futile to prove that he did so in support of a charge in respect of some other premises. Similarly, it is submitted, if a bookmaker directed his clients to send their deposit to a bank, he could be charged with using a place, to wit, the bank, for the illegal purpose (*j*).

Bucket shops, whether within the Act. The existence of the places known as bucket-shops, and the common recognition of the fact that in them the unwary and improvident are frequently fleeced, renders the consideration of their legality a matter of some importance. If these places are illegal it is because the same are used for the purpose of betting with persons resorting thereto. In aid of such a charge is the fact that the two illegal purposes are distinct and severable; and again, such purpose need not be the sole purpose for which the place is used. But the preamble of the Act presents difficulty. It cannot be said that it is clear that such premises so used are not betting-houses within the meaning of the Act. Juries would be entitled to go behind the formal disguise of the transactions, even as in the cases of civil liabilities.

Gaming on licensed premises. Many of the charges under this Act have been in respect of the user of licensed premises (*k*). But it has been thought more convenient to group those cases together as is done hereafter (*l*).

Persons liable. The statute makes the owner or occupier, or person using the place, liable for his own acts. The person

(*j*) See *post, Davis* v. *Stephenson*, 24 Q. B. D. 529; 59 L. J. Q. B. 305; 62 L. T. 436; 38 W. R. 492.

(*k*) *R.* v. *Preedie*, 17 Cox, C. C. 433.

(*l*) Chap. XIV.

who uses the place may be liable if he do so with or
without the permission of any owner or occupier.

Again, liability attaches to a person who has the care Managers.
or management of, or in any manner assists in conducting the business. But the business in which the person
assists must be the unlawful business. In *R.* v. *Cook* (*m*)
the appellant was a manager of bicycle grounds. It
was held that as such manager of a lawful business, he
could not be liable for assisting, merely because some
part of the place was used for an illegal purpose without
his assistance or care. "The Act," said Hawkins, J.,
"was not intended to apply to any person having the
care or management of a lawful business who took no
share or part in any illegality there." Mr. Justice
Smith said the correct reading of the 3rd section was
not "any person having the care or management of
any place used for betting." "If it were," he continued, "any sweeper of the cricket ground might, as a
person assisting in the management of it, be liable if
persons made bets there" (*n*).

The owners and occupiers are liable for knowingly Owners or
and wilfully permitting the illegal user of a place by permitting.
any other person. This was the charge in the case of
Reg. v. *Godfrey and others* (the recent *Newmarket case*) (*o*).
In the first place, it appeared that the prosecution were
in some difficulty in proving that the stewards of the
Jockey Club (the defendants) were the occupiers; in

(*m*) *R.* v. *Cook*, 13 Q. B. D. 377 ; 51 L. T. 21 ; 32 W. R. 796 ;
48 J. P. 694.

(*n*) See also *Jenks* v. *Turpin*, 13 Q. B. D. 505 ; 53 L. J. M. C.
161 ; 50 L. T. 808 ; 49 J. P. 20 ; 15 Cox, C. C. 486 ; *Slatter* v.
Bailey, 37 J. P. 262.

(*o*) Full reports are to be found in the "Sportsman" and
"Sporting Life," 13th and 18th February, 1895. See *ante*,
p. 234.

fact, the Jockey Club was the occupier and the defendants were the managers on behalf of the Jockey Club (*p*), and, *quâ* such managership (*q*), would have been within the above decision of *R*. v. *Cook* (*r*) ; if the defendants were occupiers, such occupation arose in virtue of their being members and not stewards of the Jockey Club. But if this point be assumed against the defendants, the prosecution then had to discharge the onus of proving that the stewards as occupiers knowingly and wilfully permitted the illegal user of the place. This the magistrates found as a fact was not done. But *non sequitur* that another bench of magistrates would not on the same evidence have arrived at the

Owner or occupier answerable for consequences of his own acts.
contrary conclusion. In *Haigh* v. *The Town Council of Sheffield* (*s*), the principle was applied that a man must be taken impliedly to be answerable for what he knows to be the consequence of what he expressly permits. In that case the occupier permitted men who made a business of betting to frequent the inclosure and to stand on stools or chairs in different spots, and to announce their willingness to bet ; that is to say, the occupier had knowledge of these acts and did not prevent the same.

Illegal advertisements. 16 & 17 Vict. c. 119, s. 7. Offences.
Section 7 of 16 & 17 Vict. c. 119, was directed against the promotion of betting by means of advertisements, and enacted that "any person exhibiting or publishing, or causing to be exhibited or published, any placard, handbill, card, writing, sign, or advertisement, whereby it shall be made to appear that any house, office, room, or place, is opened, kept, or used, for the

---

(*p*) *Wood* v. *Leadbitter*, 13 M. & W. 838 ; 14 L. J. Ex. 161.

(*q*) See *ante*, p. 234.

(*r*) *R*. v. *Cook, ante*, pp. 260, 297.

(*s*) *Haigh* v. *The Town Council of Sheffield*, L. R. 10 Q. B. 102 ; 44 L. J. M. C. 17 ; 31 L. T. 536 ; 23 W. R. 547.

purpose of making bets or wagers in manner aforesaid, or for the purpose of exhibiting lists for betting, or with intent to induce any person to resort to such house, office, room, or place, for the purpose of making bets or wagers in manner aforesaid, or any person who, in behalf of the owner or occupier of any such house, office, room, or place, or person using the same, shall invite other persons to resort thereto for the purpose of making bets or wagers in manner aforesaid, shall, upon summary conviction before two justices of the peace, forfeit and pay a sum not exceeding 30*l.*, or be sent to prison for any time not exceeding two calendar months, with or without hard labour.

It will be seen that, by this section, the persons who are liable are those who "exhibit, or cause to be exhibited, any advertisement, that any house, office, room, or place, is opened, kept, or used :— What persons liable for advertising.

1. For the purpose of betting in manner aforesaid ;
2. For the purpose of exhibiting lists for betting ;
3. To induce any person to resort thereto for the purpose of betting ;

and also any person who, on behalf of the owner or person using any house, &c., shall invite any person to resort, for the purpose of betting.

This statute did not apply to Scotland. The result was that, as betting houses were not illegal in that country, the Scotch betting houses were largely advertised in England, and the business of betting was so carried on in safety. In 1874, however, the 37 & 38 Vict. c. 15 was passed, which extended the provisions of 16 & 17 Vict. c. 119 to Scotland, with some slight procedural exceptions, and further enacted that— 16 & 17 Vict. c. 119, extended to Scotland by 37 & 38 Vict. c. 15.

Where any letter, circular, telegram, placard, handbill, card, or advertisement is sent, exhibited, or published—

Advertising information with regard to wagers.

1. Whereby it is made to appear that any person, *either in the United Kingdom or elsewhere*, will, on application, give information or advice for the purpose of or with respect to any such bet or wager, or any such bet or contingency as is mentioned in the principal Act (16 & 17 Vict. c. 119), or will make, on behalf of any other person, any such bet or wager as is mentioned in the principal Act; or

2. With intent to induce any person to apply to any house, office, room, or place, or to any person, with the view of obtaining information or advice, for the purpose of any such bet or wager, or with respect to any such event or contingency as is mentioned in the principal Act; or

3. Inviting any person to make or take any share in or in connection with any such bet or wager;

every person sending, exhibiting, or publishing, or causing the same to be sent, exhibited, or published, shall be subject to the penalties provided in the 7th section of the principal Act.

The 37 & 38 Vict. c. 15 is, however, confined to such bets as are mentioned in 16 & 17 Vict. c. 119. In the case of *Cox* v. *Andrews* (t), an information was preferred by the respondent Andrews against the appellant Cox, that he did unlawfully publish, or cause to be published, an advertisement in a newspaper called the "Licensed Victuallers' Gazette and Hotel Courier," whereby it was made to appear that he would, on application, give information and advice with respect to an

Racing tips, not illegal to advertise.

(t) *Cox* v. *Andrews*, 12 Q. B. D. 126; 53 L. J. M. C. 34; 32 W. R. 289; 48 J. P. 247.

event or contingency, as mentioned in the 16 & 17 Vict. c. 119. It was proved or admitted that the appellant was the proprietor and publisher of the newspaper, and that he published the number of the newspaper, dated the 31st March, 1883, which contained the following paragraph:—" To our readers. Special and important. ' Centaur' scored his first success of the season when he gave Knight of Burghley for the Lincoln Handicap last Tuesday. Our correspondent will use every effort to follow up his success, and those of our readers who want the most reliable and latest news from Northampton next week should not fail to avail themselves of ' Centaur's ' wire finals, sent direct from the course. They may rely on having something as good for the two principal events next week as they had in Knight of Burghley last Tuesday." The advertisement then stated the prices at which Centaur would supply information. On behalf of the appellant it was argued that the Betting Act of 1874 was intended to supplement the former Act, with which it is to be read. Both were intended to suppress betting houses or offices. The former Act dealt with bets made in such places, and the latter with advertisements relating to bets which came within the first Act, that is, bets made in a betting house; that such was not the case here, and that the conviction was therefore wrong. Mathew, J., held: " All the legislation is intended, as I think, to strike at a real mischief. The Betting Act of 1853 was intended to suppress betting houses, and it prohibits the use of ' any house, office, room, or other place,' opened, kept, or used for the purpose of betting, and imposes a penalty on the person who keeps such a house. The Betting Act of 1874 is, by section 1, to be construed as one with the prior Act ; and sub-section 1 of section 3

deals with 'any such bet or wager, or any such event
or contingency as is mentioned in the principal Act.'
The bets or wagers which are mentioned in the principal
Act are bets and wagers made in a house, office, room,
or other place kept for the purpose of betting, and these
are the bets or wagers intended to be aimed at in the
Act of 1874." The conviction was therefore quashed.

The Court had present to its mind the danger which
would be involved in the contrary decision; the Act
might prevent an advertisement giving notice that the
secretary of a club was willing to give information on
application in respect to a forthcoming race meeting.
The principal Act refers to events relating to horse
races, &c.; but it only does so as an element in the
carrying out of the second main criminal purpose of
keeping a place for receiving money on deposit. In
Form No. 9 a description is given of that which, it is
submitted, is one of the offences. There is no reported
instance in which a person had been convicted for advertising the fact that he kept a place for the purpose
of receiving money on deposit, as is mentioned in the
Act; though, possibly, he might have been convicted
under the principal Act of advertising the keeping of a
place for making wagers in that manner, and now could
be convicted under the later Act.

Advertising a foreign place.

There would be no offence in advertising the keeping
of a house in a foreign country, where such keeping
would not be an offence.

Section B.—*Soliciting Infants to Bet.*

By an Act passed in 1892 (u), everyone who for profit
invites by any document anyone whom he knows to be
an infant to enter into any wagering transaction renders

(u) 55 & 56 Vict. c. 4.

himself liable to imprisonment or fine, or to both imprisonment and fine, and if the name of anyone appears in such document as the person to whom payment is to be made, or who will give information, such person is to be deemed the sender of the document, unless he can prove that his name has been used without his knowledge or consent, and becomes liable to imprisonment or fine or both ; and anyone sending such a document to anyone at a university or school is to be deemed to have known that such a person was an infant, unless he can show good grounds that he had reason to believe such person was of full age. Power is given to anyone proceeded against under this Act to be a witness.

Section C.—*Welshing.*

A welsher is one who receives a sum of money or other valuable thing on an undertaking to return the same or the value thereof, together with other money, if an event (for example, the result of a horse race) shall be determined in a certain manner, and at the time of receiving the deposit intends to cheat and defraud the depositor. A welsher.

The existence of this fraudulent intent at the time of receiving the deposit would prevent the transfer of any property in the subject-matter of the deposit; for "a parting with the property in goods can only be effected by contract, which requires the assent of two minds" (x). In *Reg.* v. *Buckmaster* (y), Lord Coleridge, C. J., pointed out that if the depositor intended Property does not pass.

(x) 2 Russell on Crimes, 170, 5th ed., cited in *R.* v. *Walsh*, 4 Taunt. at p. 274 ; 2 Lea, C. C. pp. 1072, 1073.

(y) *Reg.* v. *Buckmaster*, 20 Q. B. D. 182; 57 L. J. M. C. 25; 57 L. T. 720; 36 W. R. 701; 52 J. P. 358; 16 Cox, C. C. 339.

to part with his money, it was only on terms which
were not the same as those whereunder the prisoner
intended to receive.   In the same judgment it is stated
that a second view was that the prosecutor never intended to pass the property, seeing that he was to have
his money back in a certain event; his intention was
solely to part with the possession.   Given such limited
intention on the part of the prosecutor, and a concurrent
intention to steal in the mind of the person who obtains
the possession, then there is evidence of larceny.

Larceny.

The crime is larceny at common law.   If the property had in fact passed in the subject of the deposit,
the charge would have been that of obtaining goods by
false pretences.

CHAPTER XIV.

Section A.—*Gaming on Licensed Premises.*
Section B.—*Betting in Public Places.*

Section A.—*Gaming on Licensed Premises.*

IN the Betting House Act, the offence on the part of the owner or occupier of a place, of knowingly and wilfully permitting the same to be used for either of the therein forbidden purposes, is created. Under the Intoxicating Liquor (Licensing) Act (35 & 36 Vict. c. 94), there is a group of sections headed " Offences against Public Order," and section 17 included therein is in terms as follows :—

" If any licensed person—

" (1) Suffers any gaming (*a*) or unlawful game to be carried on on his premises ; or

" (2) Opens, keeps, or uses, or suffers his house to be opened, kept, or used in contravention of the Act of the session of the sixteenth and seventeenth years of the reign of Her present Majesty, chapter one hundred and nineteen, intituled 'An Act for the suppression of betting houses,'

he shall be liable to a penalty not exceeding for the first offence ten pounds, and not exceeding for the second and any subsequent offence twenty pounds."

(*a*) See Chap. II. p. 39.

G.   X

By section 16, sub-sect. 3, it was further provided that any conviction for an offence under this section shall, unless the convicting magistrates shall otherwise direct, be recorded on the licence of the person convicted; but this provision has been repealed by section 13 of the Licensing Act, 1874, whereunder the justices may order the conviction to be recorded on the licence.

Sect. 17 supplemental to the Betting House Act. This section is thus supplementary to the provisions of the general Acts. As was held in the case of *Sims* v. *Pay* (*b*), having regard to section 59 (*c*) of the statute, its 17th section could not be taken to have repealed, *quoad* licensed victuallers, the provisions of the Betting House Act. The Licensing Act then extends the general Act on the offence of suffering or permitting gaming.

The question under sect. 17 The question to be considered is, whether the above-quoted section imposes an absolute liability or a qualified liability on a licensed person. If qualified only, then the extent of the qualification remains for determination.

Construction of the section. The licensed person must suffer the acts forbidden. *Primâ facie*, the word "suffer" implies feeling, from which it is only a step to knowledge. But it has been pointed out that in section 17 the word "knowingly" is omitted, whereas it is inserted in other sections of the same group, namely, in section 14 and section 16, sub-section (1). Manisty, J., considered that the omission points to an absolute prohibition (*d*), but Mathew

(*b*) *Sims* v. *Pay*, 58 L. J. M. C. 39 ; 60 L. T. 602 ; 16 Cox, C. C. 609 ; 53 J. P. 420.

(*c*) Nothing in this Act shall prevent any person from being liable to be indicted or punished under any other Act, or otherwise, so that he be not punished twice for the same offence.

(*d*) *Bond* v. *Evans*, 21 Q. B. D. 249 ; 57 L. J. M. C. 105 ; 59

and Collins, JJ., have since held that the word "knowingly," in section 14, only applies to the class of persons who are permitted to resort to the premises. Similarly in section 16 (e). The fact that the word "knowingly" was contained in the corresponding section of the repealed Act (4 Geo. IV. c. 61, sched. C.) does not point to any definite conclusion. In *Somerset* v. *Wade* it is pointed out that the word "suffers" is not distinguishable from "permits." The statute, then, is not in favour of the absolute liability which might have been imposed by saying that "If a licensed person does not prevent, then, &c." The authorities, it will be seen, support the view of qualified liability, and illustrate the extent of the qualification.

In the case of *Bosley* v. *Davies* (f), an hotel keeper had been convicted by the magistrates of suffering gaming, on evidence which failed to disclose actual knowledge or constructive knowledge on his part or on the part of his servants. The facts were—A police constable, about 12.30 P.M., being in the street outside the premises, looked into a room and saw sufficiently to lead him to enter the house; he found six men playing cards at a table on which there was a quantity of money. The players were visitors at the hotel and were in their private room. The cards belonged to them. The manageress had no knowledge of the playing, and no servant had entered the room during the play. On such facts, the case was sent back to the

Authorities on sect. 17. Bosley v. Davies.

L. T. 411; 52 J. P. 612; 36 W. R. 767; 4 T. L. R. 614; 16 Cox, C. C. 461.

(e) *Somerset* v. *Wade*, (1894) 1 Q. B. 574; 63 L. J. M. C. 126; 10 R. 105; 70 L. T. 452; 10 T. L. R. 313; 58 J. P. 231; 42 W. R. 399.

(f) *Bosley* v. *Davies*, 1 Q. B. D. 84; 45 L. J. M. C. 27; 33 L. T. 528; 24 W. R. 140; 40 J. P. 550.

justices " with an intimation of the opinion of the Court
that actual knowledge,in the sense of seeing or hearing by
the party charged, is not necessary, but that there must
be some circumstances from which it may be inferred
that he or his servants had connived at what was going
on.   Constructive knowledge will supply the place of
actual knowledge." Hence this case is an express decision that the liability is not absolute.

Responsi-
bility for
servants.   The next case illustrates the facts which may suffice
to afflict the holder of the licence with constructive
knowledge.   In *Redgate* v. *Haynes* (*g*), the appellant
was convicted for suffering gaming on her licensed premises.   It was proved by witnesses that whilst standing
in the public street of Epsom, between half-past one
and a quarter to two in the morning, they could hear
from the conversation of three persons in a room that
they were playing for money.   There was no direct
evidence that the appellant knew of the gaming : she
stated that the house was closed at 11 P.M., and that
the three persons who were staying in the house were
in their private room, and that she neither saw nor
supplied any cards, and did not know of any playing.
The hall porter closed the house and retired to his own
chair in a parlour at the extreme end of the house.   He
said that he knew nothing whatever of the gambling.
The justices, however, drew an inference from the
porter's evidence that his chair was removed to the
greatest possible distance from the guest's room in order
not to hear what passed ; they thought that the appellant
knew that gaming was intended to be carried on, and
that she purposely took pains not to know what her
guests were doing.   On such grounds they convicted

(*g*) *Redgate* v. *Haynes*, 1 Q. B. D. 89 ; 45 L. J. M. C. 65 ; 33
L. T. 779 ; 41 J. P. 86.

her, and the conviction was affirmed. It was held that she was responsible for the hall porter, and that there was evidence that he suspected and connived, and that this evidence justified the conviction. Lush, J., said, "I agree that it is not necessary that actual knowledge of the gaming should be proved. Section 17 says that the owner of licensed premises who 'suffers' gaming shall be liable to a penalty. And I think that connivance on the part of the landlady or person in charge would be quite sufficient." Blackburn, J., also said, "I agree that the mere fact that gaming was carried on on her premises would not render her liable to be convicted, because that is not 'suffering' the gaming to be carried on, and if the justices were of a different opinion they were wrong; but I think if she purposely abstained from ascertaining whether gaming was going on or not, or, in other words, connived at it, this would be enough to make her liable; and I think that where the landlady goes to bed she is still answerable for the conduct of those whom she leaves in charge of the house, and if these persons connive at the gaming she is responsible" (h).

The case of *Crabtree* v. *Hole* (i) is on all fours with the last-mentioned one; the holder's vicarial responsibility was again enforced. The holder of the licence employed a manager to live on the premises. The manager went to bed leaving "boots" to attend to the house. The justices found that "boots" knew of the gaming, but shut his eyes. It was held that "The duty imposed by the enactment is to take reasonable care that gaming is not suffered on the premises, and if

(h) See also *Mullins* v. *Collins*, L. R. 9 Q. B. 292; 43 L. J. M. C. 67; 29 L. T. 838; 22 W. R. 297; 38 J. P. 629.
(i) *Crabtree* v. *Hole*, 43 J. P. 799.

the licensed holder employs one who does not do his duty, it is the same as if he himself did not do his duty. Here 'boots' did not take reasonable care, and the licensed person must be found guilty."

Somerset v. *Hart.* Knowledge of potman.

The case of *Somerset* v. *Hart* (k) shows, however, that this responsibility does not attach in respect of the non-interference of one to whom no authority has been delegated.

In an alehouse, which was much frequented on market days, several people were present in one of the rooms and were waited upon by a potman in the service of Hart. Divers acts of gambling took place, of which the potman saw some, but he neither interfered nor told his employer. There was no evidence to show that Hart knew anything about the gaming. Lord Coleridge, C. J., said, " Here the magistrates find that there was no evidence that Hart had any actual knowledge of the gaming, or that the potman ever communicated with him on the subject, or that Hart had himself wilfully shut his eyes to what was going on. . . . Slight evidence might be sufficient to satisfy the magistrates that the landlord might have known what was taking place if he had pleased; but where no actual knowledge is shown, there must, as it seems to me, be something to show either that the gaming took place with the knowledge of some person clothed with the landlord's authority, or that there was something like connivance on his part that he might have known, but purposely abstained from knowing " (l). Hence it was held that

(k) *Somerset* v. *Hart*, 12 Q. B. D. 360; 53 L. J. M. C. 77; 48 J. P. 327; 32 W. R. 594.

(l) See comments of Manisty, J., in *Bond* v. *Evans*, 21 Q. B. D. at pp. 254, 255, and of Collins, J., in *Somerset* v. *Wade*, (1894) 1 Q. B. at pp. 577, 578.

the magistrates were right in refusing to convict on such evidence.

The case of *Bond* v. *Evans* (*m*) presents some diffi- *Bond* v. *Evans.* culty, not on account of its decision, but owing to some *obiter dicta*. In this case, the appellant, a licensed victualler, had been convicted for suffering gaming to be carried on on his premises. The evidence showed that the appellant had employed a man to manage a skittle-alley, which was attached to his premises, and had given him general directions not to permit gambling. Nevertheless, the man allowed card playing for money to take place in his presence in the alley. It was admitted that the appellant was not present, and had no actual knowledge of the card playing, and that the man had never communicated with him on the subject, but the conviction was upheld.

The decision clearly was, that the holder of the licence was properly convicted in respect of the non-interference by a man to whom he had delegated his authority. Manisty, J., after examining in detail the *Obiter dicta* of sections of the group of offences against public order, Manisty and Stephen, JJ. said, after referring to the case of *Cundy* v. *Le Cocq* (*n*), wherein it had been decided that the Act imposed an absolute liability against the sale of liquor to a drunken person, "In my opinion the principle of that decision is applicable to the present case, for I think it was intended by sect. 17 absolutely to prohibit gaming on licensed premises, and that the substantial effect is that responsibility is thrown upon any person who keeps a

(*m*) *Bond* v. *Evans*, 21 Q. B. D. 249; 57 L. J. M. C. 105; 59 L. T. 411; 52 J. P. 612; 36 W. R. 767; 4 T. L. R. 614; 16 Cox, C. C. 461.

(*n*) *Cundy* v. *Le Cocq*, 13 Q. B. D. 207; 53 L. J. M. C. 125; 51 L. T. 265; 32 W. R. 769; 48 J. P. 599.

licensed house to take proper precautions to prevent all gaming on his premises." Stephen, J., also said, " I think the meaning is, that the landlord must prevent that which the Act prohibits from being done on his premises, and if he does not prevent it, so much the worse for him." If these *dicta* go the length of meaning that proof of the fact of gaming under any circumstances establishes that proper precautions (meaning such as rebut criminal liability) have not been taken, then, it is submitted, the same are inconsistent with the foregoing cases. Again, in answer to Stephen, J., it may be said that the Act does not prevent gaming on licensed premises, but only the suffering of gaming therein.

However, in the recent case of *Somerset* v. *Wade* (o), the earlier case of *Somerset* v. *Hart* was approved, and the case of *Bond* v. *Evans* (p) was explained. The offence alleged in *Somerset* v. *Wade* was permitting drunkenness; there was a drunken female on the licensed premises, but the respondent Wade did not know that she was drunk. Mathew, J., commenting on *Somerset* v. *Hart*, said, " It comes to this, that a licensed person cannot be convicted of suffering gaming, in the absence of knowledge, or connivance, or carelessness on his part." Collins, J., concurred. Of course, the licensed holder can connive or be careless in the person of those to whom he has delegated his authority.

Conclusion.   Thus, then, the liability imposed is not absolute. The foregoing cases will serve to illustrate to what extent it is qualified.

(o) *Somerset* v. *Wade*, (1894) 1 Q. B. 574; 63 L. J. M. C. 126; 10 R. 105; 70 L. T. 452; 10 T. L. R. 313; 58 J. P. 231; 42 W. R. 399.

(p) *Bond* v. *Evans*, *ante*, p. 311.

But given actual knowledge on the part of the licensed person, it is seemingly impossible for him to withstand a charge under section 17. Thus, he may not even play any game for money with his personal friends as distinguished from customers. In the case of *Patten* v. *Rhymer* (q), an innkeeper invited some friends to come as his guests and play cards, which they did after prohibited hours. They were in the habit of visiting each other's houses and playing for small stakes. They accepted the invitation and played in a private room. The innkeeper, however, was convicted. Wightman, J., said, "It appears that the licence makes it a condition that the innkeeper shall not knowingly suffer any unlawful games, nor any gaming whatsoever, in his house —words quite wide enough to include the present case. The appellant may have acted *bonâ fide*, and there may have been no improper gambling. He may have invited some of his private friends, and they may only have been playing a friendly game of cards for a small stake. But he has permitted playing cards for money, and that is gaming on his licensed premises, and the case comes within the letter of the licence, and it may well be that it was intended to forbid all playing at cards for money in order to prevent an evasion of the licence, as it would be exceedingly easy, under pretence of a lawful game at cards with pretended friends of the landlord, to introduce and cloak unlawful gaming."

By the 30th section of the Act of 1874 (37 & 38 Vict. c. 49), a licensed person was allowed to supply intoxicating liquors after the hours of closing, to private friends *bonâ fide* entertained by him, at his own expense;

(q) *Patten* v. *Rhymer*, 3 El. & El. 1; 29 L. J. M. C. 189; 6 Jur. 1030; 2 L. T. 352; 8 W. R. 496; 24 J. P. 342.

lawful (*y*); but restrictions have been placed on the keeping of public places for the purposes of playing thereat. In Chapter VII., the sections of the statute 8 & 9 Vict. c. 109, which regulate the licensing of such places for the purpose, were mentioned, but not otherwise dealt with.

Power to license public places. Section 10 of the statute gives the justices at the annual general licensing meeting authority to grant licences to persons to keep public billiard tables or bagatelle boards, or instruments used in any game of the like kind, such licence to cost in all the sum of six shillings, and to continue in force for one year. Sec-*Licence necessary.* tion 11 requires that a licence shall be taken out for every house, room, or place kept for public billiard playing, or where a public billiard table or bagatelle board, or instrument used in any game of the like kind, is kept, at which persons are admitted to play, and requires that the words, "Licensed for billiards," shall be put up in some conspicuous place near the door on *Innkeepers do not require licence.* the outside. People holding victuallers' licences under 9 Geo. IV. c. 61, are exempted from the necessity of procuring the above licence.

Restrictions as to times of play. But, by section 13 of 8 & 9 Vict. c. 109, everyone keeping such public table is prohibited from allowing play to take place after one and before eight o'clock in the morning, and on Sundays, Christmas Day, and Good Friday, or any day appointed to be kept as a public fast or thanksgiving, and persons holding victuallers' licences are only to permit play during such times as they are allowed to keep open for the sale of liquors.

Residents may not play billiards after hours, though may be supplied with drink. By 37 & 38 Vict. c. 49, s. 10, the powers of licensed victuallers were expressly extended to allow them at all times to sell intoxicating liquors to persons residing in their houses; but, curiously, no mention is made as to

(*y*) *Parsons* v. *Alexander*, 24 L. J. Q. B. 277; 1 Jur. N. S. 660; 5 E. & B. 263.

billiard or bagatelle playing. In the case of *Ovenden* v.
Raymond (*z*), the appellant Ovenden was charged with
allowing billiards to be played after the prohibited
hours. It was contended on his behalf that, as the
players were lodgers, within the meaning of section 10
of the Act of 1874 (37 & 38 Vict. c. 49), and as that
Act allowed a licensed victualler to sell intoxicating
liquor to lodgers after prohibited hours of closing, he
was justified in allowing them to play billiards. But
the Court, consisting of Bramwell, B., and Grove, J.,
held : " We think that this point is not arguable, and
that the appellant is clearly wrong. No doubt it is a
casus omissus in the statute, and a great anomaly; but
it is clear that the section 10 of the Act of 1874 does
not tend to exempt persons playing billiards after the
closing hours, though they may be able to obtain a
drink after those hours."

No appeal lies in respect of a refusal by the justices *Appeal.*
to grant such a billiard licence (*a*). In respect of convictions for contravention of the foregoing provisions, a
right of appeal is conferred by section 20 of the statute
8 & 9 Vict. c. 109. The section is in terms similar to
the corresponding sections of the Betting and Gaming
House Acts ; the informant and the witnesses are to be
bound over, and expenses allowed, such expenses to be
repaid by the appellant if the appeal be dismissed.

Section B.—*Betting in Public Places.*

By the Metropolitan Streets Act, 30 & 31 Vict. c. 134, Metropolitan
s. 23, any three or more persons assembled together in betting in.

(*z*) *Ovenden* v. *Raymond*, 34 L. T. 698 ; 40 J. P. 727.
(*a*) *R.* v. *Devonshire JJ.*, 21 J. P. 773 ; *S. C.*, nom. *Ex parte
Chamberlain*, 8 E. & B. 644.

any part of a street within the metropolis for the purpose of betting, are to be deemed to be obstructing the
street, and each of such persons is liable to a penalty
not exceeding 5*l.* Power is also given to constables to
take into custody without warrant any person who may
commit such offence in view of such constable.

Gaming in public places.

In 1873, an Act was passed to amend the Vagrants
Act, 5 Geo. IV. c. 83, and to repeal the Vagrants Act
Amendment Act of 1868, and, by section 3 thereof, the
provisions of the first-mentioned Act were extended so
that every person playing or betting by way of wagering or gaming in any street, road, highway or other
open and public place, or in any open place to which
the public have or are permitted to have access, at or
with any table or instrument of gaming, or any coin,
card, token or other article used as an instrument or
means of such wagering or gaming at any game or
pretended game of chance (*b*), shall be deemed a rogue
and a vagabond, and may be convicted and punished
under the provisions of 5 Geo. IV. c. 83, or in the discretion of the justice or justices trying the case in lieu
of such punishment by a penalty for the first offence
not exceeding 2*l.*, and for the second or any subsequent
offence not exceeding 5*l.*

Cases of street betting are continually coming before
the metropolitan police magistrates, and on conviction
the maximum penalty of 5*l.* seems to be almost invari-
ably imposed.

(*b*) For game of chance, see *Jenks* v. *Turpin*, 13 Q. B. D. 505;
53 L. J. M. C. 161; 50 L. T. 808; 49 J. P. 20; 15 Cox, C. C.
486; *Dyson* v. *Mason*, 22 Q. B. D. 351; 58 L. J. M. C. 55;
60 L. T. 265; 53 J. P. 262; *Tollett* v. *Thomas*, L. R. 6 Q. B.
514; 40 L. J. M. C. 209; 19 W. R. 246; 24 L. T. 508; *Fairtlough*
v. *Whitmore*, 64 L. J. Ch. 386; W. N. (1895) 52.

(319)

CHAPTER XV.

LOTTERIES AND GAMES OF CHANCE.

In Chapter IV. an account was given of the series of statutes impos-
ing criminal liability in respect of lotteries and games of chance;
the object of that chapter was to afford a foundation for the consideration of civil obligations connected with illegal gambling. In this
chapter the various offences will be set out in the form of a Schedule.

Offence.	*Penalty.*
[1699] I.—10 & 11 Will. III. c. 17 (see p. 62).	

[After preamble, see p. 63.]

Lotteries declared nuisances.]—All such lotteries, and all other lotteries, are common and public nuisances.

The keeper is indictable for a mis-demeanor, although the other sec-tions impose specific penalties (a).

Prohibition of keeping lottery.]—Sect. 2. No person shall publicly or privately exercise, keep, open, show, or expose to be played at, drawn at, or thrown at, or shall draw, play, or throw at any such lottery, either by dice, lots, cards, balls, or any other numbers or figures, or any other way whatsoever.

For every such offence the person shall forfeit £500 ; one-third to the Crown, one-third to poor of parish, one-third to informer ; and the per-son so offending shall be prose-cuted as a common rogue.

Penalty on playing at such lotteries.]—Sect. 3. Every person who shall play, throw, or draw at any such lottery, play, or device, or other lotteries,

Shall—
Forfeit the sum of £20 ; applica-tion as in offence under sect. 2.

[1710]   II.—9 Anne, c. 6 (see page 63).

Person advertising.]—Every person who shall by writing or printing publish the setting up any such unlawful lottery, with intent to have such lottery drawn,

Shall—
Forfeit for every such offence £100 ; application as in the pre-viously mentioned offences.

(a) *R. v. Crawshaw*, 1 Bell, C. C. 303.

Offence.	*Penalty.*

[1711] **III.—10 Anne, c. 26** (see page 64).

Setting up offices for improvement of small sums of money under divers denominations.]—Sect. 108. Every person who shall erect, set up, or keep any office or place under the denominations of sale of gloves, of fans, of cards, of numbers, of the Queen's picture, for the improvement of small sums of money, or the like offices or places under the pretence of improving small sums of money,

Shall—
Forfeit for every such offence £500.

Advertising such offices.]—Every printer or person who shall by writing or printing publish the setting up or keeping any such office or place, under any of the denominations aforesaid, or like denominations for the improvement of small sums of money,

Shall—
Forfeit for every such offence £100.

[1718] **IV.—5 Geo. I. c. 10** (see page 64).

Sect. 43. An offence arising out of the existence of public lotteries.

[1721] **V.—8 Geo. I. c. 2** (see page 65).

The like offices under divers other denominations.]—Sect. 36. Every person who shall erect, set up, continue, and keep, or shall cause to be erected, set up, continued and kept, any office or place under the denominations of sales of houses, lands, advowsons, presentations to livings, plate, jewels, ships, goods, or other things for the improvement of small sums of money :

Sale of houses, &c. by lot.]—Or shall sell or expose for sale any houses, &c. by way of lottery or lots, tickets, numbers, or figures :

Advertising.]—Or shall make, print, or publish, or cause to be made, printed, or published, any proposal or scheme of the like nature and kind whatsoever, under any denomination or title whatsoever :

Shall—
Be liable to forfeit for every such offence £500 over and above any penalties inflicted by former Acts.

Contributing.]—Sect. 37. Any person contributing to the sales, &c.

Shall—
Be liable to forfeit for every such offence twice the sum contributed.

Offence.   *Penalty.*

[1722]   VI.—9 Geo. I. c. 19 (see page 65).

Prevention of foreign lotteries in the kingdom :
i. *Setting up.*]—Sect. 4. Any person who shall,
by virtue or colour of any grant or authority
from any foreign prince, state, or government
whatsoever, erect, set up, continue, or keep, or
shall cause or procure to be erected, set up, continued, or kept, any lottery or undertaking in
the nature of a lottery under any denomination
whatsoever :

ii. *Advertising.*]—Or who shall make, print, or
publish, or cause to be made, printed, or published, any proposal or scheme for any such   *Shall—*
lottery or undertaking :   Be liable to forfeit £200 over

iii. *Sale of tickets.*]—Or who shall within this   and above any penalties inflicted by
kingdom sell or dispose of any ticket or tickets   former Acts against unlawful lot-
in any foreign lottery: -   teries. Application as under I. (*b*).

[1733]   VII.—6 Geo. II. c. 35.

The last statute supplemented : i. *Sale of a ticket
in a foreign lottery.*]—Sect. 29. Any person who
shall sell, procure, or deliver any ticket, receipt,
chance, or number in or belonging to any foreign
lottery, or pretended foreign lottery, or in or
belonging to any class, part or division of such
lottery, or pretended lottery, or in or belonging
to any undertaking whatsoever in the nature of
a lottery :

ii. *Sale of a ticket in a duplicate of a foreign
lottery.*]—Or who shall sell, procure, or deliver,
any ticket, receipt, chance, or number in or
belonging to any duplicate, or pretended duplicate of any foreign lottery, or pretended foreign
lottery :

iii. *Receipt of money on such contingencies.*]—Or
who shall receive, or cause to be received, any
money whatsoever for any such ticket, receipt,
chance, or number, or for or in consideration for
any money to be repaid in case any ticket or
tickets, number or numbers, in any foreign   *Shall—*
lottery, or pretended foreign lottery, or any class,   For every such offence forfeit
part, or division thereof, shall prove fortunate :   £200. Application as before (*b*).

(b) See now, *post*, p. 329.

Offence.   *Penalty.*

[1738]   VIII.—12 Geo. II. c. 28 (see page 66).

After reciting 10 & 11 Will. IV. c. 17; 9
Anne, c. 6; 8 Geo. I. c. 2, s. 36, enacts:—

i. *Keeping a lottery.*]—Sect. 1. Any person who
shall erect, set up, continue, or keep any office or
place under the denomination of a sale or sales
of houses, lands, advowsons, presentations to
livings, plate, jewels, ships, goods, or other
things by way of lottery, or by lots, tickets,
numbers or figures, cards or dice:

ii. *Sale by means of chance.*]—Or who shall expose to sale any houses, lands, advowsons, presentation to livings, plate, jewels, ships, or other
goods by any game, method or device whatso-   *Shall—*
ever, depending upon or to be determined by any   Forfeit £200. Application, one-
lot or drawing, whether it be out of a box or   third to informer, remainder to
wheel, or by cards or dice, or by any machine,   poor of parish.
engine, or device of any kind whatsoever:

Setting up of ace of hearts, &c.]—Sect. 2. Ace of
hearts, pharaoh, basset and hazard, declared to
be lotteries by cards or dice within 9 Anne, c. 6;
8 Geo. I. c. 2, s. 36.

And any person who shall set up, maintain, or   *Shall—*
keep the said games of the ace of hearts, pharaoh, Be liable to forfeit £200 as for
basset and hazard: keeping any lottery mentioned in
                                                   the Act.

Liability of adventurers.]—Sect. 3. Any person
who shall be an adventurer in any of the said   *Shall—*
games, lottery or lotteries, sale or sales: Forfeit £50, or in default of pay-
Or who shall play, set at stake, or punt at   ment, imprisonment not exceeding
either of the said games of the ace of hearts, &c.: six months.

[1740]   IX.—13 Geo. II. c. 19.

Recites lastly hereinbefore mentioned statute.
Declares that—

*Game of passage, and other games with dice, ex-
cept backgammon, to be lotteries.*]—The game of
passage, and all and every other game and

Offence.   *Penalty.*

games invented, or to be invented, with one or
more die or dice, or with any other instrument,
engine or device in the nature of dice, having
one or more figures or numbers thereon (backgammon and the other games now played with
the backgammon tables only excepted), are games
or lotteries by dice, within the lastly hereinbefore
mentioned Act.

i. *Setting up a place for the same.*]—And any
person who shall set up, maintain, or keep any   *Shall—*
office, table, or place for the said game of passage,   Forfeit as for setting up a game,
or for any other such game or games as aforesaid   &c. within the lastly hereinbefore
(backgammon, &c. only excepted):   mentioned Act.

ii. *Adventurers.*]—Or any person who shall   *Shall—*
play, set at stake, or adventure at the said   Forfeit respectively as in the
game of passage, or at any other such game as   lastly hereinbefore mentioned Act
aforesaid (backgammon, &c. excepted):   is inflicted on any one who shall
                                                        play, &c. at any of the games
                                                        therein mentioned.

[1745]   X.—18 Geo. II. c. 34 (see page 67).

12 *Geo. II. c. 28, supplemented.* i. *Keeping a
place for roulet.*]—Sect. 1. Any person who shall
keep any house, room, or place for playing, or
permit or suffer any person or persons whatsoever within any such house, room or place, to
play at the said game of roulet, otherwise roly-
poly, or at any other game with cards or dice
already prohibited by law:

ii. *Permit the play.*]—Or who shall permit or
suffer any person or persons as aforesaid to play   *Shall—*
at the said game of roulet, otherwise roly-poly,   Be liable to the penalties for the
or at any other game with cards or dice already   corresponding offences in the lastly
prohibited by law: hereinbefore mentioned Act.

iii. *Players, liability of.*]—Sect. 2. Any person   *Shall—*
who shall play at the said game of roulet, other-   Be liable to the penalties directed
wise roly-poly, or at any game or games with   by the lastly hereinbefore men-
cards or dice already prohibited by law: tioned Act.

Y 2

Offence.   *Penalty.*

[1802]   **XI.—42 Geo. III. c. 119** (see page 68).

The suppression of little goes.]—Declares all such games or lotteries called Little Goes to be common and public nuisances.   See *Reg.* v. *Crawshaw (b).*

i. *Keeping a place for purpose of any lottery.*]— Sect. 2. Any person who shall publicly or privately keep any office or place to exercise, keep open, show, or expose to be played, drawn, or thrown at or in, either by dice, lots, cards, balls, or by numbers or figures, or by any other way, contrivance, or device whatsoever, any game or lottery called a Little Go, or any other lottery whatsoever not authorized by Parliament:

ii. *Suffering a game to be played in a place.*]— Or who shall knowingly suffer to be exercised, kept open, shown, or exposed to be played, drawn or thrown at or in, either by dice, lots, cards, balls, or by numbers or figures, or by any other way, contrivance, or device whatsoever, any such game or lottery in his or her house, room, or place:

Shall—
Forfeit £500, and shall be punishable as a rogue and vagabond, under 17 Geo. II. c. 5.
And (sect. 3) if no information be laid for penalties, shall be punishable as a rogue and vagabond, under 17 Geo. II. c. 5 ; 27 Geo. III. c. 1.

iii. *An executive power.*]—Sect. 4. Justices are empowered on information to authorize persons to break open doors of places (if at night with a police officer) where such offences are committed, and apprehend offenders:

iv. *Forcible obstruction of searchers.*]—And any person who shall forcibly obstruct, oppose, molest, or hinder any such officer or officers, or others acting in his or their aid or assistance, in due execution of their duty, or in the due entering into such house, or place, or in seizing, detaining, or conveying before such justice or justices any such offenders or persons as aforesaid:

Shall—
On so obstructing, opposing, molesting, or hindering as aforesaid, be fined, imprisoned, and publicly whipped, as the Court may deem fit.

(*b*) *Reg.* v. *Crawshaw,* 1 Bell, C. C. 303 ; 8 Cox, C. C. 375.

Offence.	*Penalty.*

v. *Liability of employer of assistant.*]—And any person, although discovered in such house or place as aforesaid, who shall employ or cause to be employed any person or persons in carrying on any of the transactions aforesaid, or in aiding or assisting any such person or persons :

Shall—
Be deemed a rogue and a vagabond : 27 Geo. III. c. 1.

vi. *Liability for agreeing to pay money, &c. on an event relative to such lottery.*]—Sect. 5. Any person who shall on or under any pretence, device, form, denomination, or description whatsoever, promise or agree to pay any sum or sums, or to deliver any goods or to do or forbear doing anything for the benefit of any person or persons, whether with or without consideration, on any event or contingency relative or applicable to the drawing of any ticket or tickets, lot or lots, numbers or figures in any such game or lottery :

vii. *Offence of publishing any proposal for, &c.*]—Or who shall publish any proposal for any of the purposes aforesaid :

Shall—
For every offence forfeit £100; application, one-third to Crown, one-third to informer, one-third to person apprehending offender.

[1836]   **6 & 7 Will. IV. c. 66.**

Advertising foreign lotteries.]—Enacts that if any person shall print or publish, or cause to be printed or published, any advertisement or other notice of or relating to the drawing or intended drawing of any foreign lottery, or of any lottery or lotteries not authorized by some Act of Parliament; or if any person shall print or publish, or cause to be printed or published, any advertisement or other notice of or for the sale of any ticket or tickets, chance or chances, or of any share or shares of any ticket or chance of or in any such lottery or lotteries as aforesaid, or any advertisement or notice concerning or in any manner relating to any such lottery or lotteries, or any ticket, chance, or share, tickets, chances, or shares thereof or therein : for every such offence—

Shall—
Forfeit £50, to be recovered with full costs by action of debt, bill, plaint, or information in any of His Majesty's Courts at Westminster (one moiety to use of His Majesty, and the other moiety to the person who shall inform or sue for the same).

From the foregoing tabular statement, it appears that the criminal proceedings may be by indictment, or on information, for penalties, or on information as against a person as a rogue and a vagabond.

I. Public nuisances.

I. Informations for a common misdemeanor may be founded as follows :—Lotteries within 10 & 11 Will. III. c. 17 (including sweepstakes) ; ace of hearts, &c., under 12 Geo. II. c. 28 ; games of passage, &c., under 13 Geo. II. c. 19 ; keeping a place for roulet, under 18 Geo. II. c. 34 ; little goes, under 42 Geo. III. c. 119.

In the case of *Reg.* v. *Crawshaw* (c), the defendant was indicted for a public nuisance, to wit, for setting up a certain lottery, contrary to 10 & 11 Will. III. c. 17, s. 1. It was contended on his behalf that the proper remedy was under the 2nd section of that statute. But it was held "that the principle has prevailed, and been acted upon without qualification, that when the legislature declares an act to be a public nuisance, the person doing the act is indictable" (d), and that, accordingly, the counts framed upon the Lottery Act were not bad.

But the proceeding by indictment is not of much general utility, having regard to the other proceedings which are available.

II. Informations for penalties.

II. Informations for penalties may be grounded in respect of the different offences, as follows :—

Keeping a place for, &c.

(A.) *For keeping a place* : under the pretence of improving small sums of money (10 Anne, c. 26, s. 108, or under 8 Geo. I. c. 2, s. 36) ; or under denomination of a sale of, &c., by way of lottery (12 Geo. II. c. 28) ; or for the game of passage, &c. (13 Geo. II. c. 19, s. 9) ; or for the purpose of any little go (42 Geo. III. c. 119, s. 2).

(c) *Reg.* v. *Crawshaw*, 1 Bell, C. C. 303 ; 8 Cox, C. C. 375.
(d) *R.* v. *Gregory*, 5 B. & Ad. 555.

There is an offence of a nature ancillary to the fore- Advertising.
going, namely, advertising : advertising the offices (10
Anne, c. 26, s. 108) ; or publishing a scheme to be conducted in such place (8 Geo. I. c. 2) ; or publishing
any proposal for using a place contrary to the Act,
42 Geo. III. c. 119 (s. 5).

All such offences of keeping a place for the forbidden
purpose imply a number of acts committed, or intended
to be committed, and might lead to some difficulty in
establishing.   Doubtless the decisions cited in Chapters
IV. and XIV. would apply, that such illegal purpose
need not be the sole and exclusive purpose.   The diffi- "Place."
culty of the meaning of the term "place" has been met $\begin{smallmatrix}4 \text{ Geo. IV.} \\ \text{c. 60, s. 60.}\end{smallmatrix}$
by a statutory explanation.   By section 60 of the statute
4 Geo. IV. c. 60, it is stated that doubts had arisen
whether, under and by virtue of the former Act (42
Geo. III. c. 119), the word "place" mentioned in the
said Act was meant to describe any place used for the
purpose of drawing the illegal lottery or little go, or
in anywise relating thereto, be the same an inclosed
building or not ; it was therefore thereby declared and
enacted that the word "place," when and where used
in the said Act and the several above recited Acts, relating to the drawing of the said illegal lottery called
little go, or the assembling of persons for any of the
illegal purposes mentioned therein, or for the purpose
of any little go or lottery insurance, shall be taken to
extend to and mean any place in or out of an inclosed
building or premises, whether upon land or water, where
such illegal practices, or anything relating thereto, shall
be carried on or attempted to be carried on.

(B.) There are, however, the series of offences, not
involving an actual or contemplated series of acts as is
implied in keeping a place for a purpose ; in respect of

these offences, the Acts go much beyond—for example,

Exercising or setting up. the Betting House Act. Such offences are as follows :
—Publicly or privately exercise a lottery (10 & 11
Will. IV. c. 17) ; offer a house, &c., for sale by lottery
(8 Geo. I. c. 2, s. 36 ; 12 Geo. II. c. 28) ; sell a ticket
in a foreign lottery (9 Geo. I. c. 19, s. 4 ; 6 Geo. II.
c. 35, s. 29) ; set up the game of hazard, &c. (12 Geo. II.
c. 28, s. 2), or any little go (42 Geo. III. c. 119, s. 2).

Permitting. Further, there are the ancillary offences:—permitting a
person to play roulet (18 Geo. II. c. 34, s. 1); knowingly

Playing. to suffer a little go (42 Geo. III. c. 119, s. 2); playing
at a lottery (10 & 11 Will. III. c. 17, s. 3) ; contributing
to a sale by chance (8 Geo. I. c. 2, s. 37) ; receiving
money on the contingency of a foreign lottery (6 Geo. II.
c. 35, s. 29); adventuring in such game (12 Geo. II.
c. 28, s. 3) ; playing at passage, &c. (13 Geo. II. c. 19,
s. 9), or at roulet or other forbidden game with dice
(18 Geo. II. c. 34, s. 2). Again, there are offences

Assisting. connected with assisting :—a person exercising a little
go, or employing or causing others to be so employed
(42 Geo. III. c. 119, s. 4). There are also the offences

Advertising. of advertising :—the setting up of a lottery (9 Anne,
c. 6, s. 57); publishing a proposal or scheme (8 Geo. I.
c. 2, s. 36, and 9 Geo. I. c. 19, s. 4), or a little go
(42 Geo. III. c. 119, s. 5).

The main offences and the chief ancillary ones are
well defined. This somewhat chaotic mass of statutes
might with advantage be repealed, and re-enacted in
one well-arranged Act.

Jurisdiction of magistrates. The magistrates have no power to inflict on persons
the pecuniary penalties attached to the different offences
heretofore mentioned. It has been enacted by the
statute 46 Geo. III. c. 148, that no information shall
be prosecuted to recover penalties against any law con-

THE LOTTERY ACTS, OFFENCES. 329

cerning lotteries, save in the name of the Attorney- Present appli-
General, and that such penalties when recovered shall penalties.
be applied to the use of the Crown. With regard to
proceedings against proprietors of newspapers for advertising lotteries, it has been separately enacted that the
proceedings must be in the name of the Attorney-
General (e).

In *Taylor* v. *Smetten* (f), the appellant had been
convicted before the justices that he unlawfully did
publicly keep in a tent a lottery to be drawn by lots and
by coupons by a certain contrivance, to wit, the distributing of a quantity of parcels of tea with coupons in
· certain of such parcels, such being a lottery not authorized by law, to wit, a lottery for clocks and other articles.
The justices convicted, and imposed a fine of 20s.
Hawkins, J., said, that if he had simply been convicted
of keeping a lottery and fined 20s. for so doing, under
42 Geo. III. c. 119, s. 2, then the above-mentioned
Act, 46 Geo. III. c. 148, s. 59, applied, and the conviction could not be upheld (g). The sole offences
over which the justices have jurisdiction are those in
respect of which the offender may be dealt with as a
rogue and a vagabond.

III. Information as against a rogue and a vagabond.
—This information lies in respect of the offences of
keeping lotteries within section 2 of the statute 10 & 11
Will. III. c. 17; but whilst section 3 of that Act
subjects adventurers to penalties, it does not allow of
their conviction as rogues, and they are, therefore,
punishable only on the information of the Attorney-
General. Again, by section 2 of the Act 42 Geo. III.

(e) 8 & 9 Vict. c. 74.
(f) *Taylor* v. *Smetten*, 11 Q. B. D. at p. 212.
(g) *Reg.* v. *Tuddenham*, 9 Dowl. 937; 10 L. J. M. C. 163.

c. 119, it is provided that, in respect of the offences therein described, keeping a place for exercising a lottery, or knowingly suffering a lottery to be exercised in a place, and, by section 4 of the same Act, in respect of the offences therein of employing, or causing to be employed, or aiding and abetting, the offender may be dealt with as a rogue and a vagabond.

Appeal against summary conviction. With regard to an appeal against a summary conviction as a rogue and a vagabond, two cases arise : either the penalty is imprisonment without the option of a fine, or a fine is imposed. Where there is imprisonment without the option of a fine, then, under section 19 of the Summary Jurisdiction Act, 1879, an appeal to quarter sessions lies where the defendant has not pleaded guilty. Where there is no imprisonment, or only imprisonment in default of payment of a fine, then a question of some difficulty arises as to the effect of section 7 of the statute 42 Geo. III. c. 119. Under that section, all pains, forfeitures, fines, and penalties, and all provisions, powers, authorities, rules, regulations, restrictions, exemptions, and exceptions, clauses, matters, and things contained in 17 Geo. II. c. 5 (the then Vagrant Act) were incorporated. The statute 5 Geo. IV. c. 83, has been substituted for the Act 17 Geo. II. c. 5. In the present Vagrant Act, an express power of appeal is, under section 14, conferred on a person aggrieved. But such power of appeal is a special provision, and on the whole it would appear that the general words of section 7 of the Little-go Statute do not incorporate such special provision (*h*).

However, the circumstances which mostly lead to

(*h*) *R.* v. *Surrey JJ.*, (1892) 2 Q. B. 719 ; 61 L. J. M. C. 200 ; 66 L. T. 578 ; *R.* v. *Stone*, 6 East, 514 ; *R.* v. *Hanson*, 4 B. & Ald. 519 ; *R.* v. *Worcester JJ.*, 7 Dowl. 789.

appeals in connection with these offences are such as raise questions of law whereunder it has to be decided whether a given transaction or scheme is a lottery. Such question is proper subject-matter for a special case. The essentials of a lottery have been discussed in Chapter IV. (*i*).

(*i*) Pages 79 *et seq.*

Appendix.

---◆---

FORMS.

No. 1.—Example of Information.

In the County of ——, Petty Sessional Division of ——
Borough of ——
City and County of the City of ——

The —— day of ——, one thousand eight hundred
and ninety ——

The information (a) of C. D. [address, description], who **First offence**
upon oath [or affirmation] states that A. B., of [address, **under 16 & 17 Vict. c. 119,**
description (b)], on the —— day of ——, and on **s. 3.**
divers other days between that date and the date of
laying this information, being the owner of a certain
house and premises situate at **X. Street, in ——, then
and there opened, kept, and used the same for the
purpose of betting with persons resorting thereto,** contrary to the statute in that case made and provided.

      Taken before me,   (L.S.)

        (Signed)   X. Y.,

Justice of the Peace for the [County, or
Borough, or City] aforesaid.

(a) If complaint, strike out word "information," and insert "complaint."

(b) The address and description of the offender, as well as the place
at which the offence was committed, may sufficiently appear from
the statement of the offence, as in the above example.

*** *The black type is inserted by way of illustration of particular offences.*

No. 2.—Search Warrant.

County of {} To the Constable.

WHEREAS it appears to me, J. P., one of the justices of
our lady the Queen, assigned to keep the peace in the said
county, by the information on oath of A. B., of ———, in
the county of ———, ———, that the house [room *or*
place] known as [*here insert a description of the house,
room, or place by which it may be readily known and
found*], is kept and used as a common gaming house
within the meaning of an Act passed in the ———
year of the reign of her Majesty Queen Victoria, intituled [*here insert the title of this Act*] :

This is, therefore, in the name of our lady the Queen,
to require you, with such assistants as you may find
necessary, to enter into the said house [room *or* place],
and, if necessary, to use force for making such entry,
whether by breaking open doors or otherwise, and there
diligently to search for all instruments of unlawful gaming
which may be therein, and to arrest, search, and bring
before me, or some other of the justices of our lady the
Queen assigned to keep the peace within the county
of ———, as well the keepers of the same as also the
persons there haunting, resorting, and playing, to be
dealt with according to law ; and for so doing this shall
be your warrant.

                    J. P.,   (L.S.)

Given under my hand and seal at ———, in the county
of ———, this ——— day of ———, in the ——— year
of the reign.

No. 3.—Example of Summons to Defendant.

In the County of ———, Petty Sessional Division of ———
Borough of ———
City and County of the City of ———.

To A. B. ——— of ———

Information on oath [or affirmation] has been laid this day by C. D., for that you on the ——— day of ——— and on divers other days, between that date and the date of the said information, being the occupier of a certain house and premises situate at X. Street, in ———, then and there opened, kept, and used the same for the purpose of receiving money as and for the consideration for certain assurances, undertakings, promises and agreements to pay and give thereafter certain sums of money on certain events and contingencies of and relating to certain horse races, contrary to the statute, &c. Second offence, under 16 & 17 Vict. c. 119, s. 3.

You are therefore hereby summoned to appear before the Court of Summary Jurisdiction, sitting ——— on ———day, the ——— day of ———, at the hour of ——— in the forenoon, to answer to the said information.

Dated the ——— day of ———, one thousand eight hundred and ninety ———

(L.S.)

(Signed)   J. P.
Justice of the Peace for the [County or Borough or City] aforesaid.

No. 4.—Example of Summons to a Witness.

In the County of ———, Petty Sessional Division of ———
Borough of ———
City and County of the City of ———

To E. F.

A. B. has been charged by C. D. for that he on the ——— day of ———, being the owner (a) of a certain house and Offence under section 4,

⁎ The black type is inserted by way of illustration of particular offences.

16 & 17 Vict. premises situate at No. ——— Street, ———, opened, kept,
c. 119.   and used for the purpose of betting with persons resorting thereto, unlawfully did receive of X. Y. the sum of
£5 as a deposit on a certain bet, on condition of paying
a sum of money to the said X. Y. on the happening of an
event or contingency of and relating to a certain horse
race, to wit, on a horse named "Acrobat," thereafter to
run in a race known as the Lincoln Handicap, contrary to
the statute, &c.

And it appearing to me by the oath [or affirmation] of
———, that you are likely to give material evidence
therein on behalf of the informant [or defendant], and will
not voluntarily appear for that purpose.

You are therefore hereby summoned to appear before
the Court of Summary Jurisdiction sitting at ———, on
———day the ——— day of ——— at the hour of ———
in the ———noon, to testify what you know of such matter.

Dated the ——— day of ———, one thousand eight
hundred and ———

(L.S.)

(Signed)   J. P.

Justice of the Peace for the [County or
Borough or City] aforesaid.

(a) Or occupier, or person acting for or on behalf, &c. (as the case
may be).

No. 5.—Example of Warrant for Apprehension of Defendant.

In the County of ———, Petty Sessional Division of ———
Borough of ———
City and County of the City of ———

To each and all of the Constables of ———

Information on oath [or affirmation] has been laid on
the ——— day of ———, by C. D.—that A. B., hereinafter

⁎ The black type is inserted by way of illustration of particular offences.

called the defendant, being a person then having the care and management of an unlawful business, conducted in a certain house and premises, situate at ——, **by opening, keeping, and using the same for the purpose of receiving money on deposit by or on behalf of a certain person, as and for the consideration for assurances, undertakings, promises, and agreements to pay certain sums of money on events or contingencies of and relating to horse races, did, on the —— day of ——, receive of X. Y. the sum of £5 as a deposit on a certain bet, on condition of paying a sum of money to the said X. Y. on the happening of an event or contingency of and relating to a certain horse race, to wit, on a horse named "Ladas," thereafter to run in a race known as the Derby,** contrary to the statute.

Charge against a manager, under sect. 4 of 16 & 17 Vict. c. 119.

[*Where the defendant has been summoned and has not appeared, add—*

And the defendant was thereupon summoned to appear before the Court of Summary Jurisdiction, sitting at ——, on ——day, the —— day of ——, at the hour of —— in the ——noon, to answer the said charge.

And oath [*or* affirmation *or* declaration] has been made that the defendant was duly served with the summons, but did not appear, and that such information is true.]

You are therefore hereby commanded to bring the defendant before the Court of Summary Jurisdiction, sitting at —— forthwith [*or* on ——, the —— day of ——, at the hour of —— in the ——noon], to answer to the said information.

Dated the —— day of ——, one thousand eight hundred and ninety ——.

(Signed)   J. P.,   (L.S.)
Justice of the Peace for the [County *or* Borough *or* City aforesaid].

⁂ The black type is inserted by way of illustration of particular offences.

———————————

No. 6.—Example of Warrant for Apprehension of Witness.

In the County of ——, Petty Sessional Division of ——
    Borough of ——
    City and County of the City of ——
    To each and all the constables of ——.

E. F. was duly summoned to appear before the Court of Summary Jurisdiction, sitting at ——, on ——day, the —— day of ——, at the hour of —— in the —— noon, to testify what he should know concerning a certain information against A. B. :

And he has neither appeared thereto nor offered any just excuse for his neglect :

And it has been proved on oath [or affirmation] that the summons has been duly [indorsed and] served on him, and that a reasonable sum has been paid [or tendered] to him for his costs and expenses in that behalf.

You are therefore hereby commanded to bring him before the Court of Summary Jurisdiction, sitting at ——, forthwith [or on ——day, the —— day of ——, one thousand eight hundred and ninety ——].

(Signed)   J. P.,   (L.S.)
Justice of the Peace for the [County or
Borough or City aforesaid].

No. 7.—Example of Warrant for Apprehension of Witness in First Instance.

In the County of ——, Petty Sessional Division of ——
    Borough of ——
    City and County of the City of ——
    To each and all of the constables of ——.

Offence of wilfully permitting.
16 & 17 Viot. c. 119, s. 3.

A. B. has been charged by C. D., for that he, **being the owner** [or occupier] **of a certain place, to wit, an enclosure** situate at, &c., and known as the —— Ring, **unlawfully and knowingly and wilfully did permit the said place,**

₊ *The black type is inserted by way of illustration of particular offences.*

on ———— the ———— day of ————, one thousand eight hundred and ninety————, to be used by G. H. and others for the purpose of betting with persons resorting thereto, contrary to the statute, &c. :

And it appearing to me by the oath [*or* affirmation] of ————, that E. F. is likely to give material evidence concerning the said matter, and that it is probable that he will not attend to give evidence concerning the said matter unless compelled so to do,

You are therefore hereby commanded to bring him before the Court of Summary Jurisdiction sitting at ————, forthwith [*or* on ————day the ———— day of ————, one thousand eight hundred and ninety ————].

(Signed)   J. P., (L.S.)

Justice of the Peace for the [County *or* Borough *or* City aforesaid].

No. 8.—Example of Commitment on Remand.

In the County of ————, Petty Sessional Division of ————
Borough of ————
City and County of the City of ————.

To each and all the constables of ————, and to the governor of her Majesty's prison at ————.

A. B., hereinafter called the defendant, being brought before the Court of Summary Jurisdiction sitting at ————, charged with having—**unlawfully exhibited and published** on the ———— day of ————, at ————, a certain placard and advertisement, whereby it was made to appear that a certain house and premises, situate and known as No. —, ———— Street, aforesaid, was then and there opened, kept, and used by him for the purpose of betting with persons resorting thereto, contrary to the statute, &c. :

Offence under 16 & 17 Vict. c. 119, s. 7.

The hearing of the case being adjourned :

You, the said constables, are therefore hereby commanded to convey the defendant to the said prison, and

---

₊ *The black type is inserted by way of illustration of particular offences.*

z 2

there to deliver him to the governor thereof, together with this warrant, and you, the governor of the said prison, to receive him into your custody and keep him until the ———— day of ————, and on that day to convey him before the Court of Summary Jurisdiction sitting at ————, at the hour of ———— in the ————noon, to be further dealt with according to law.

Dated the ———— day of ————, one thousand eight hundred and ninety ————.

> (Signed)   J. P., (L.S.)
> Justice of the Peace for the [County *or* Borough *or* City aforesaid].

[*Indorsement where Bail allowed.*]

I hereby certify that I consent to the defendant being bailed, himself in ———— pounds, and ———— sureties in ———— pounds each.

No. 9.—Example of Conviction for Penalty.

In the County of ————, Petty Sessional Division of ————
     Borough of ————
     City and County of ————
     Before the Court of Summary Jurisdiction sitting at ————.

The ———— day of ————, one thousand eight hundred and ninety ————.

A. B., hereinafter called the defendant, is this day convicted for that he on the ———— day of ————, at ———— aforesaid, **unlawfully in a certain newspaper, to wit, ————, published an advertisement whereby it was made to appear that C. D. would, on application, give information with respect to certain events, to wit, events whereon E. F., being the occupier of a certain house and premises situate and known as No. —, ———— Street, then and**

Advertising offence under 37 & 38 Vict. c. 15.

₊ The black type is inserted by way of illustration of particular offences.

there opened, kept, and used by the said E. F., for the
purpose of receiving money as and for the consideration
for agreements to give thereafter sums of money on events
relating to horse races, was willing to receive deposits as
mentioned in the statute 16 & 17 Vict. c. 119, contrary to
section 3 of the statute 37 & 38 Vict. c. 15.

And it is adjudged that the defendant for his said
offence do forfeit and pay the sum of 30*l.*, and do also
pay the further sum of 5*l.* for costs forthwith.

And in default of payment it is adjudged that the
defendant be imprisoned in her Majesty's prison at ——
and there kept to hard labour for the space of two calendar
months, unless the said sums, and all costs and charges of
the said commitment and of his conveyance to the said
prison, be sooner paid.

(Signed)   J. P.,   (L.S.)
Justice of the Peace for the [County *or*
Borough *or* City aforesaid].

———————

No. 10.—Example of Notice of Appeal.

In the County of ——, Petty Sessional Division of ——
City and County of the City of ——
Borough of ——

To the Clerk of the Court of Summary Jurisdiction
sitting at ——, and to [*naming the other party*].

Take notice that I, A. B., of ——, intend at the next
General Quarter Sessions of the Peace to be holden in and
for —— at —— in the said ——, to appeal against
a certain conviction, for that —— [*set out the offence and
date and adjudication*], and that the grounds of such appeal
are that—

(1.) I am not guilty of the said offence.
(2.) That the sentence was excessive.

Dated the ——.

Signed by Appellant.

•.• *The black type is inserted by way of illustration of particular offences.*

No. 11.—Recognizance of Appellant.

——— ⎱ Be it remembered, that on the ——— day
to wit. ⎰ of ———, 18—, A. B., of ———, C. D., of
———, and E. F., of ———, personally came before me, the undersigned, one of Her Majesty's justices of the peace acting in and for ———, and severally acknowledged themselves to owe to our sovereign lady the Queen the sum of fifty pounds of good and lawful money of Great Britain, to be made and levied on their several goods and chattels, lands, and tenements respectively to the use of our said lady the Queen, her heirs and successors, if he the said A. B. shall fail in the condition hereunder written.

(Signed)   A. B.
C. D.
E. F.

Taken and acknowledged at ⎱
the ———, before me,   ⎰ ———, Justice.

The condition of the above-written recognizance is such that if the said A. B. shall appear at the next General Quarter Sessions of the peace to be holden in and for the said ———, and there enter and prosecute an appeal against a certain conviction, bearing date the ———, and made by and before a Court of Summary Jurisdiction for the said ——— sitting at the Court House therein on that day, for that he within six months then last past did unlawfully, &c. [*setting out offence*], contrary to the statute, for which offence the said A. B. was adjudged to forfeit and pay the sum of fifty pounds and costs. And further, that if the said A. B. shall abide the judgment and determination of the Quarter Sessions, and pay such costs as shall be then and there awarded, then the said recognizance to be void, or else to remain in full force and virtue.

No. 12.—Example of Special Case.

In the High Court of Justice,
Queen's Bench Division.

Between A. B....................Appellant.
and
C. D....................Respondent.

to wit. }

1. This is a Case stated by ——, the undersigned, being —— of Her Majesty's justices of the peace in and for ——, and being a Court of Summary Jurisdiction, sitting as a Court of Summary Jurisdiction, on the application in writing of the appellant, who was dissatisfied with our determination as being erroneous in point of law, as hereinafter stated:—

2. [*Sets out the information, and the hearing and the adjudication.*]

3. [*States request to state a case, pursuant to, &c., and the fact that a recognizance has been duly entered into.*]

4. Now we do hereby state and sign the following Case:—

Paragraphs 1 to 4, introductory.

20 & 21 Vict. c. 43, and 42 & 43 Vict. c. 49, s. 33.

CASE.

5. The material facts [*which were proved to the satisfaction of the justices, and for convenience of reference, if long, in sub-paragraphs (a), (b), (c), &c.*].

6. [*Evidence tendered upon behalf of the appellant.*]

7. [*Set out a list of the cases cited at the hearing.*]

OPINION.

8. **We find, in the first place, that the charge against C. D. of betting with non-members within the club premises had not been established.**

We were of the opinion, in the second place, that the words in the Act, **"betting with persons resorting thereto"** apply to persons who are distinct from the owners or occupiers of the premises.

Conclusion of fact.

Conclusion of law.

*** *The black type is inserted by way of illustration of particular offences.*

Consequently, on the facts as found by us, we dismissed the aforesaid charge.

QUESTION.

The Question.

9. The question upon which the opinion of the said Court is required is, **Whether the said justices came to a correct decision in point of law upon the above statement of facts, and if not, what should be done in the premises?**

Dated, &c.

NOTE.—The recognizance to be entered into prior to the stating of a case is, in substance, as in Form No. 11.

** *The black type is inserted by way of illustration of particular offences.*

INDEX.

ART UNIONS,
lotteries, 69.
conditions of legality, 69.

ASSIGNEE, OFFICIAL, 216. See *Stock Exchange.*

AUTREFOIS ACQUIT OR CONVICT, 230, 231, 234. See *Criminal Procedure.*
occasion for such plea under Betting Houses Act, 265, 266.

BACKGAMMON, games played on table, lawful, 67.

BACKWARDATION,
what is, 209, 210.
occasion for, 209, 210.

BAGATELLE, public tables, licences for, 138, 316, 317.

BANK, user of, in contravention of Betting Houses Act, 296.

BANKER, acting as such in gaming house, liability, 244.

BANKRUPTCY,
of principal, determines agent's authority, 176.
sanction in hazardous speculation, 215, 216.

BANK SHARES,
sale and purchase of, 217 *et seq.*
contracts for, 217.
object of Leeman's Act, 217.
provisions of, 217, 218.
unreasonable usage of Stock Exchange, 218, 219.
negligence of brokers, 219, 220.
no indemnity of broker against his principal, 220.
 secus, where principal has actual knowledge, 220, 221.
inserting false numbers or names, misdemeanour, 218.
actual transfer of, 221.

BARNARD'S ACT. See *Stock Exchange.*

BASSET,
illegal game (lottery), 66, 255, 256, 322.
offences relating to, 66, 322.

BAZAAR, EASTERN, lottery, 72.

BEARS, speculative sellers, 208. See also *Stock Exchange.*

BETTING. See *Wagering Contracts.*

BETTING HOUSES ACT (16 & 17 VICT. c. 119),
object of—
business of betting offices, 260.
enacting parts of Act go beyond preamble, 261.

DEPOSITS,
on wagering contracts,
recovery of, from,
    (1) other principal, possible when, 171, 172, 173, 174.
    (2) personal representative of other principal, 172, 173.
    (3) stakeholder, on rescission, 190, 191, 192, 193.
distinguished from winnings, 194.
              plates, prizes, or added money, 155—164.
made in pursuance of illegal transactions,
recovery of,
    on rescission, when possible, 116, 117, 118, 119.
    by oppressed from oppressor, 119, 120.
    where *delictum impar*, 120, 121, 266.
       secus, where *delictum par*, 122, 123.
    from stakeholder on rescission, 127, 128, 129.
criminal offences relating to, 264, 265. See *Betting Houses Act.*

DICE,
games of, under 33 Hen. VIII. c. 9...44.
    illegal, 67, 322, 333.
        except backgammon, 67, 322, 333.

DIFFERENCE TRANSACTIONS,
description of, 12.
when wagers,
    mutual intention of parties, 12, 13.
    test, 13, 14, 15.
    evidence of intention,
        course of dealing, 13.
        documents may be fictitious, 14, 15, 18.
        documents to be read together, 19.
    question for the jury, 13.
in bucket shops,
    cases on, 14, 17, 18, 19, 20.
on Stock Exchange,
    result of speculative sales and purchases, 8, 9, 208 *et seq.*
    forbidden by rules when wagers, 109, 207, 210.
relation to,
    options, 212, 213.
    sale of prospective dividends, 213, 214.
sometimes called time bargains,
    user of terms, 11.

DIVIDENDS,
sale of prospective, 7.
    valid at law, 7, 214.
    forbidden by rules of Stock Exchange, 213.
    division of, by lot, 77.

ENTRANCE MONEY, 154.

A A 2

GAMES—*continued.*
unlawful—*continued.*
within meaning of 33 Hen. VIII. c. 9, as repealed by 8 &
9 Vict. c. 109...136, 256.
includes games of skill and chance, 256, 257.
e. g., baccarat, 257.
chemin de fer, 257.
games of chance, 164, 257.
within the Lottery Acts,
includes all kinds of lotteries, 62—79, 319—324.
includes specific games of chance,
ace of hearts, 66, 322.
pharaoh, 66, 322.
basset, 66, 322.
hazard, 66, 322.
passage, 67, 322, 323.
roulet, 67, 322, 333.
dice, 67, 322, 333.
because of cruelty,
cock-fighting, &c., 60, 61.
lawful,
games of skill, 164, 256.
within the proviso of sect. 18 of 8 & 9 Vict. c. 109...164.
may be used for unlawful gaming, 258.
See *Gaming Houses*, sub-tit. *Unlawful Gaming; Gaming
on Licensed Premises.*

GAMING,
playing a game for money, 38.
contracts by way of, valid at common law, 35.
question, when stakes excessive, 35, 36, 37, 241, 242.
cheating at, indictable at common law, 39.
statutory provisions as to,
fraudulent and excessive, 45 *et seq.*
statute 16 Car. II. c. 7...45, 46, 47.
aim of, 45.
penalties on dishonest, 46.
honest but excessive, 46.
above limit, contracts and securities void, 46.
statute 9 Anne, c. 14,
extended 16 Car. II. c. 7...47.
avoided all securities, 47.
penalty on excessive play, 48.
limit, 49.
fraudulent gaming, 50.
living by gambling, 50.
quarrels at gaming, 50.
transactions within 16 Car. II. and 9 Anne,
games, sports, and pastimes, 50.
examples—
horse races, 51.
cricket, 51.
foot race, 51.

OCCUPIER. See *Betting Houses Act; Gaming Houses.*

OFFICES, for sale of re-disguising lotteries, 64, 66.

OFFICIAL ASSIGNEE. See *Assignee.*

OPPRESSED, right against oppressor in illegal transactions, 119, 120.

OPTIONS,
nature of, 212.
puts and calls, 212.
continuation of puts and calls, 213.
grantor of, not entitled to shares, &c., 213.
contract for sale of, may be wager, 213.

PACKETS with prizes, lotteries, 73.

PARTITION, by lot, 67.

PARTNERSHIP,
in illegal transactions—
    general rule, no action, 130.
    validity of collateral contracts, 130.
rights of partners *inter se*, 130.
    losses paid, no contribution, 130.
    profits received, no shares, 130.
    no action of account maintainable, 131.
    Sharp v. *Taylor* considered, 131 *et seq.*
    personal representative of deceased partner liable to
        account to beneficiaries, 135.
in void wagering transactions—
rights of partners *inter se*—
    recovery of share of winnings, 188, 195, 196.
    instances of, 194.
    account stated, action on, at law, 195.
        why maintainable, 195.
    cheque given by one partner to another for winnings,
        195, 196.
    dissolution of, action for, in Chancery Division, 197.
    probable effect of Gaming Act, 1892, on, 205, 206.
    legality of, recognized, 195, 196.

PASSAGE,
illegal game, lottery, 67, 255, 256, 322.
offences, 66, 322.

PAYMENT,
by personal representative, 166.
of debt by wager, 170.
by third persons in respect of wagering contract, 199, 200.
    estoppel, remedial effect of, 201, 202.

SECURITIES,
  statutory provisions as to—
    the statutes 16 Car. c. II. 7, and 9 Anne, c. 14—
      sections of, cited, 46,.47.
      what securities are within—
        for payment of money won by gaming or wagering
          at—
          cards, 47. .
          dice tables, 47.
          tennis, 47.
          bowles, 47.
          or other game or games, 47. .
          games within statute, 50.
            cricket, 51.
            foot-racing, 51.
            horse-racing, 51.
        for money won by betting on sides or hands of players
          at such games, 47.
        for repayment of money knowingly lent for such
          gaming or betting, 47.
        for money lent or advanced at the time and place of
          such play to persons gaming or betting, 47.
  all such securities null and void, 46, 47, 80.
  null and void securities illustrated—
    i. Notes and bills of exchange, 80 *et seq.*
      negotiability destroyed, 80.
      bonâ fide holder for value, hardship on, 80.
        action on indorsement, 81.
      cases illustrating, 81, 82, 83, 84.
      second security substituted for original, 84.
    ii. Judgments, voluntary only, 84.
    iii. Bonds, 84, 85.
    iv. Mortgages, 85.
      assignability, 85, 87.
      examples, 86.
      divesting estate, 88.
  estoppel—
    remedial operation of, 88.
    bonds, 89.
  grantor of null security, usual relief, 89, 90.
  the statute 5 & 6 Will. IV. c. 41—
    operates on same securities as earlier ones, 90.
    such securities deemed to be for illegal consideration, 91.
    securities for illegal consideration—
      i. **Notes and bills of exchange,** 92 *et seq.*
        cheques included, 97.
        onus of proof of illegality, 92.
        codification by Bills of Exchange Act, 1882—
          holder in due course, 93.
          defective title, 93.
          person claiming through holder in due course,
            93.
            exemplified, 95.

STAKE HOLDERS,
  are severally agents of the several depositors, 189, 190.
  several bailments not single trust, 190.
  in illegal transactions—
    rescission by principal, 127.
    notice by principal of rescission, 128.
      effectual till actual payment over, 128, 129.
  in void transactions—
    cannot sue for stake, 194.
    rescission by principal, of authority of, 190.
      after event before actual payment over, 191, 192, 193.
      rights in such rescissions, 191, 192, 193, 194.
        See *Agent*.

STAKES,
  excessive, at common law, 35 *et seq.*, 164.
    in equity, 36, 37.
    under statutes, 45 *et seq.*, 55, 138, 241.

STATUTES,
  Betting Houses,
    16 & 17 Vict. c. 119 (betting houses), 260 *et seq.*
    37 & 38 Vict. c. 15 (Scotland), 299 *et seq.*
  Billiards,
    8 & 9 Vict. c. 109 (licence), 315 *et seq.*
  Cock Fighting,
    5 & 6 Will. IV. (penal), 60.
    2 & 3 Vict. c. 47 (search), 61.
    12 & 13 Vict. c. 92 (penal), 62, 253.
  Games and Gaming,
    33 Hen. VIII. c. 9 (unlawful games), 42, 43, 44.
    16 Car. II. c. 7 (fraudulent and excessive gaming), 45, 46, 47, 51.
    9 Anne, c. 14 (fraudulent and excessive gaming), 47 *et seq.*
    2 Geo. II. c. 28 (executive powers), 44.
    18 Geo. II. c. 34 (excessive and deceitful gaming), 55, 56.
    8 & 9 Vict. c. 109 (repealing), 136—139.
  Gaming Houses,
    33 Hen. VIII. c. 9 (gaming houses), 242, 243.
    2 Geo. II. c. 28 (search), 243.
    2 & 3 Vict. c. 47 (search, metropolitan), 246, 248.
    8 & 9 Vict. c. 109 (gaming houses), 243 *et seq.*
    17 & 18 Vict. c. 38 (gaming houses), 249 *et seq.*
  Gaming Securities,
    16 Car. II. c. 7 (effect on securities), 80 *et seq.*
    9 Anne, c. 14 (effect on securities), 80 *et seq.*
    5 & 6 Will. IV. c. 41 (effect on securities), 88, 90 *et seq.*
    8 & 9 Vict. c. 109 (wagering and gaming contracts), 103, 104, 139 *et seq.*
    36 & 37 Vict. c. 66 (procedure), 104.
    45 & 46 Vict. c. 61 (bills and notes), 93 *et seq.*

VOID TRANSACTIONS—*continued.*
securities for payment,
   i. under 5 & 6 Will. IV. c. 41...90 *et seq.*
     See *Securities for Illegal Consideration;* and *Securities.*
   ii. void consideration of, 168.
     illustrated by bill of exchange, 169.
        mortgage by deposit, 169.
   wager by way of payment, no discharge, 170.
   rescission of, where no agent, 171.
deposits not voluntary payments, 171, 172.
   recovery of, on rescission, 171, 172, 173, 175.
pleading, facts to be stated, 175.
agency in, 175 *et seq.* See *Agents; Stakeholders.*

WAGERING CONTRACTS,
characteristics of, 1, 26.
consideration, 1, 27, 28.
uncertain event, future or past, 2, 3.
distinguished from—
   i. warranties and liquidated damages, 4.
     contracts of guarantee, 5.
   ii. sales conditional as to price, 5.
   iii. speculative sales, 6, 7, 8, 9.
illustrated by reference to—
   I. sports, &c., 9.
   II. stocks and shares, 10.
     difference transactions, 11.
     time bargains, 11.
   III. insurance, life, 24.
substance not form in all cases, 20.
written documents may be fictitious, 14, 27.
   form of action at common law, 27.
illegal at common law as tending to—
   breach of peace, 30.
   immorality, 31.
   interests of third parties, 31.
   contrary to public policy, 32.
whether any still illegal, 142, 143, 145.
excessive amounts for, at common law, 34.
     under statutes, 45 *et seq.*
void by section 18, 8 & 9 Vict. c. 109...139. See *Statutes* (8 & 9 Vict. c. 109).
   (1) agents in. See *Agency; Agents.*
   (2) deposits, recovery of. See *Deposits.*
   (3) partnership in. See *Partnership.*
   (4) rescission of. See *Rescission.*
   (5) securities for. See *Securities.*
   (6) stakeholders in. See *Stakeholders.*
   (7) winnings. See *Winnings on Wagers.*
   no payment by, 170.

WARRANTIES, distinguished from wagers, 4.

G.   C C

LONDON: PRINTED BY C. F. ROWORTH, GREAT NEW STREET, FETTER LANE, E.C.

www.ingramcontent.com/pod-product-compliance
Lightning Source LLC
Chambersburg PA
CBHW032340280326
41935CB00008B/394